THOR
Son of Asgard

WRITER: Akira Yoshida
PENCILER: Greg Tocchini
COLORIST: Guru eFX
LETTERERS: Virtual Calligraphy's Randy Gentile & Dave Sharpe
COVER ARTIST: Jo Chen
EDITOR: MacKenzie Cadenhead
CONSULTING EDITOR: Ralph Macchio

COLLECTION EDITOR: Jennifer Grünwald
SENIOR EDITOR, SPECIAL PROJECTS: Jeff Youngquist
DIRECTOR OF SALES: David Gabriel
PRODUCTION: Jerry Kalinowski
BOOK DESIGNER: Carrie Beadle
CREATIVE DIRECTOR: Tom Marvelli

EDITOR IN CHIEF: Joe Quesada
PUBLISHER: Dan Buckley

Worthy

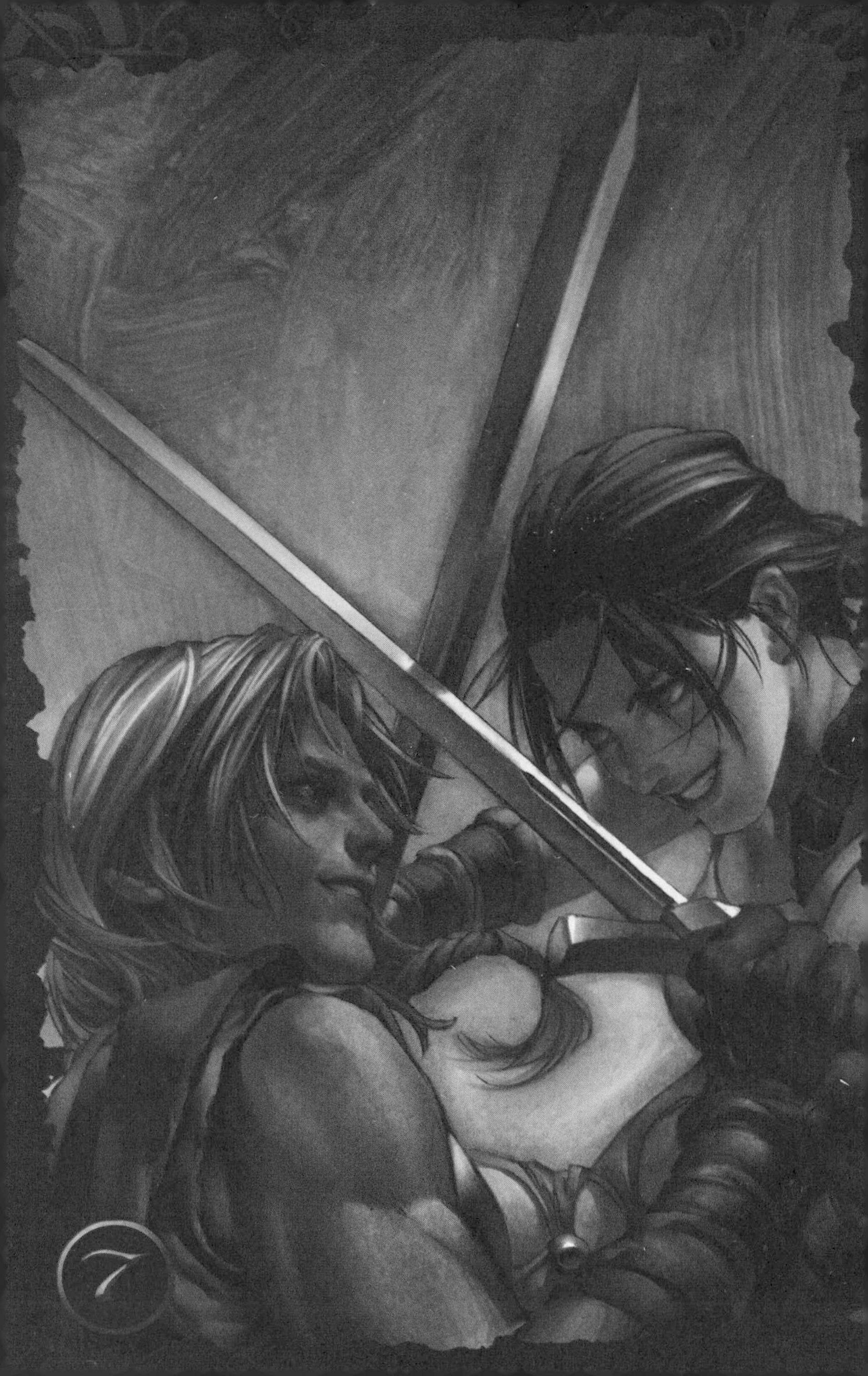
7

Welcome to a Tale of Asgard...

On their arduous journey across the wilds of Asgard, Thor, Balder and Sif fought dragons, trolls and magical creatures of all kinds in order to obtain four mystical objects requested by Lord Odin himself. But once they completed their task against all odds, the trio returned home only to find the city of Asgard under attack by the forces of the Norn Queen Karnilla. By successfully defending the city and surviving a near-death experience, the three teens have proven themselves to be brave and noble warriors.

However, a warrior's training never ends... so it is back to school for the young Asgardians!

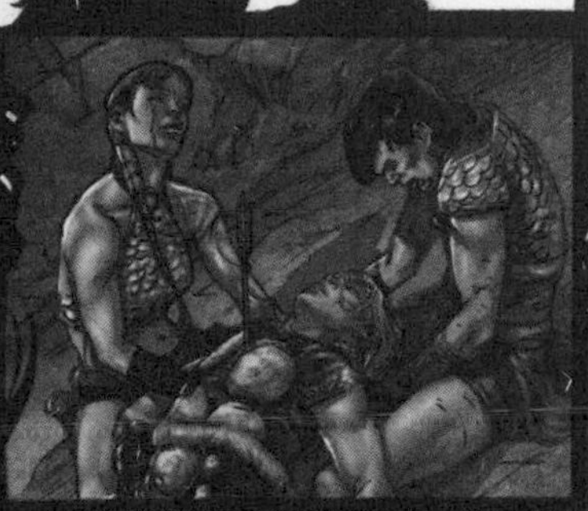

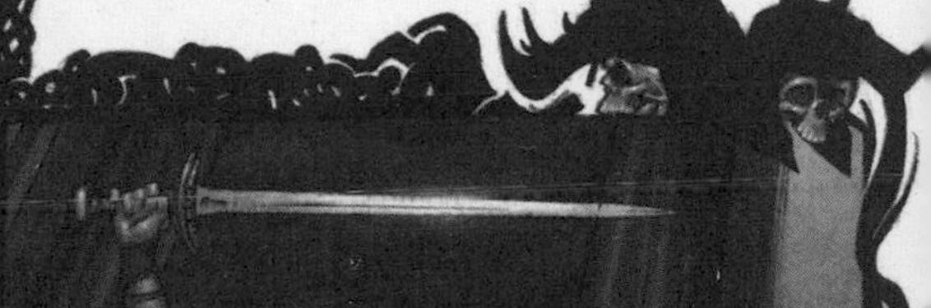

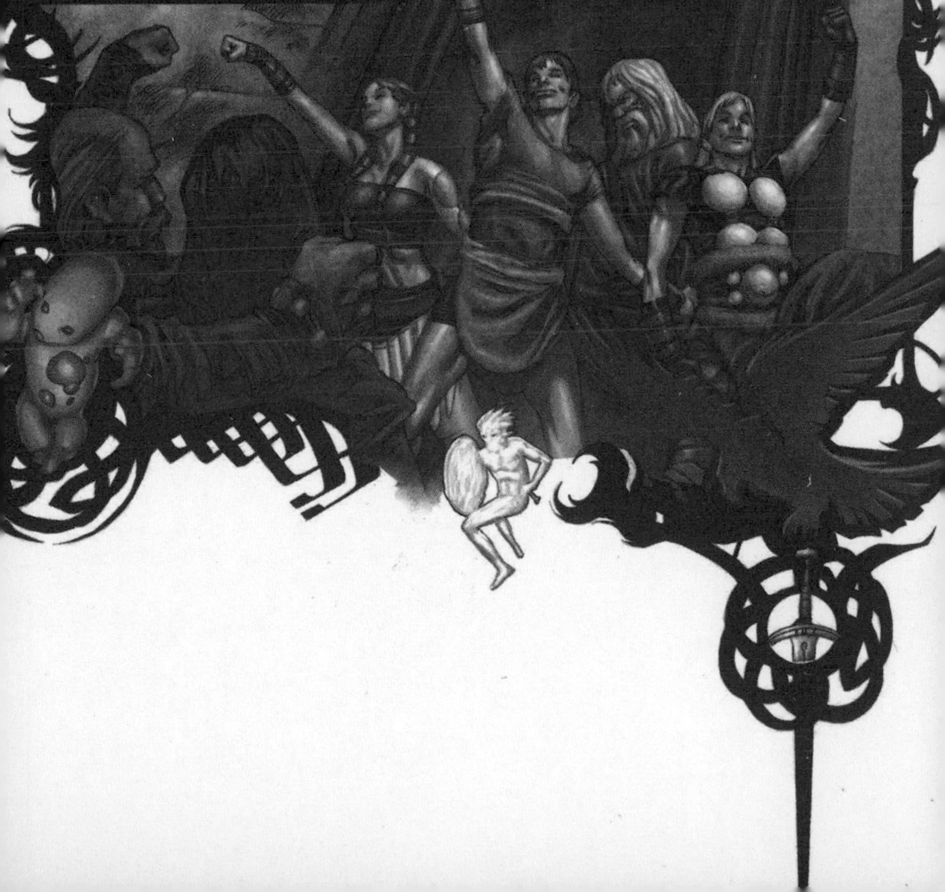

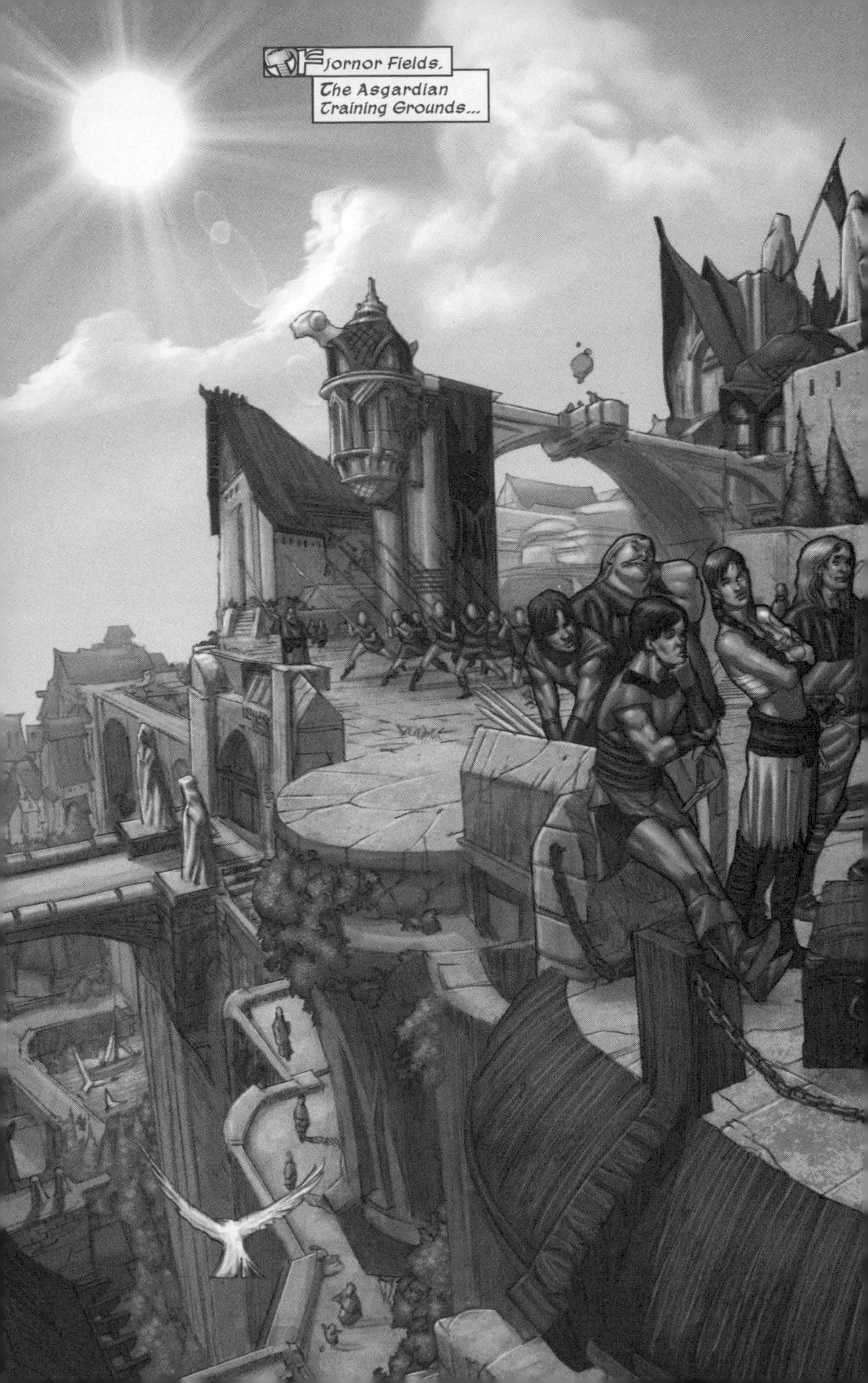
Fjornor Fields,
The Asgardian Training Grounds...

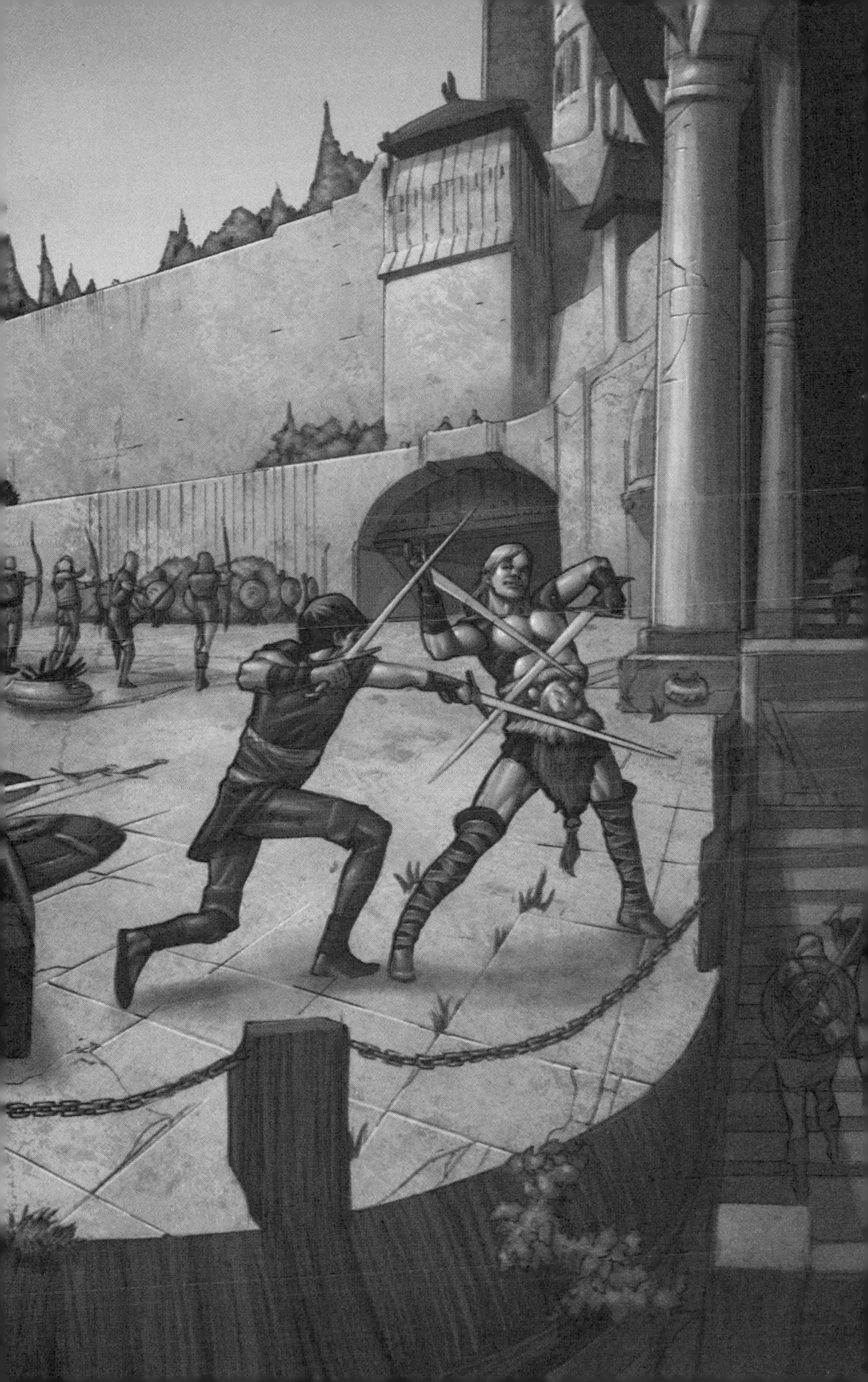

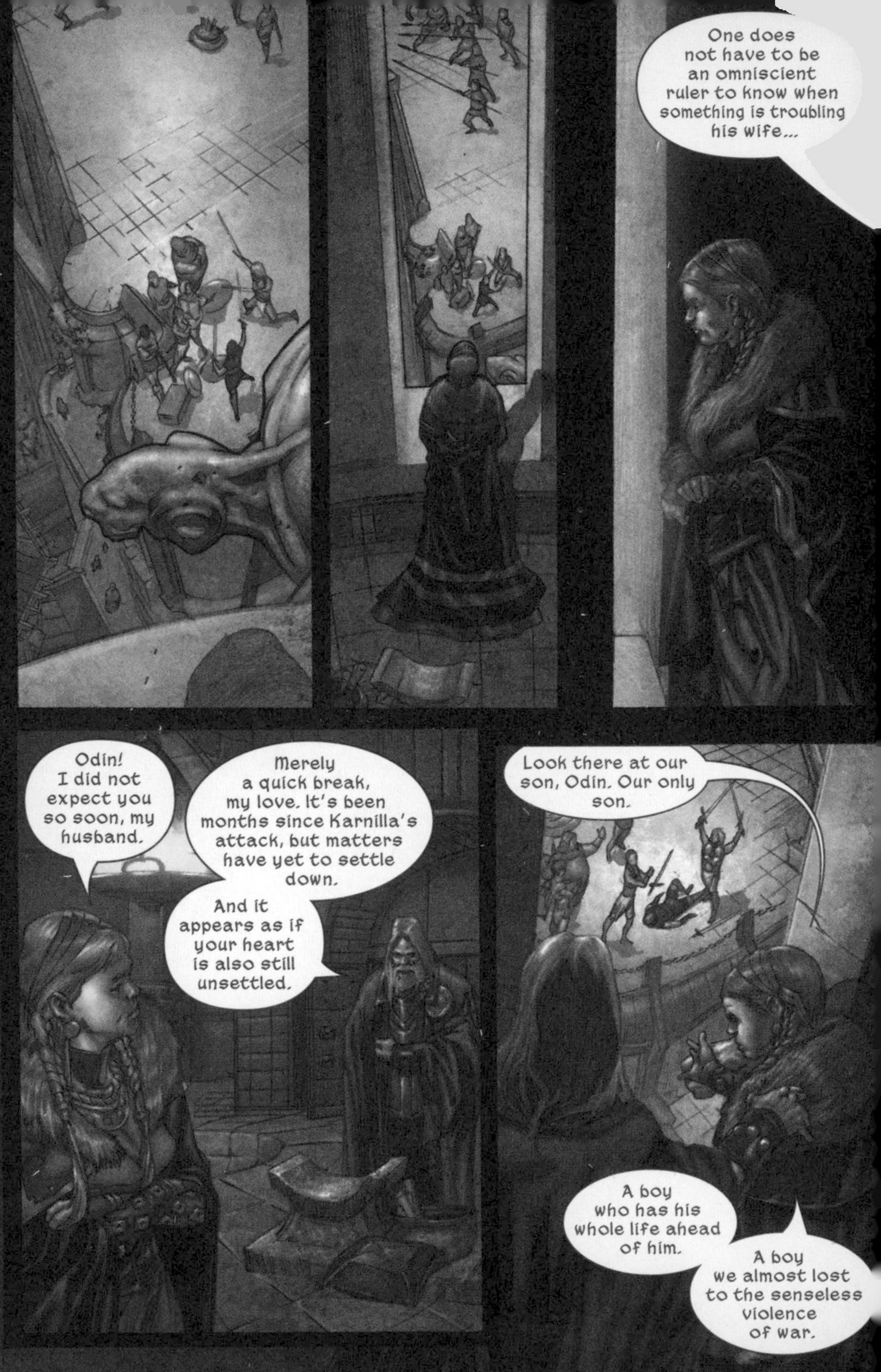
One does not have to be an omniscient ruler to know when something is troubling his wife...
Odin! I did not expect you so soon, my husband.
Merely a quick break, my love. It's been months since Karnilla's attack, but matters have yet to settle down.
And it appears as if your heart is also still unsettled.
Look there at our son, Odin. Our only son.
A boy who has his whole life ahead of him.
A boy we almost lost to the senseless violence of war.

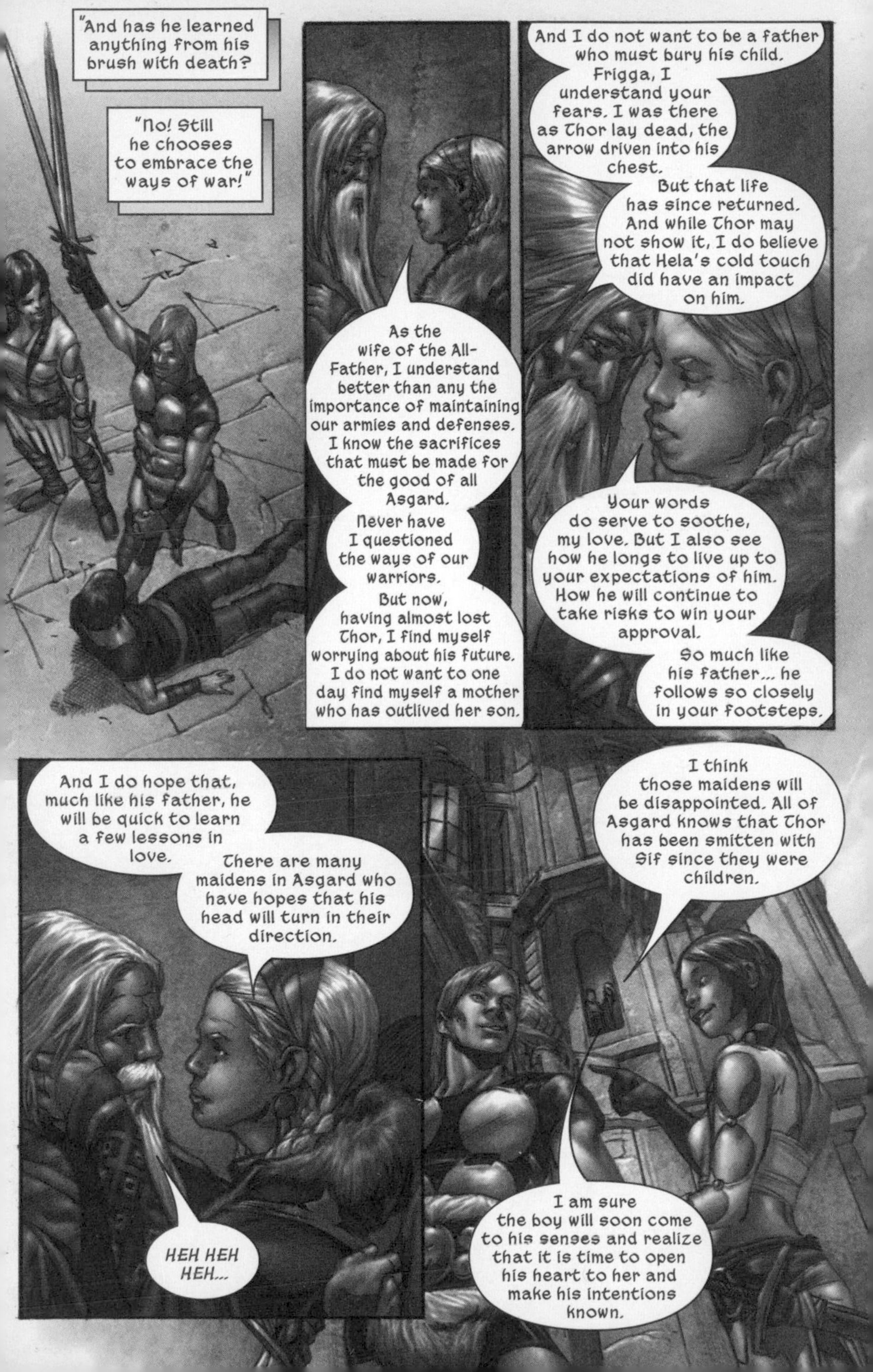
"And has he learned anything from his brush with death?
"No! Still he chooses to embrace the ways of war!"
As the wife of the All-Father, I understand better than any the importance of maintaining our armies and defenses. I know the sacrifices that must be made for the good of all Asgard.
Never have I questioned the ways of our warriors.
But now, having almost lost Thor, I find myself worrying about his future. I do not want to one day find myself a mother who has outlived her son.
And I do not want to be a father who must bury his child.
Frigga, I understand your fears. I was there as Thor lay dead, the arrow driven into his chest.
But that life has since returned. And while Thor may not show it, I do believe that Hela's cold touch did have an impact on him.
Your words do serve to soothe, my love. But I also see how he longs to live up to your expectations of him. How he will continue to take risks to win your approval.
So much like his father... he follows so closely in your footsteps.
And I do hope that, much like his father, he will be quick to learn a few lessons in love.
There are many maidens in Asgard who have hopes that his head will turn in their direction.
HEH HEH HEH...
I think those maidens will be disappointed. All of Asgard knows that Thor has been smitten with Sif since they were children.
I am sure the boy will soon come to his senses and realize that it is time to open his heart to her and make his intentions known.

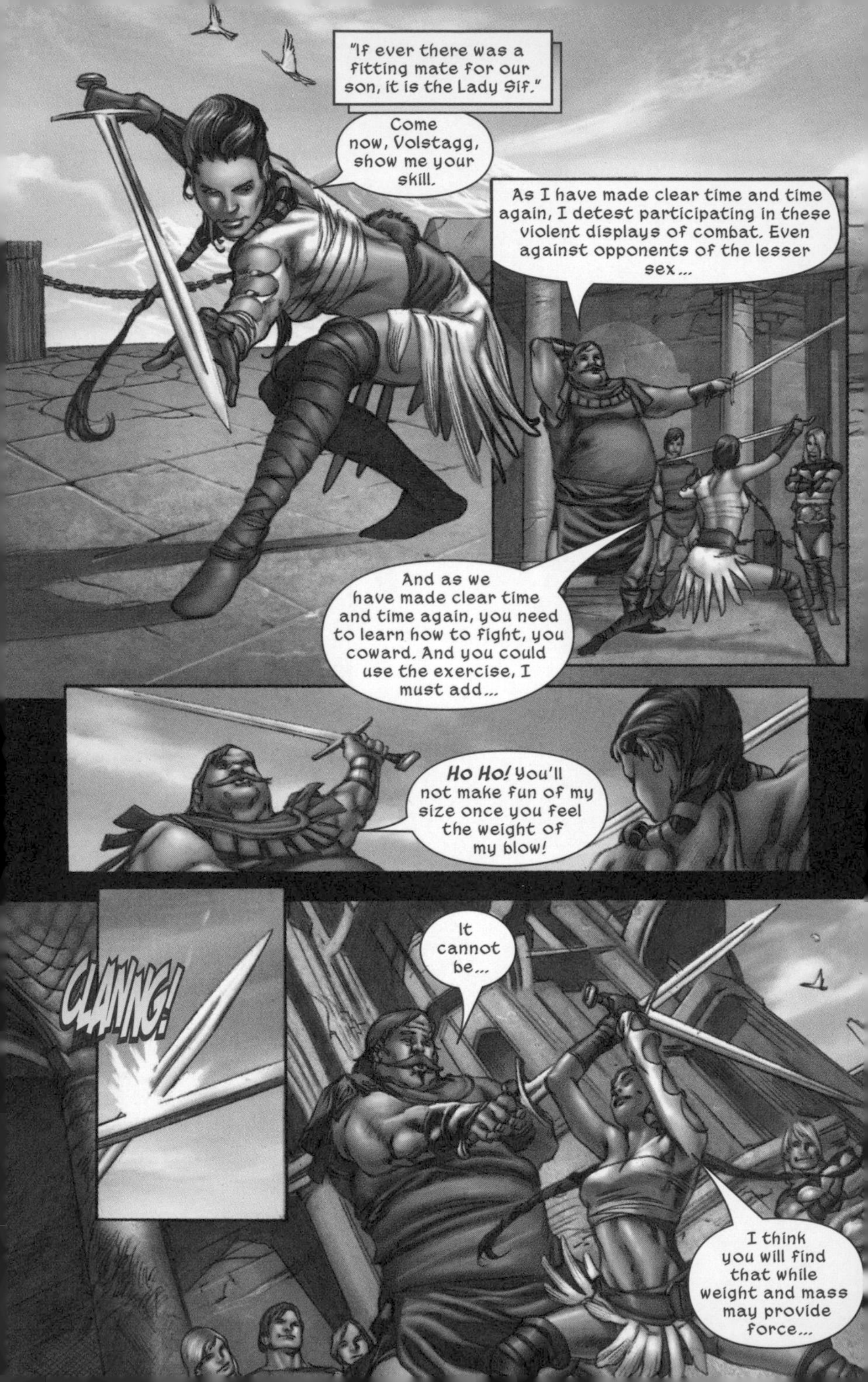
"If ever there was a fitting mate for our son, it is the Lady Sif."
Come now, Volstagg, show me your skill.
As I have made clear time and time again, I detest participating in these violent displays of combat. Even against opponents of the lesser sex...
And as we have made clear time and time again, you need to learn how to fight, you coward. And you could use the exercise, I must add...
HO HO! You'll not make fun of my size once you feel the weight of my blow!
CLANNG!
It cannot be...
I think you will find that while weight and mass may provide force...

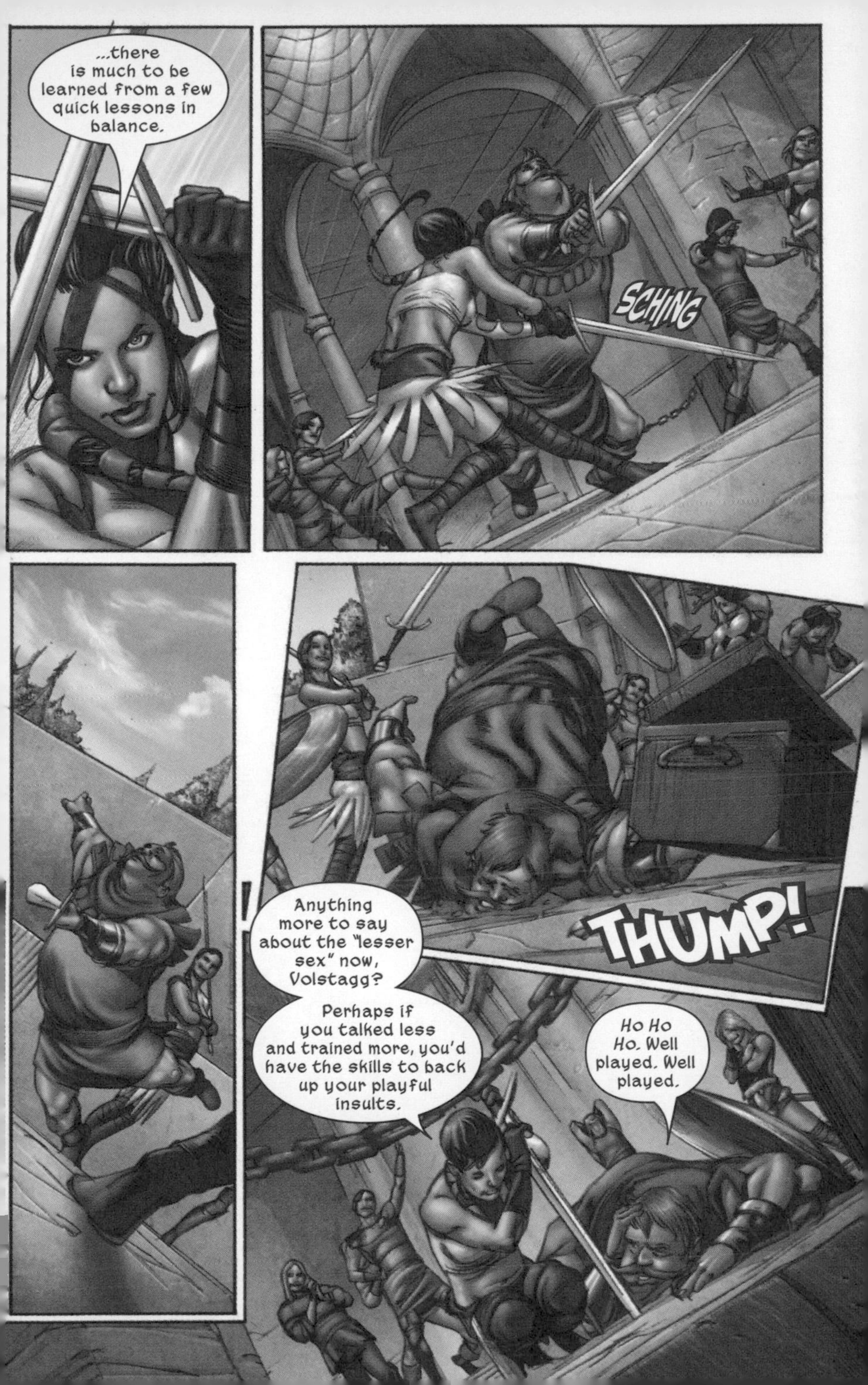
...there is much to be learned from a few quick lessons in balance.
SCHING
THUMP!
Anything more to say about the "lesser sex" now, Volstagg?
Perhaps if you talked less and trained more, you'd have the skills to back up your playful insults.
Ho Ho Ho. Well played. Well played.

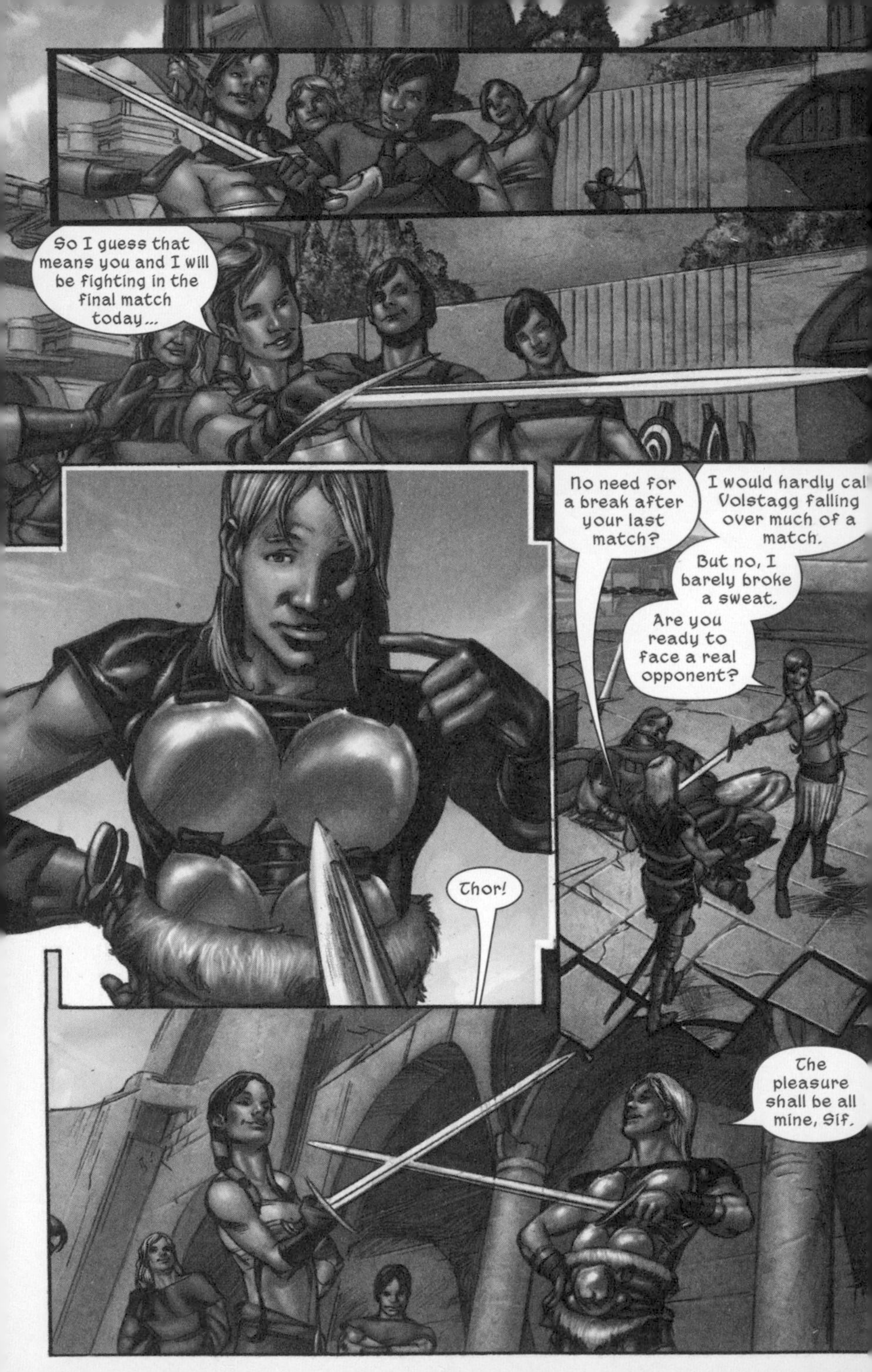
So I guess that means you and I will be fighting in the final match today...
No need for a break after your last match?
I would hardly cal Volstagg falling over much of a match.
But no, I barely broke a sweat.
Are you ready to face a real opponent?
Thor!
The pleasure shall be all mine, Sif.

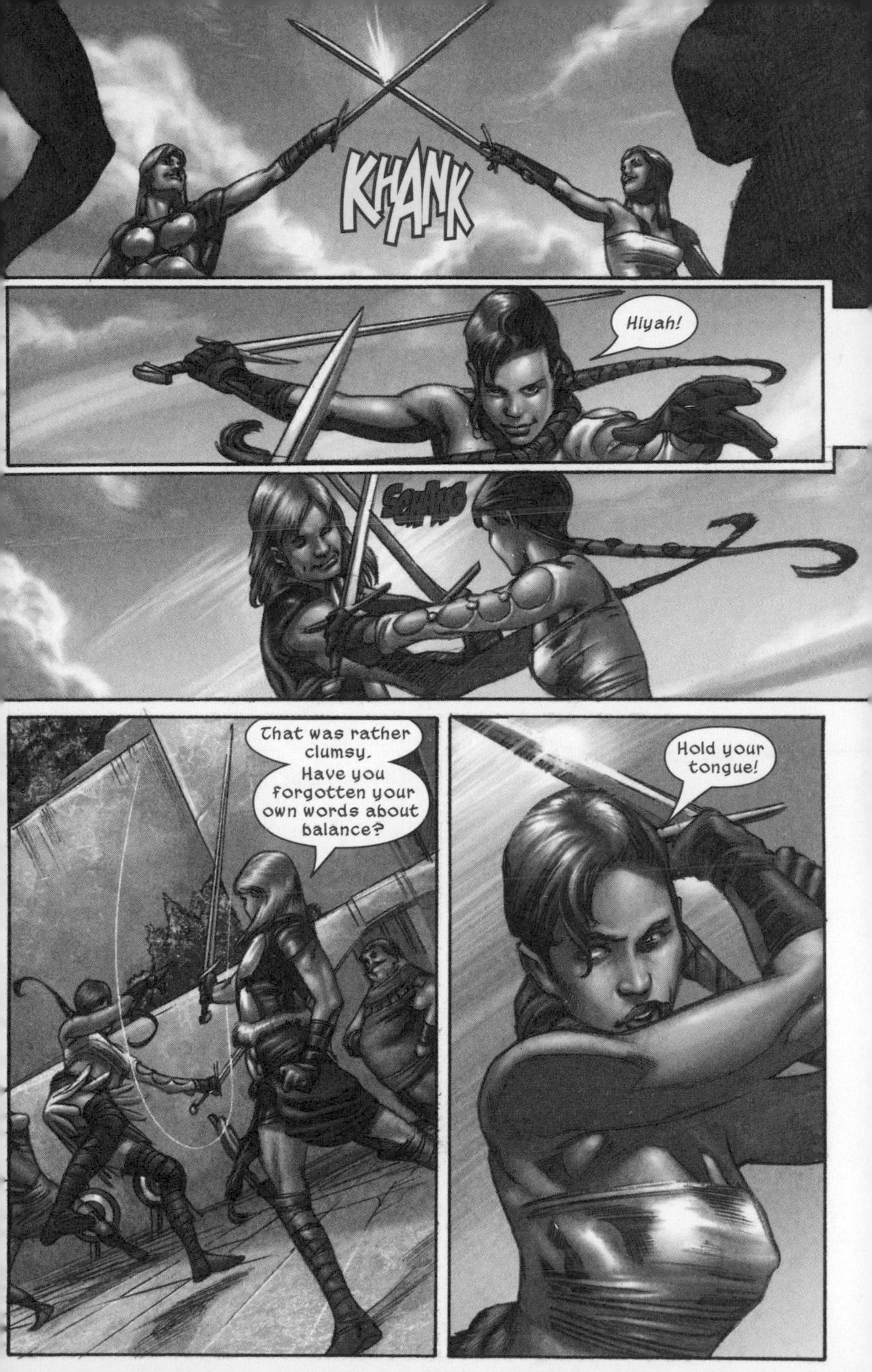
KHANK
Hiyah!
That was rather clumsy. Have you forgotten your own words about balance?
Hold your tongue!

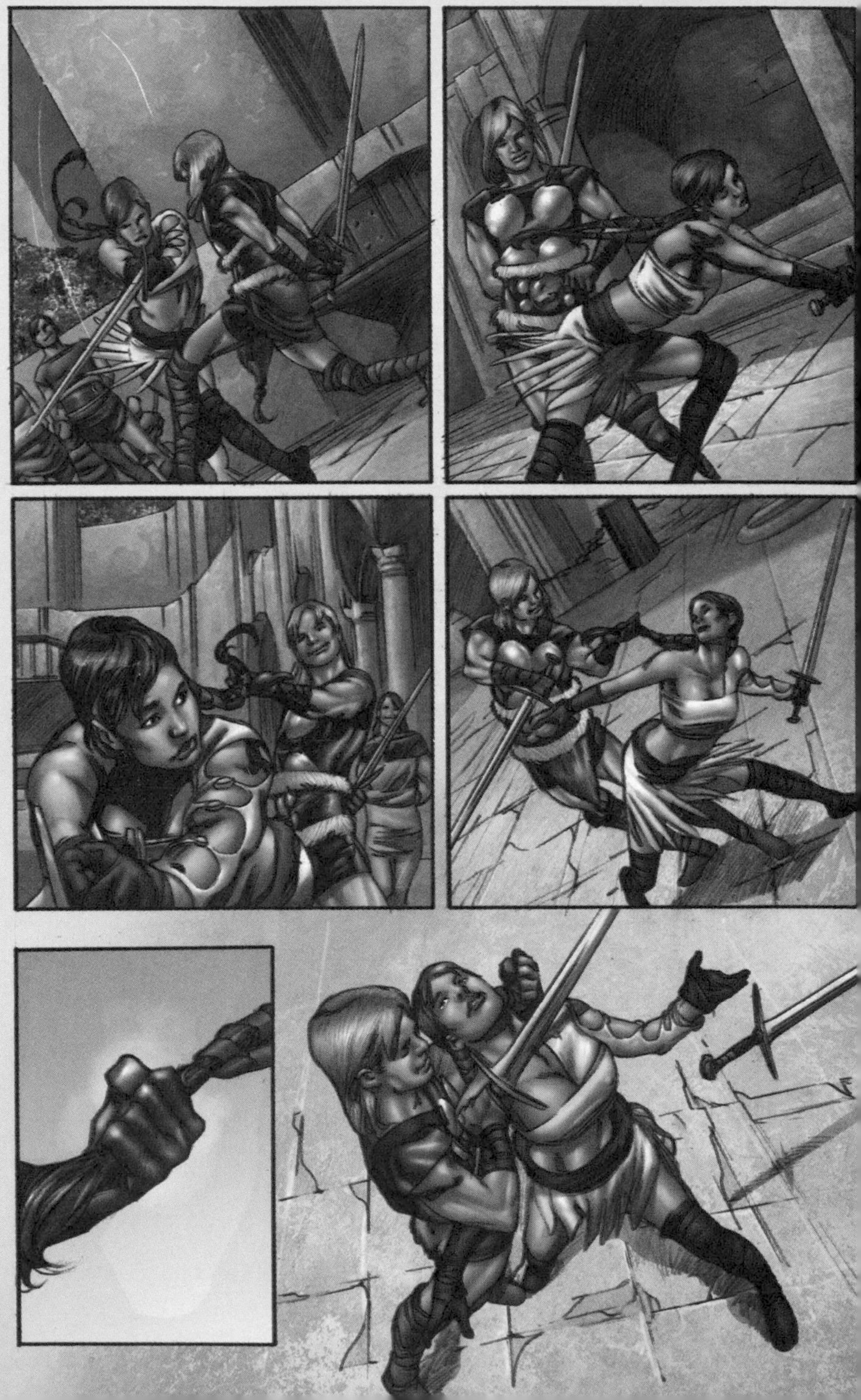

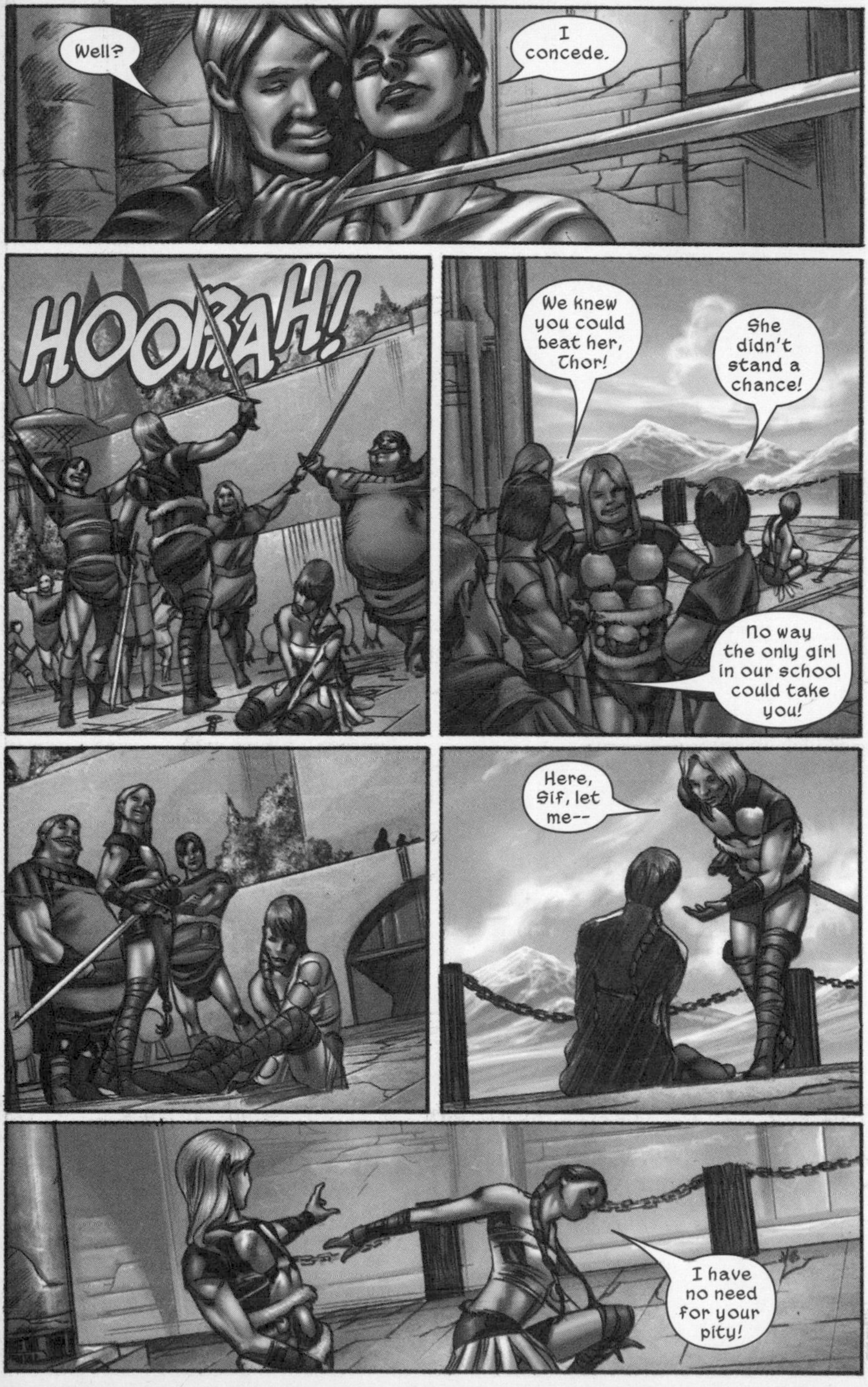
Well?
I concede.
HOORAH!
We knew you could beat her, Thor!
She didn't stand a chance!
No way the only girl in our school could take you!
Here, Sif, let me--
I have no need for your pity!

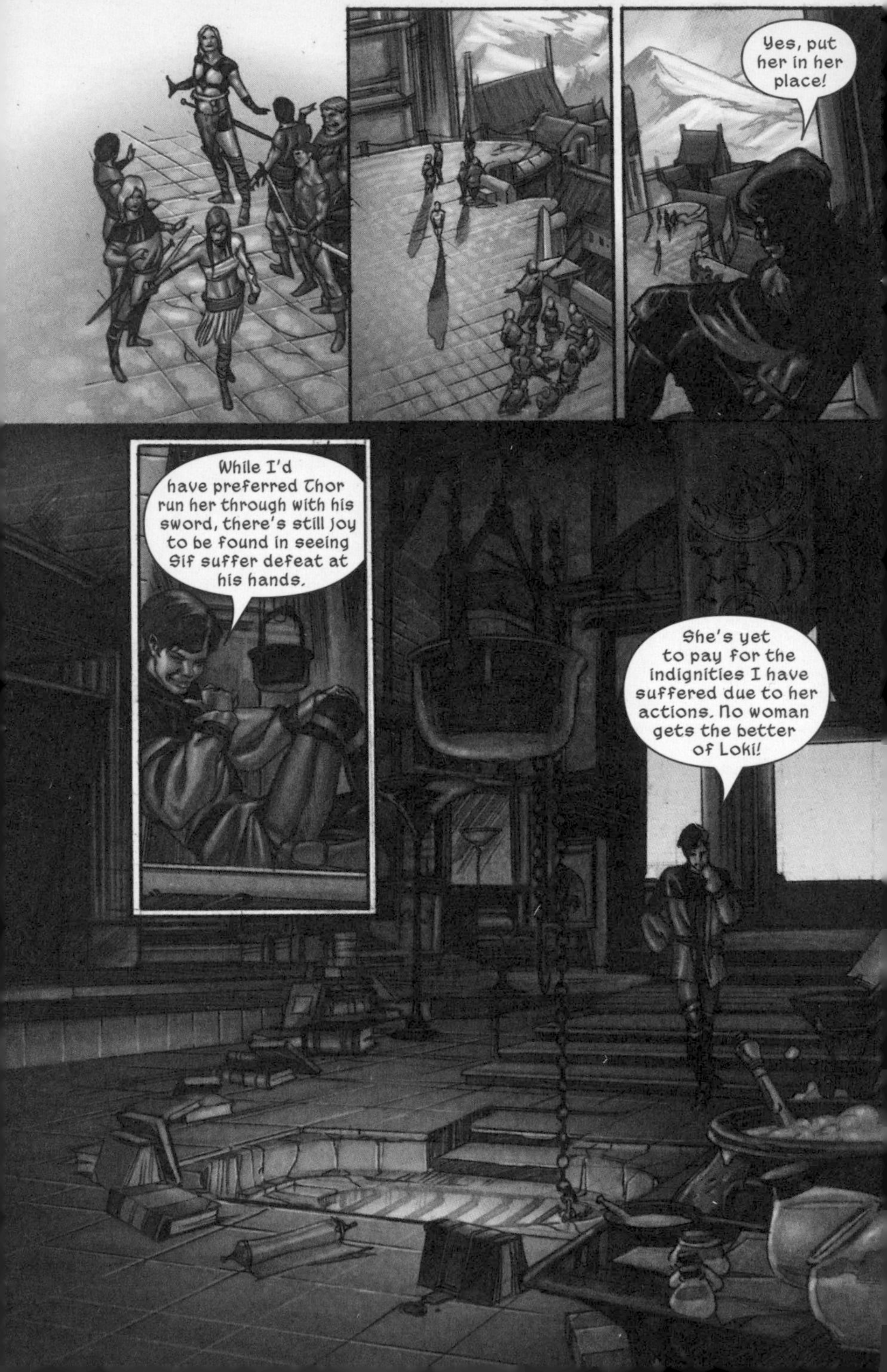
Yes, put her in her place!
While I'd have preferred Thor run her through with his sword, there's still joy to be found in seeing Sif suffer defeat at his hands.
She's yet to pay for the indignities I have suffered due to her actions. No woman gets the better of Loki!

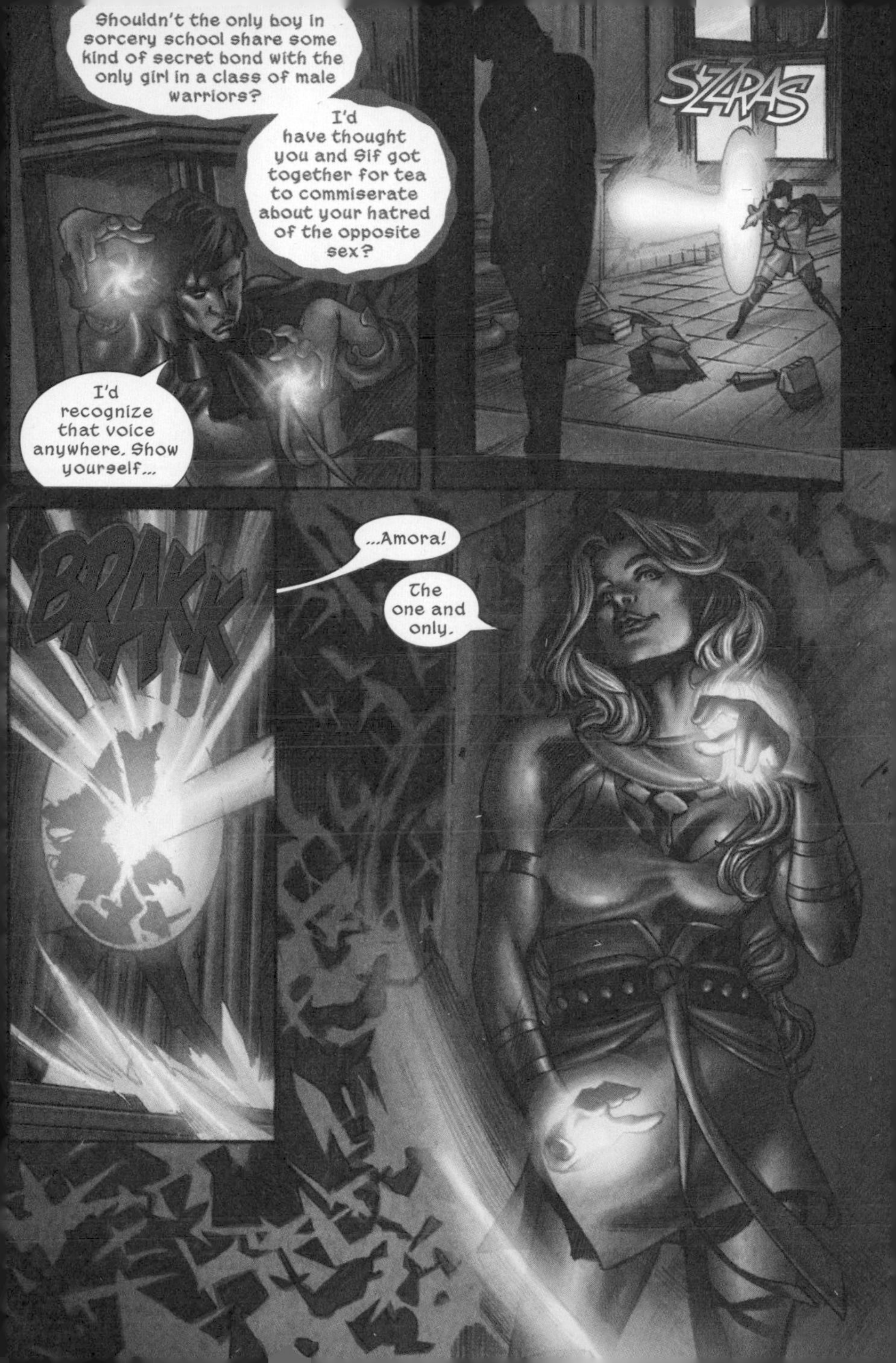
Shouldn't the only boy in sorcery school share some kind of secret bond with the only girl in a class of male warriors?
I'd have thought you and Sif got together for tea to commiserate about your hatred of the opposite sex?
I'd recognize that voice anywhere. Show yourself...
SZARAS
BRAKK
...Amora!
The one and only.

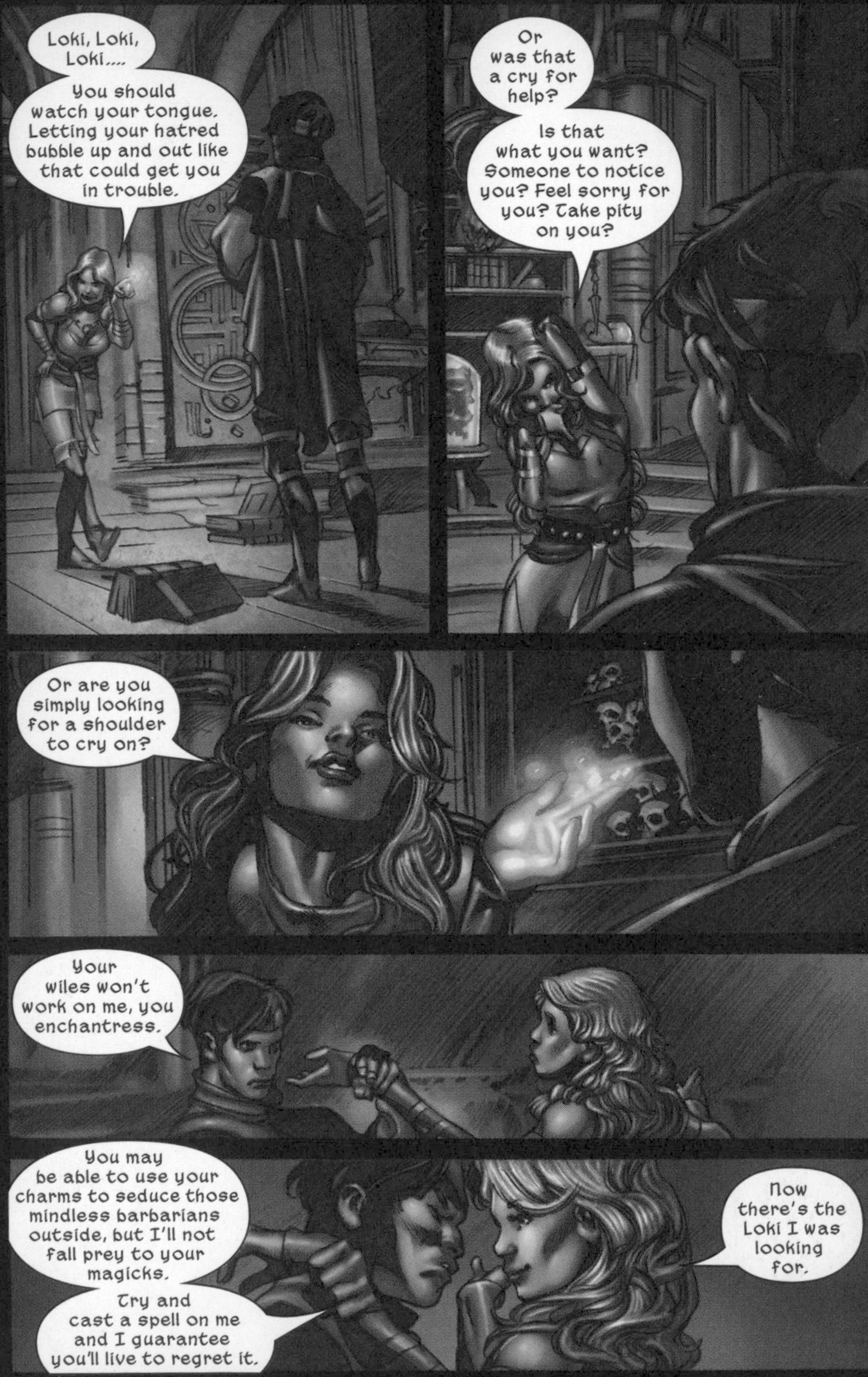
Loki, Loki, Loki....
You should watch your tongue. Letting your hatred bubble up and out like that could get you in trouble.
Or was that a cry for help?
Is that what you want? Someone to notice you? Feel sorry for you? Take pity on you?
Or are you simply looking for a shoulder to cry on?
Your wiles won't work on me, you enchantress.
You may be able to use your charms to seduce those mindless barbarians outside, but I'll not fall prey to your magicks.
Try and cast a spell on me and I guarantee you'll live to regret it.
Now there's the Loki I was looking for.

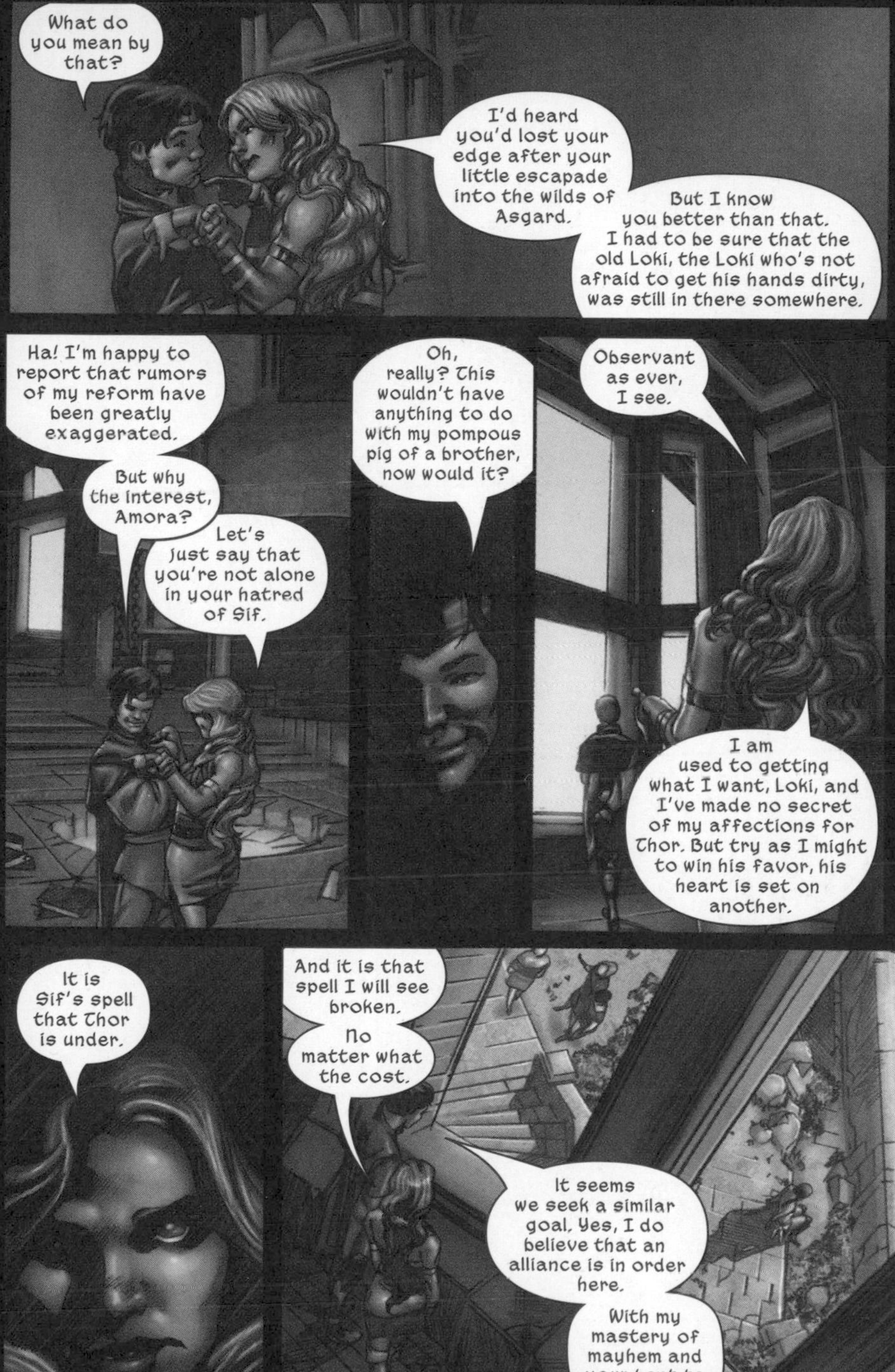
What do you mean by that?
I'd heard you'd lost your edge after your little escapade into the wilds of Asgard.
But I know you better than that. I had to be sure that the old Loki, the Loki who's not afraid to get his hands dirty, was still in there somewhere.
Ha! I'm happy to report that rumors of my reform have been greatly exaggerated.
But why the interest, Amora?
Let's just say that you're not alone in your hatred of Sif.
Oh, really? This wouldn't have anything to do with my pompous pig of a brother, now would it?
Observant as ever, I see.
I am used to getting what I want, Loki, and I've made no secret of my affections for Thor. But try as I might to win his favor, his heart is set on another.
It is Sif's spell that Thor is under.
And it is that spell I will see broken.
No matter what the cost.
It seems we seek a similar goal. Yes, I do believe that an alliance is in order here.
With my mastery of mayhem and your bent to bewitch...

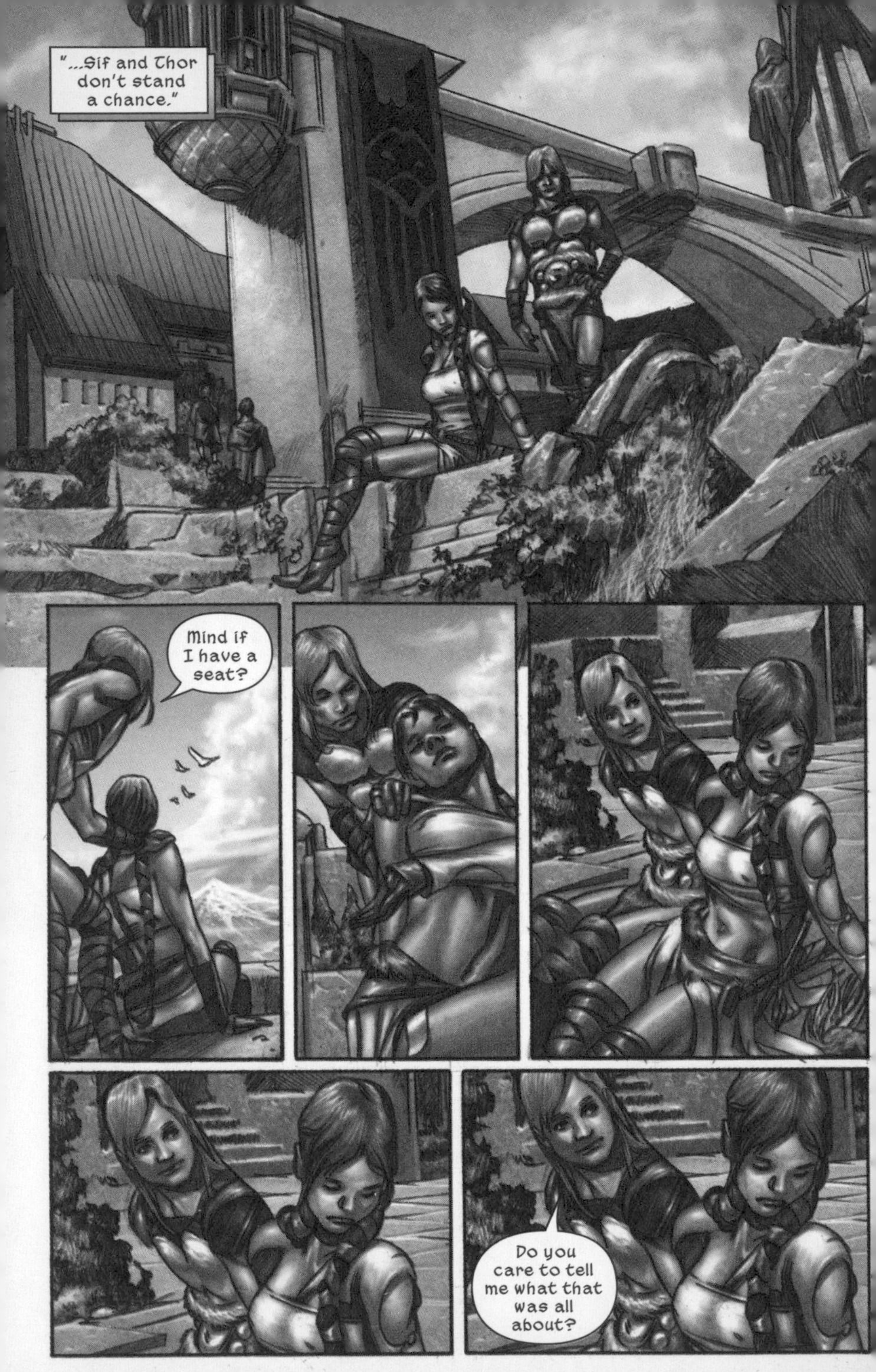
"...Sif and Thor don't stand a chance."
Mind if I have a seat?
Do you care to tell me what that was all about?

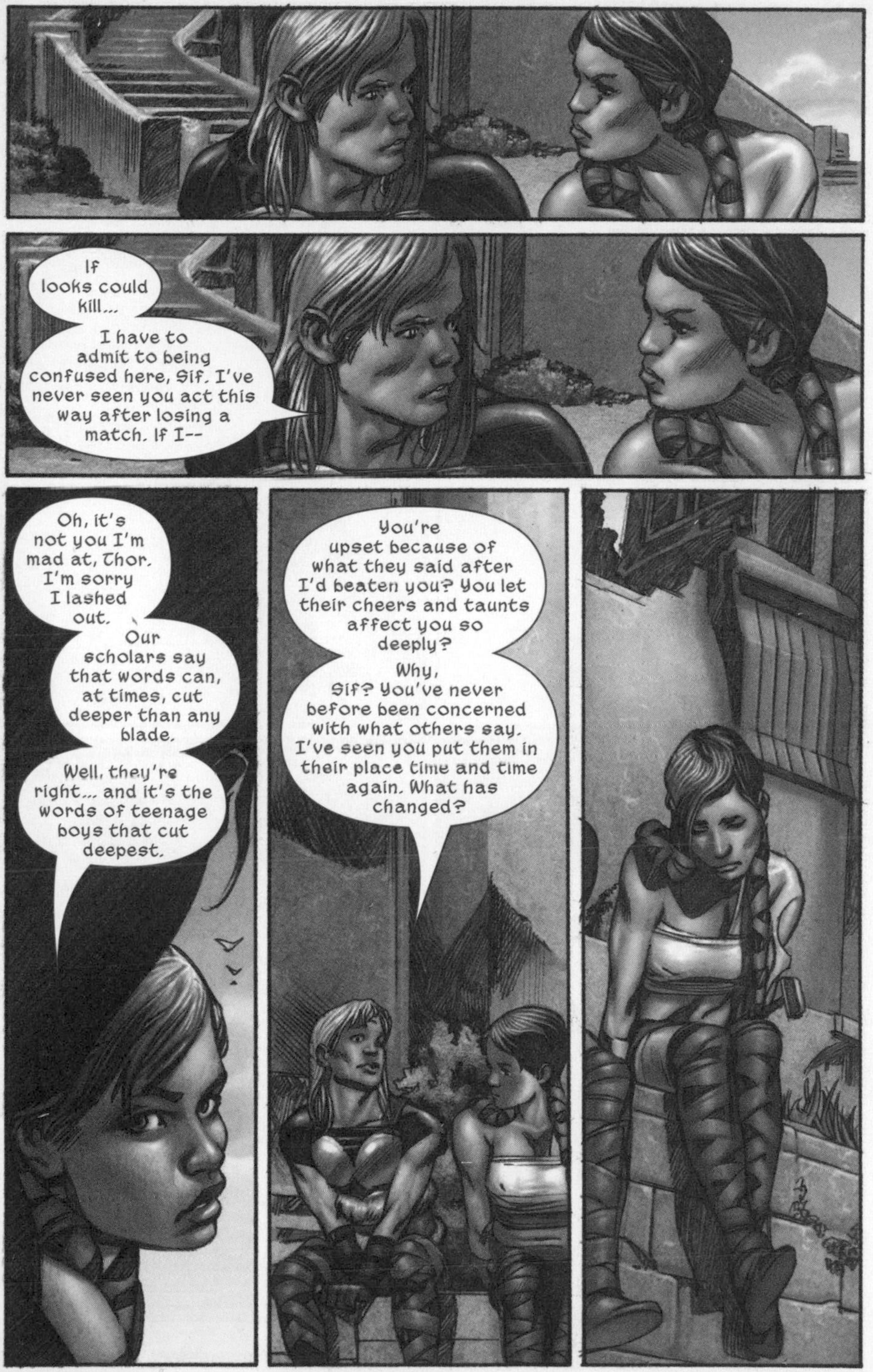
If looks could kill...
I have to admit to being confused here, Sif. I've never seen you act this way after losing a match. If I--
Oh, it's not you I'm mad at, Thor. I'm sorry I lashed out.
Our scholars say that words can, at times, cut deeper than any blade.
Well, they're right... and it's the words of teenage boys that cut deepest.
You're upset because of what they said after I'd beaten you? You let their cheers and taunts affect you so deeply?
Why, Sif? You've never before been concerned with what others say. I've seen you put them in their place time and time again. What has changed?

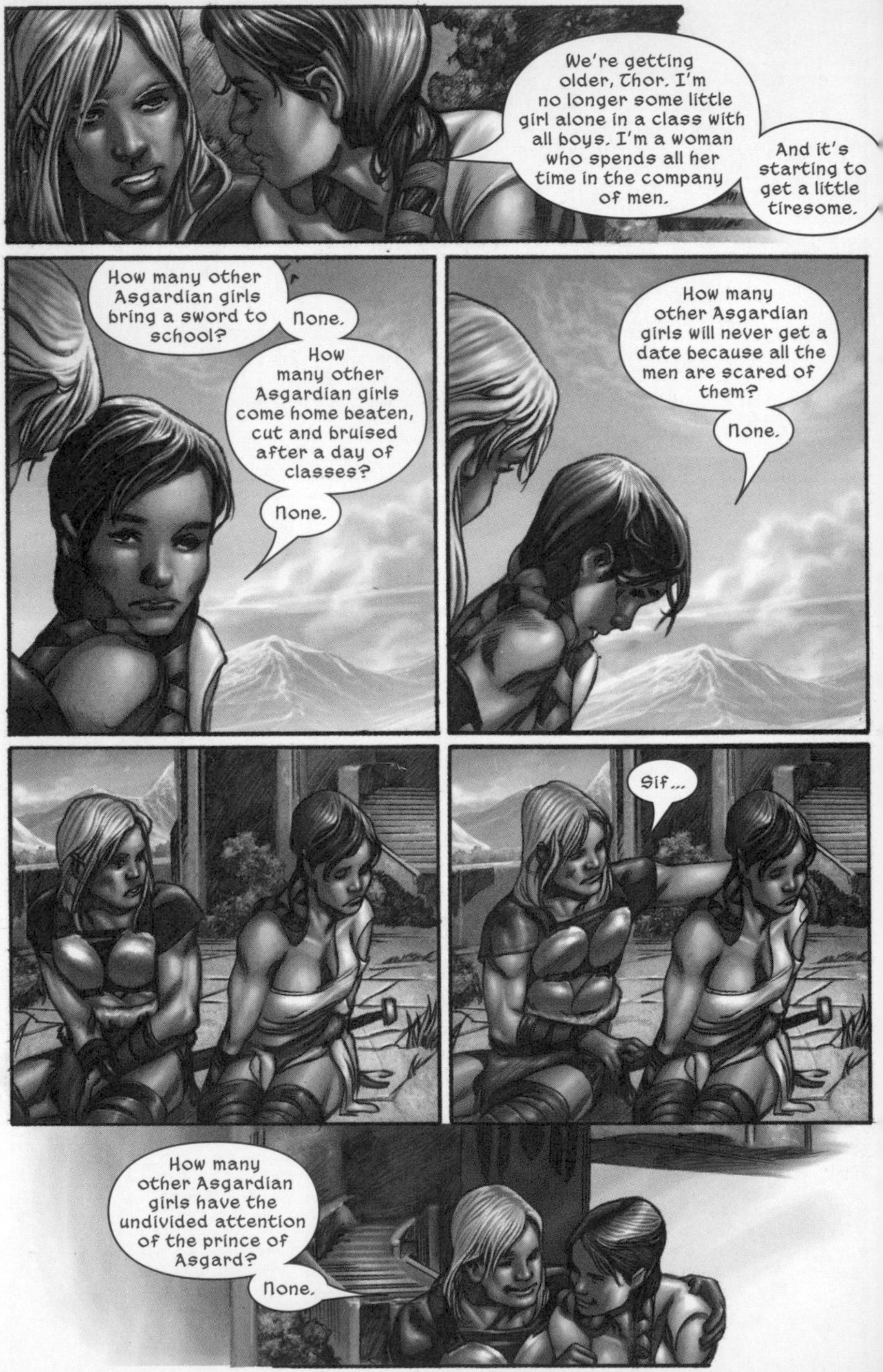

We're getting older, Thor. I'm no longer some little girl alone in a class with all boys. I'm a woman who spends all her time in the company of men.
And it's starting to get a little tiresome.
How many other Asgardian girls bring a sword to school?
None.
How many other Asgardian girls come home beaten, cut and bruised after a day of classes?
None.
How many other Asgardian girls will never get a date because all the men are scared of them?
None.
Sif...
How many other Asgardian girls have the undivided attention of the prince of Asgard?
None.

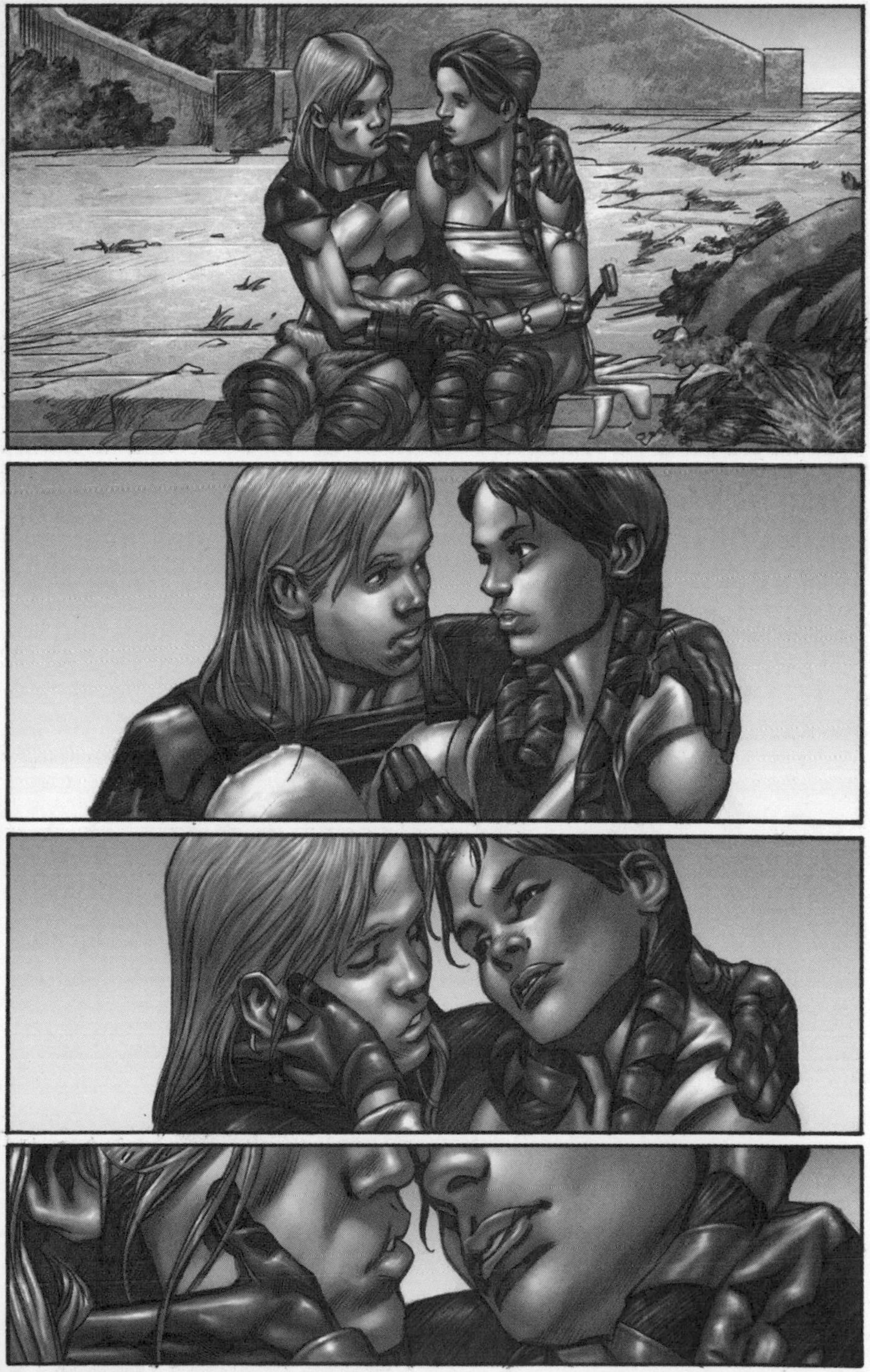

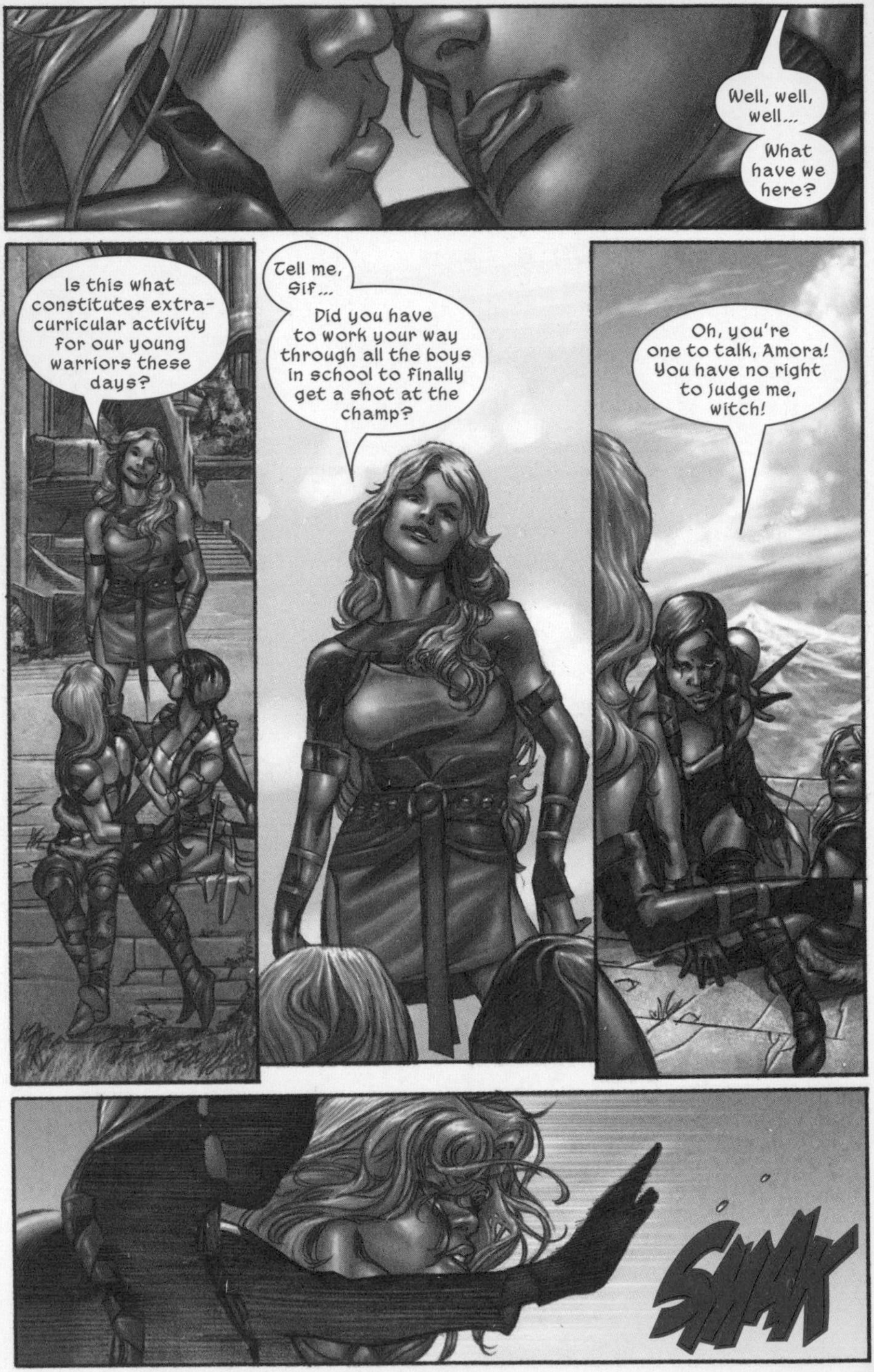
Well, well, well...
What have we here?
Is this what constitutes extra-curricular activity for our young warriors these days?
Tell me, Sif...
Did you have to work your way through all the boys in school to finally get a shot at the champ?
Oh, you're one to talk, Amora! You have no right to judge me, witch!
SHAK

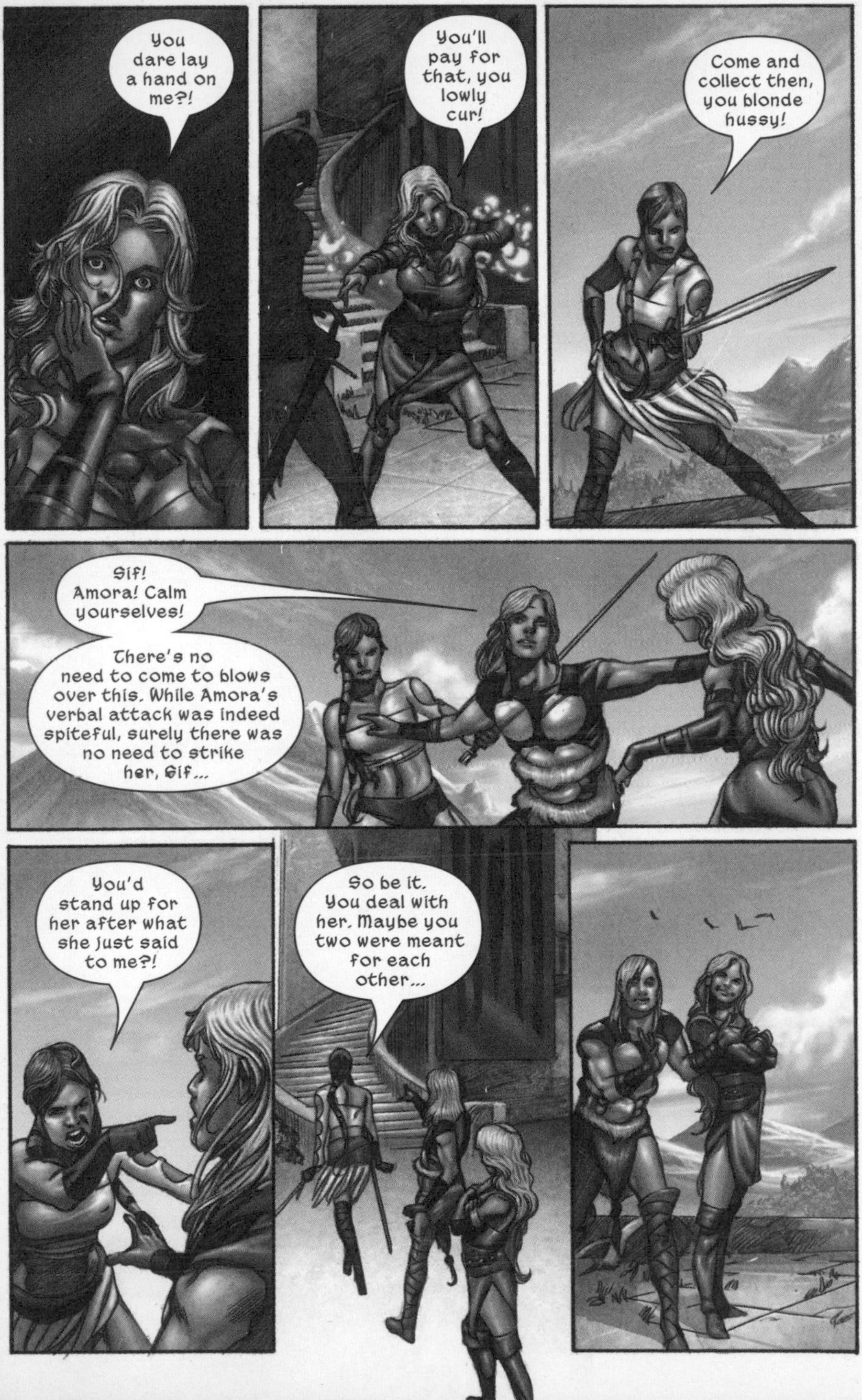
You dare lay a hand on me?!
You'll pay for that, you lowly cur!
Come and collect then, you blonde hussy!
Sif! Amora! Calm yourselves!
There's no need to come to blows over this. While Amora's verbal attack was indeed spiteful, surely there was no need to strike her, Sif...
You'd stand up for her after what she just said to me?!
So be it. You deal with her. Maybe you two were meant for each other...

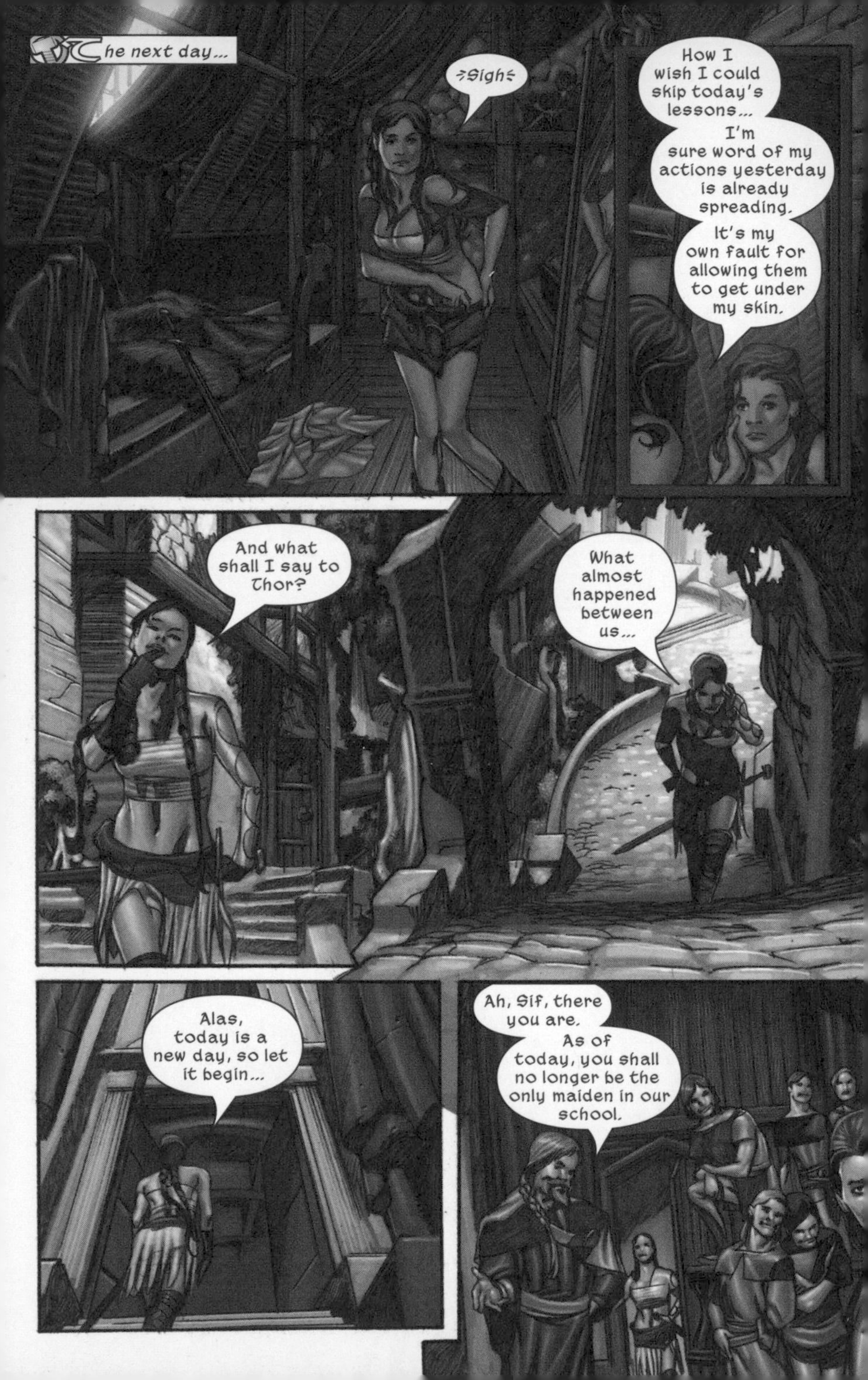
The next day...
⇌Sigh⇌
How I wish I could skip today's lessons...
I'm sure word of my actions yesterday is already spreading.
It's my own fault for allowing them to get under my skin.
And what shall I say to Thor?
What almost happened between us...
Alas, today is a new day, so let it begin...
Ah, Sif, there you are.
As of today, you shall no longer be the only maiden in our school.

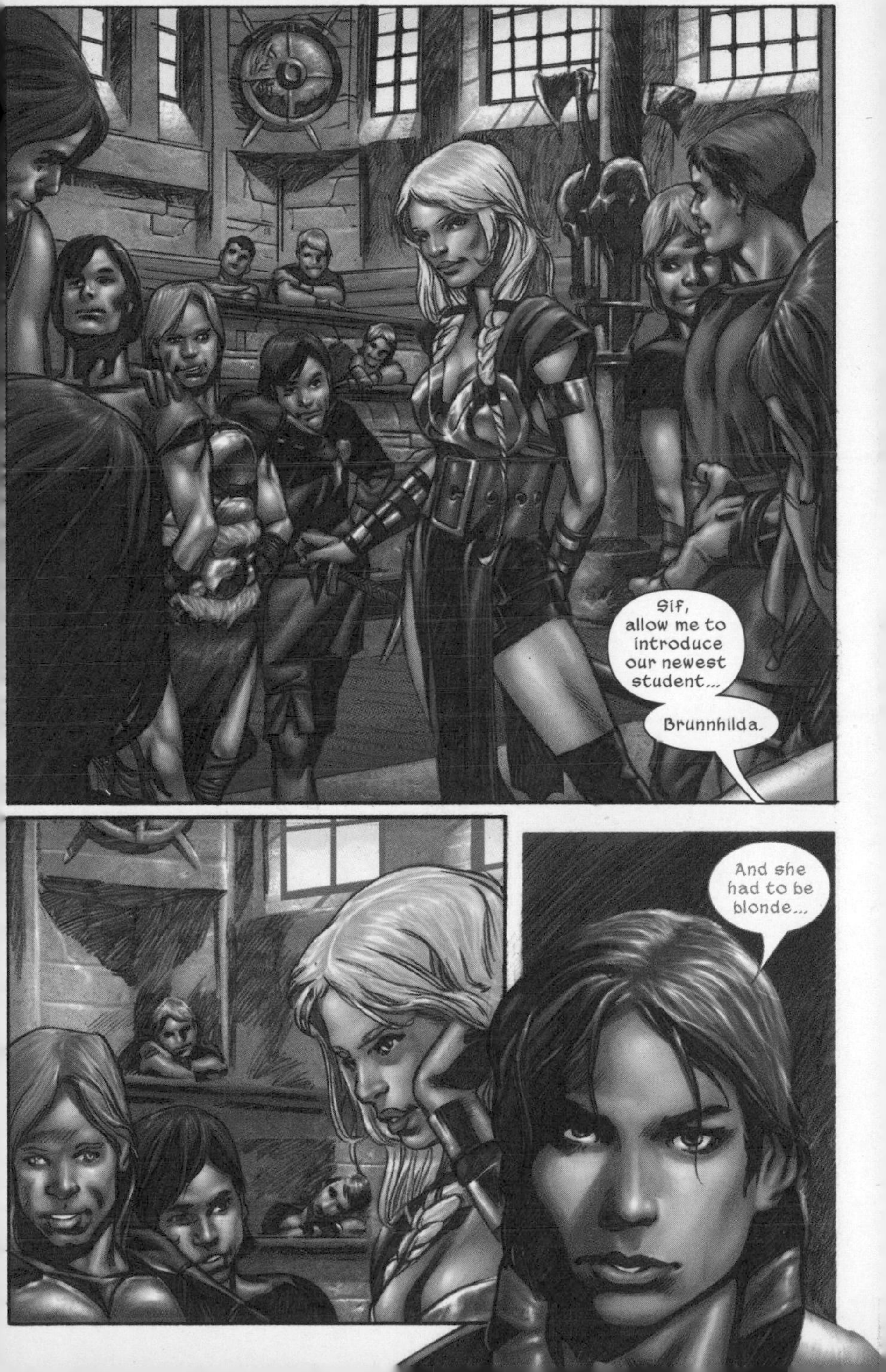
Sif, allow me to introduce our newest student...
Brunnhilda.
And she had to be blonde...

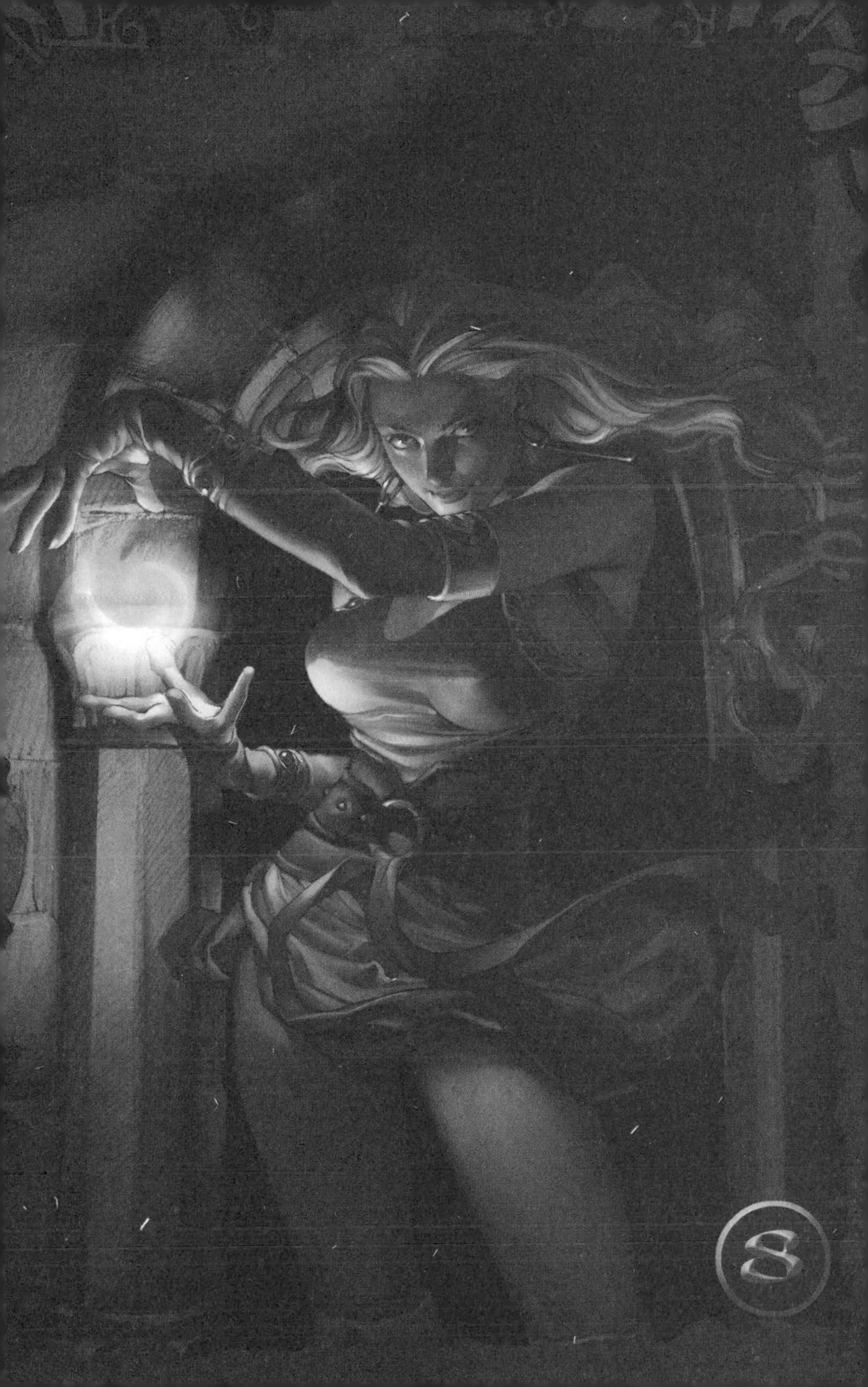
8

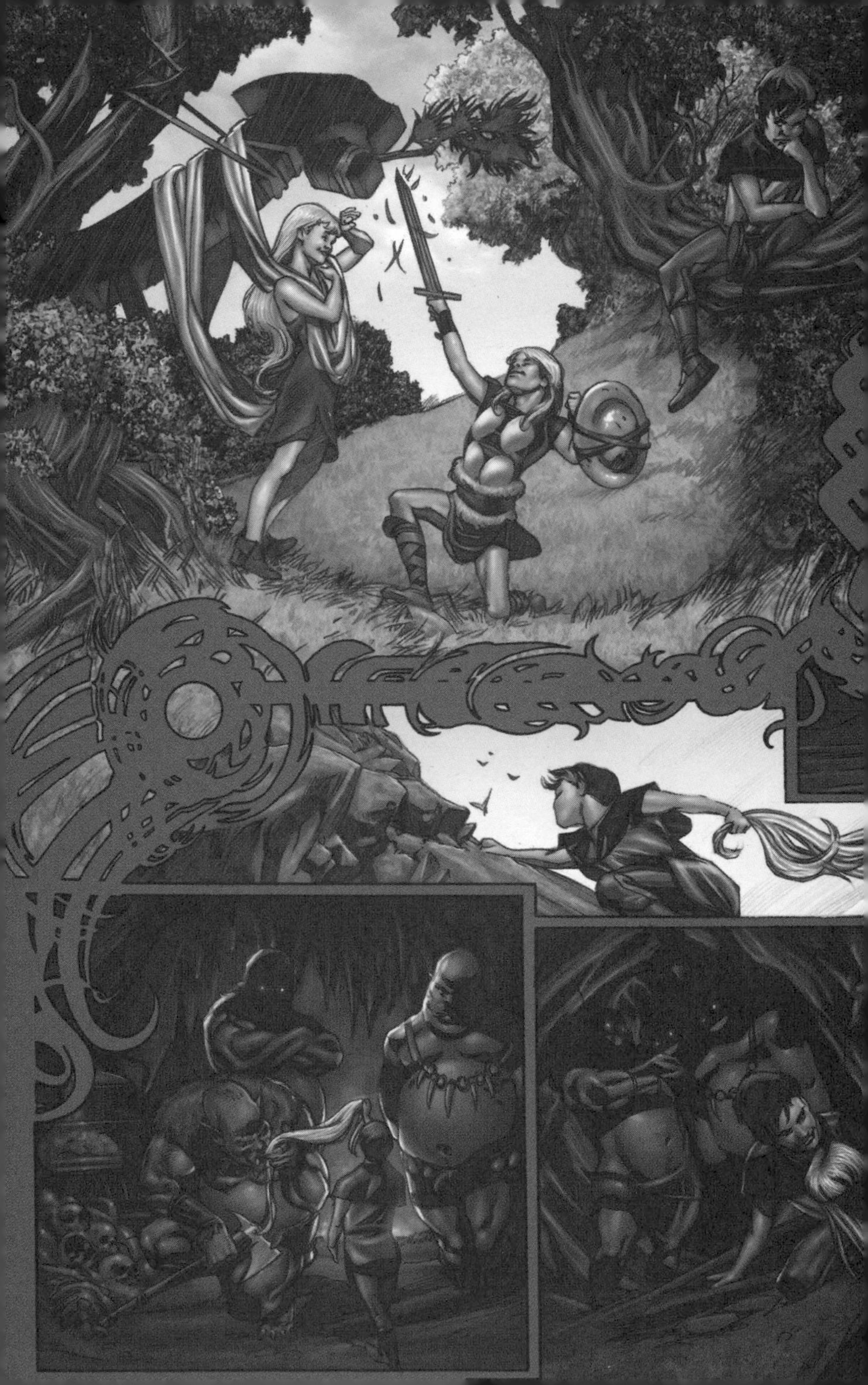

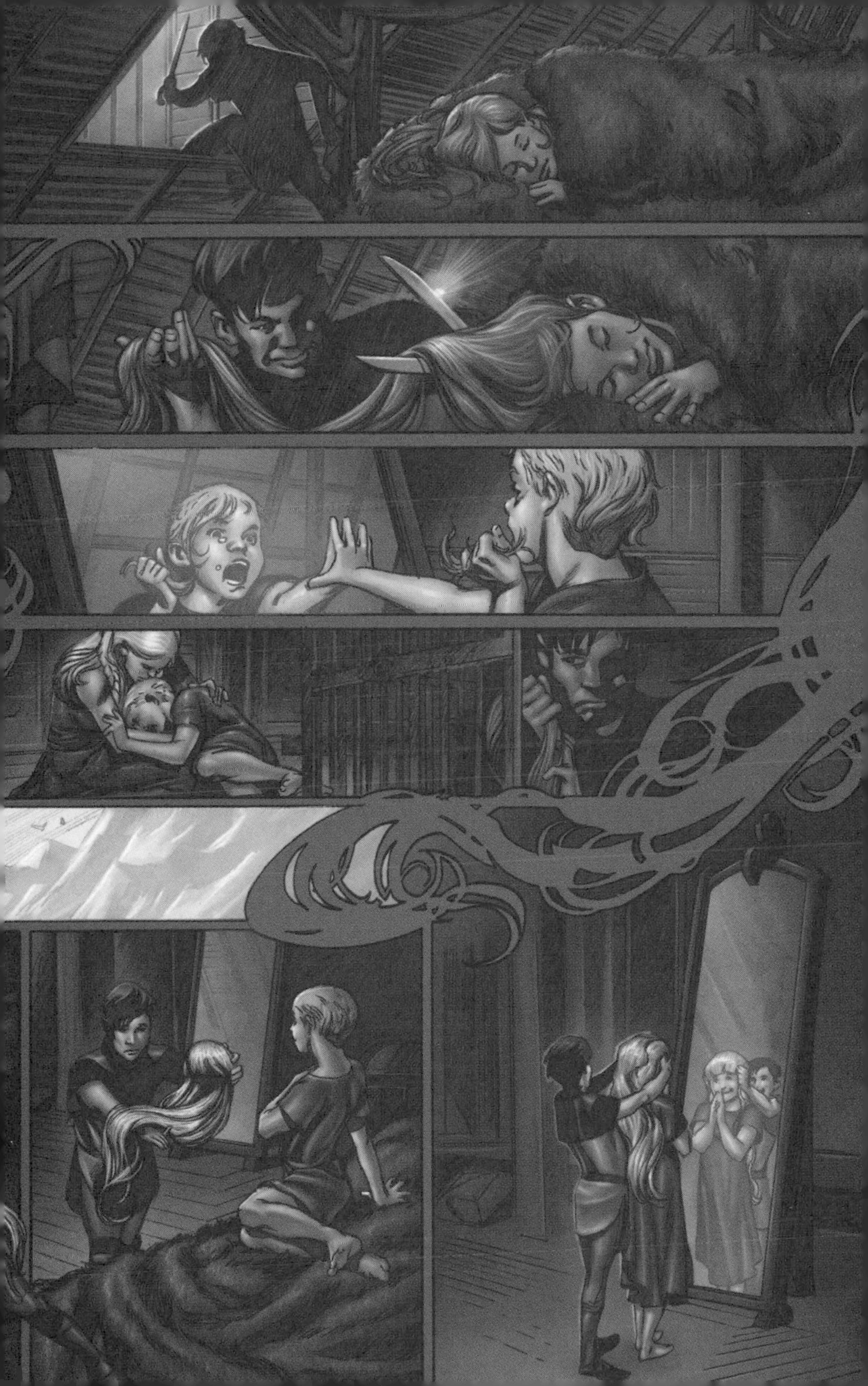

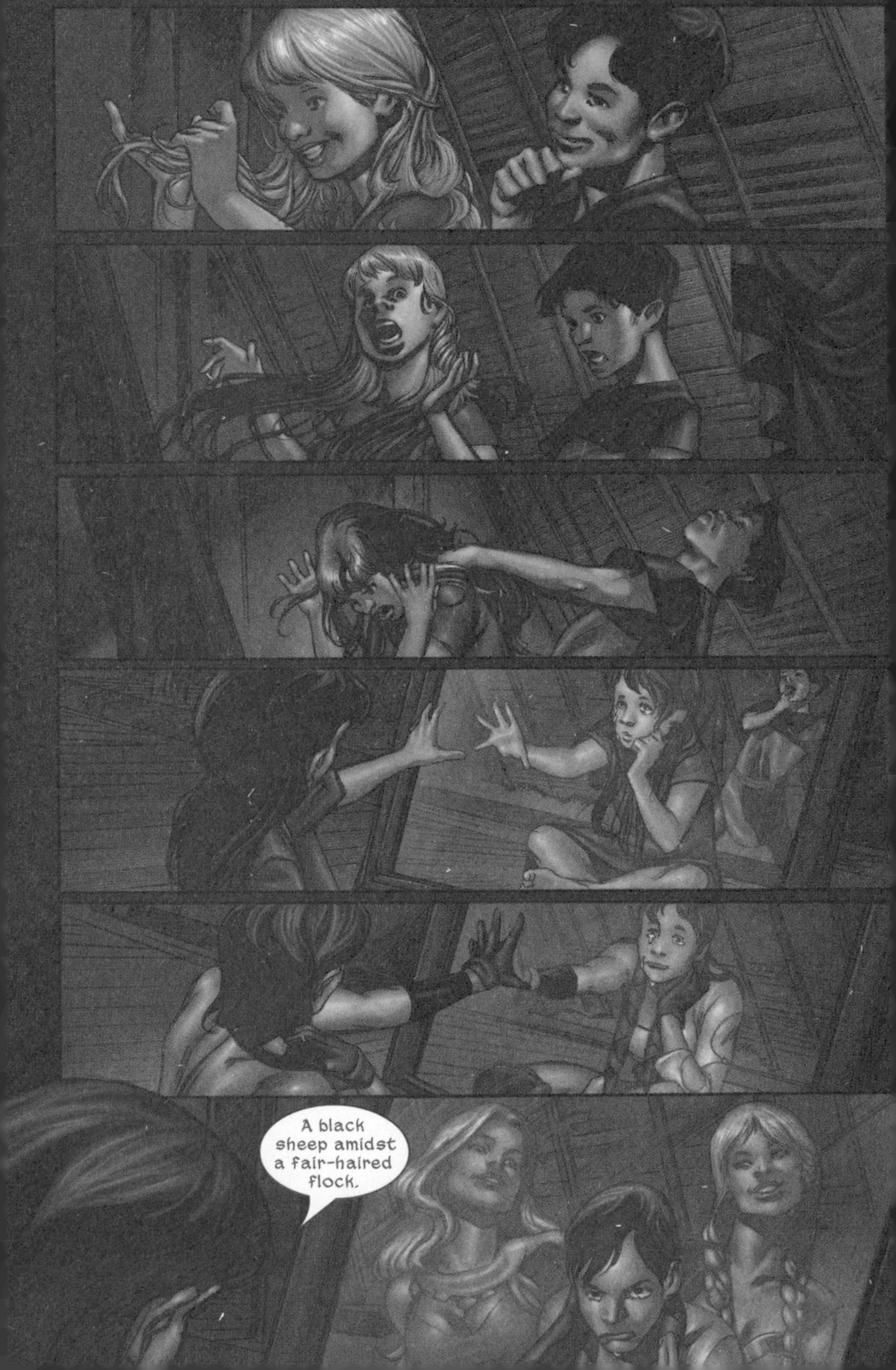
A black sheep amidst a fair-haired flock.

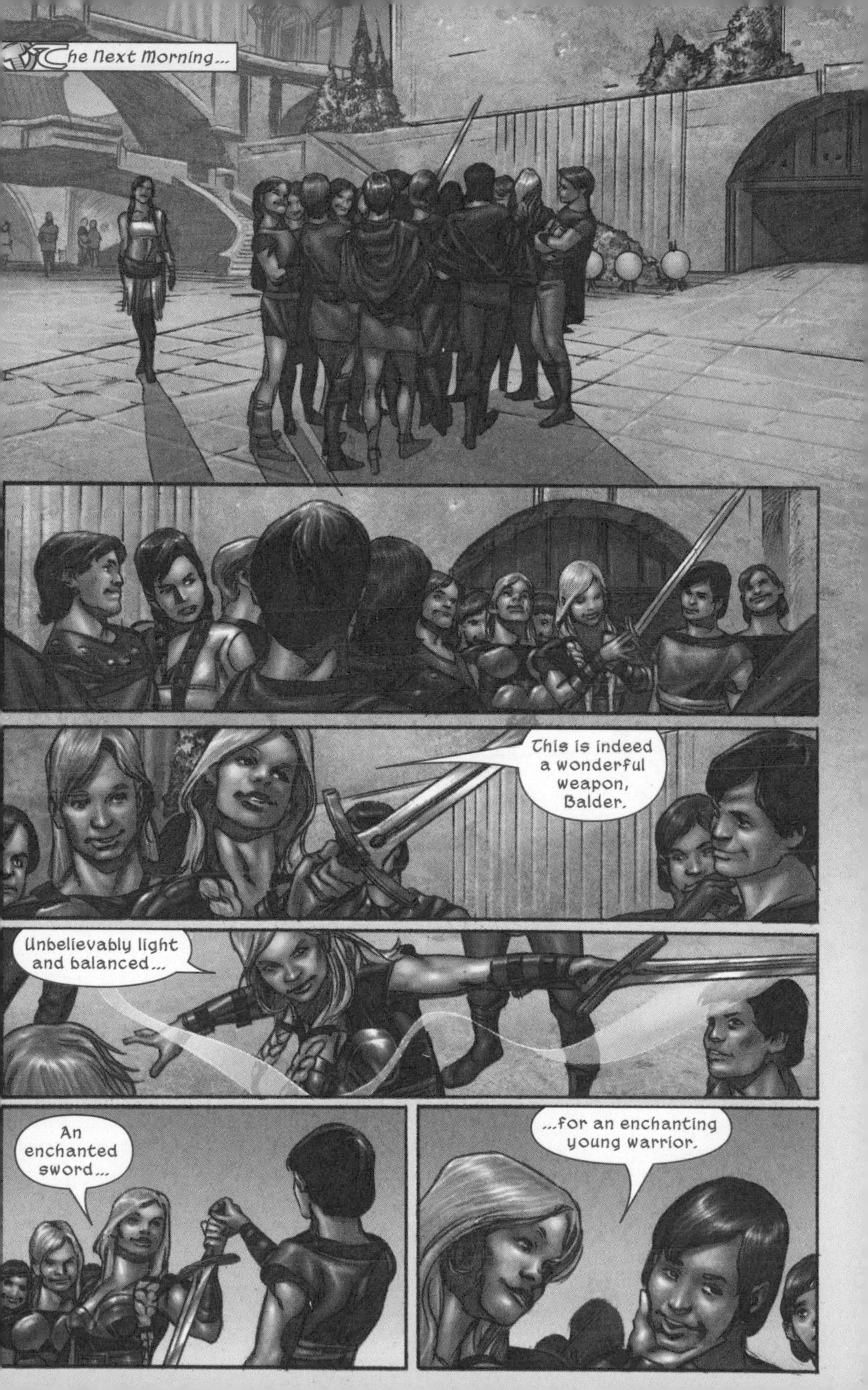
The Next Morning...
This is indeed a wonderful weapon, Balder.
Unbelievably light and balanced...
An enchanted sword...
...for an enchanting young warrior.

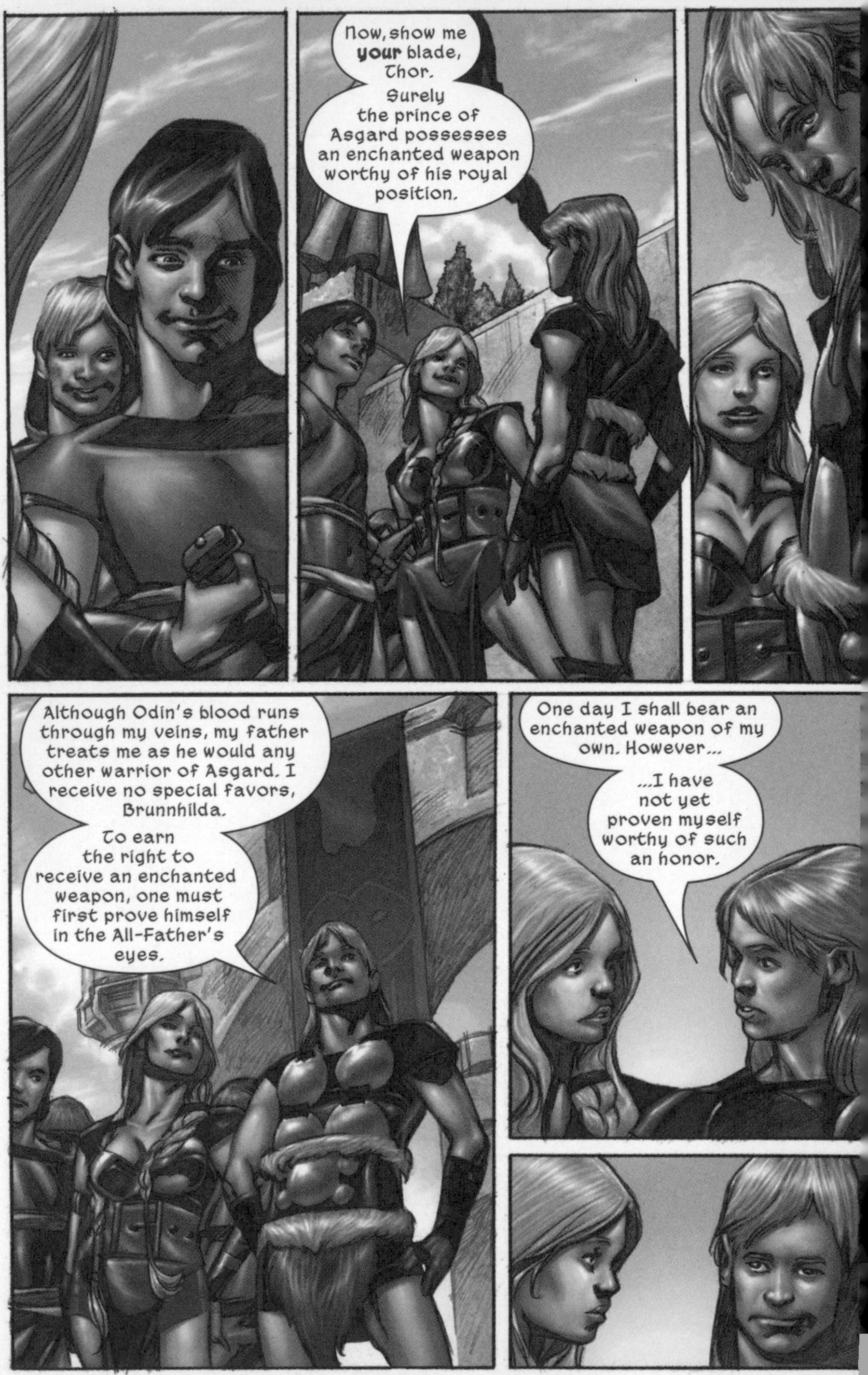
Now, show me **your** blade, Thor.
Surely the prince of Asgard possesses an enchanted weapon worthy of his royal position.
Although Odin's blood runs through my veins, my father treats me as he would any other warrior of Asgard. I receive no special favors, Brunnhilda.
To earn the right to receive an enchanted weapon, one must first prove himself in the All-Father's eyes.
One day I shall bear an enchanted weapon of my own. However...
...I have not yet proven myself worthy of such an honor.

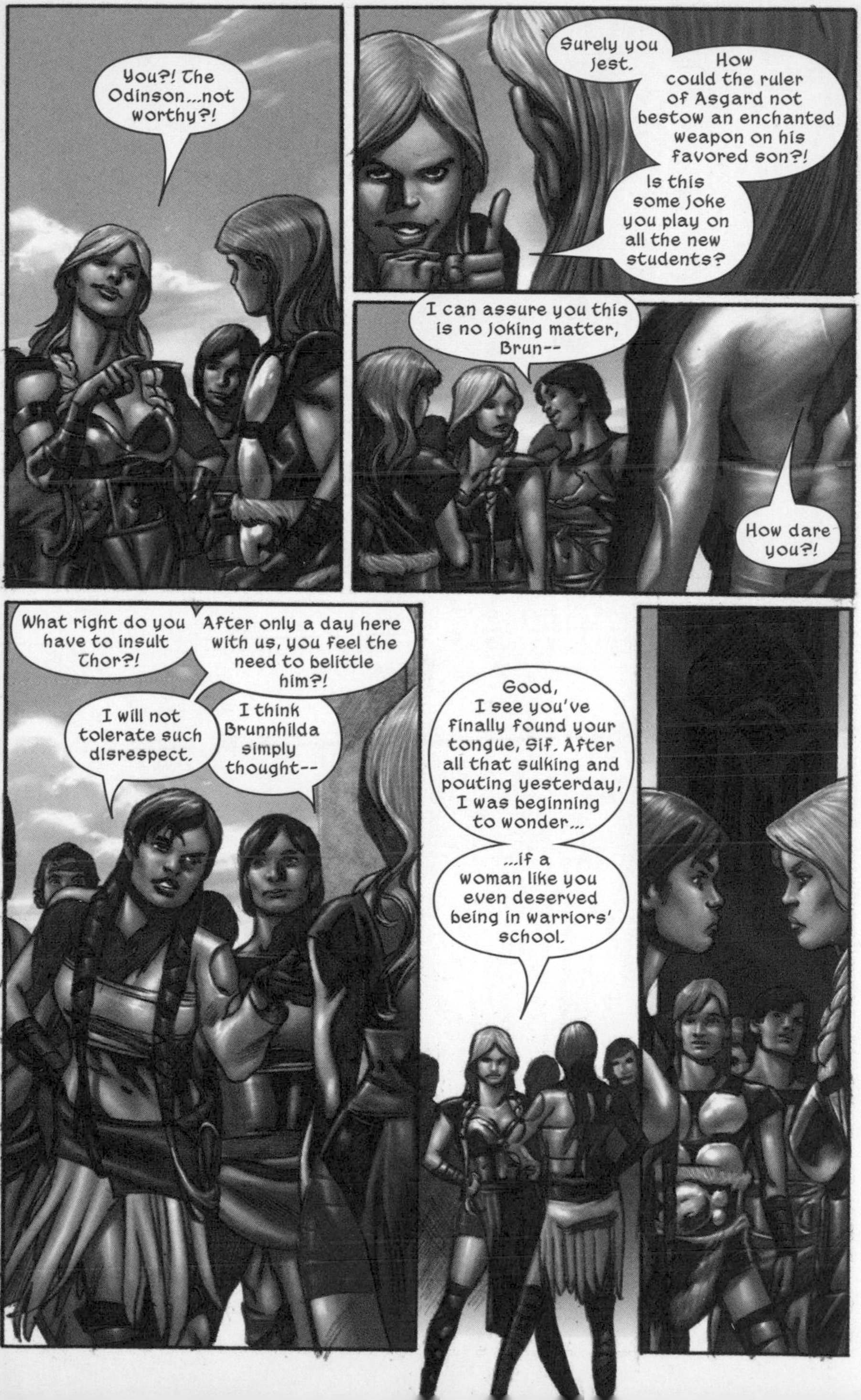
You?! The Odinson...not worthy?!
Surely you jest.
How could the ruler of Asgard not bestow an enchanted weapon on his favored son?!
Is this some joke you play on all the new students?
I can assure you this is no joking matter, Brun--
How dare you?!
What right do you have to insult Thor?!
After only a day here with us, you feel the need to belittle him?!
I will not tolerate such disrespect.
I think Brunnhilda simply thought--
Good, I see you've finally found your tongue, Sif. After all that sulking and pouting yesterday, I was beginning to wonder...
...if a woman like you even deserved being in warriors' school.

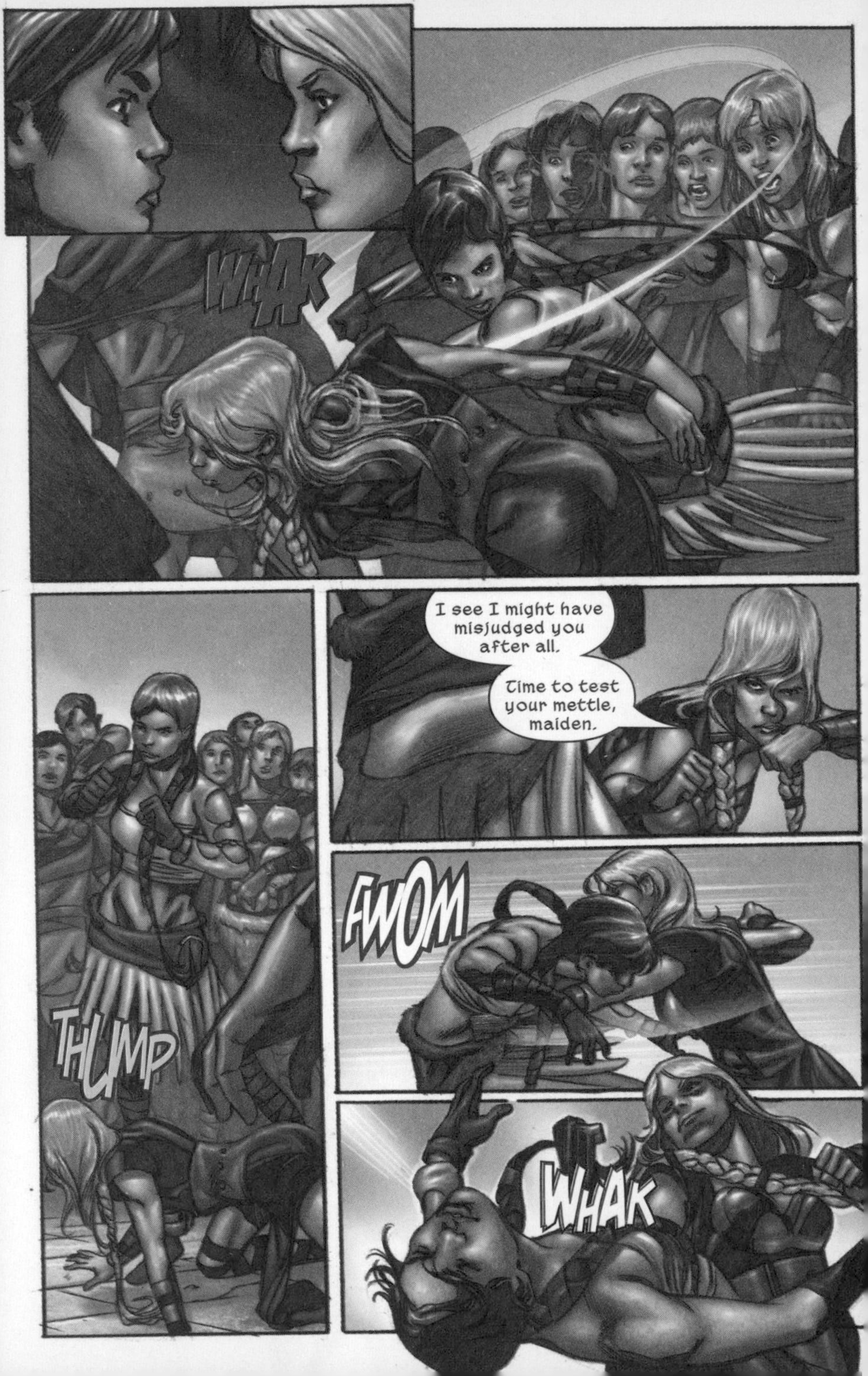
WHAK
I see I might have misjudged you after all.
Time to test your mettle, maiden.
THUMP
FWOM
WHAK

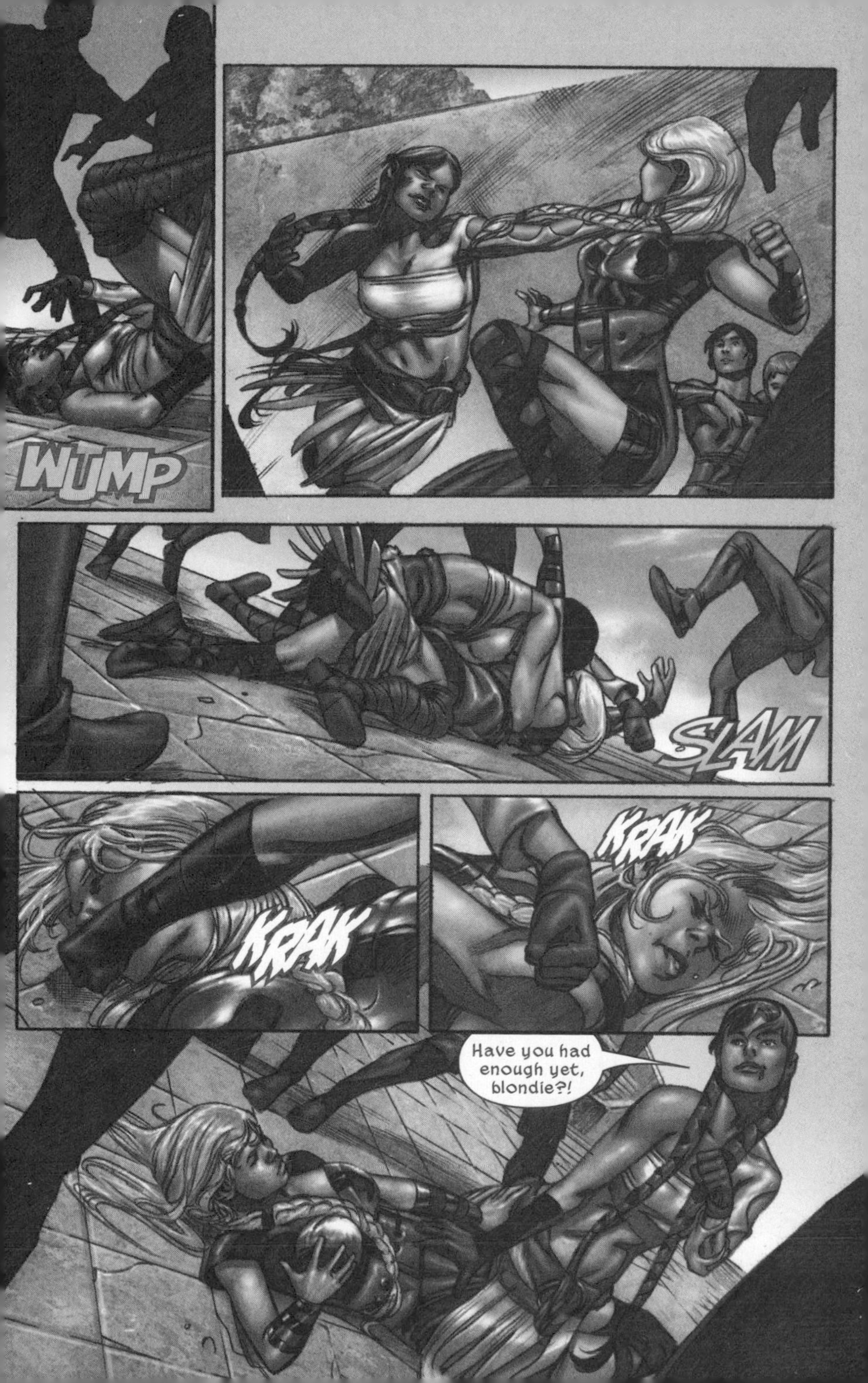
WUMP
SLAM
KRAK
KRAK
Have you had enough yet, blondie?!

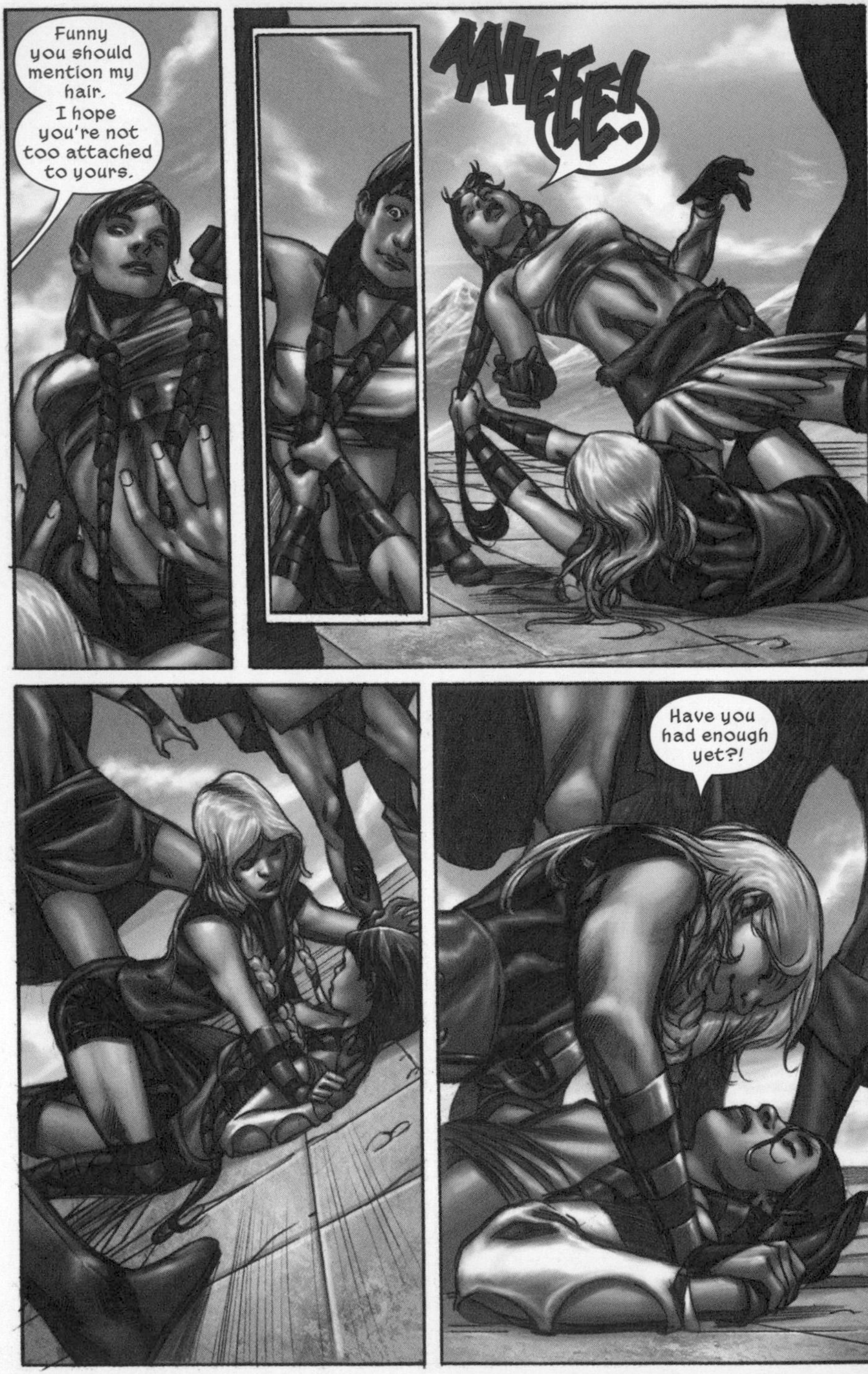

Funny you should mention my hair. I hope you're not too attached to yours.
AAHIEEEE!
Have you had enough yet?!

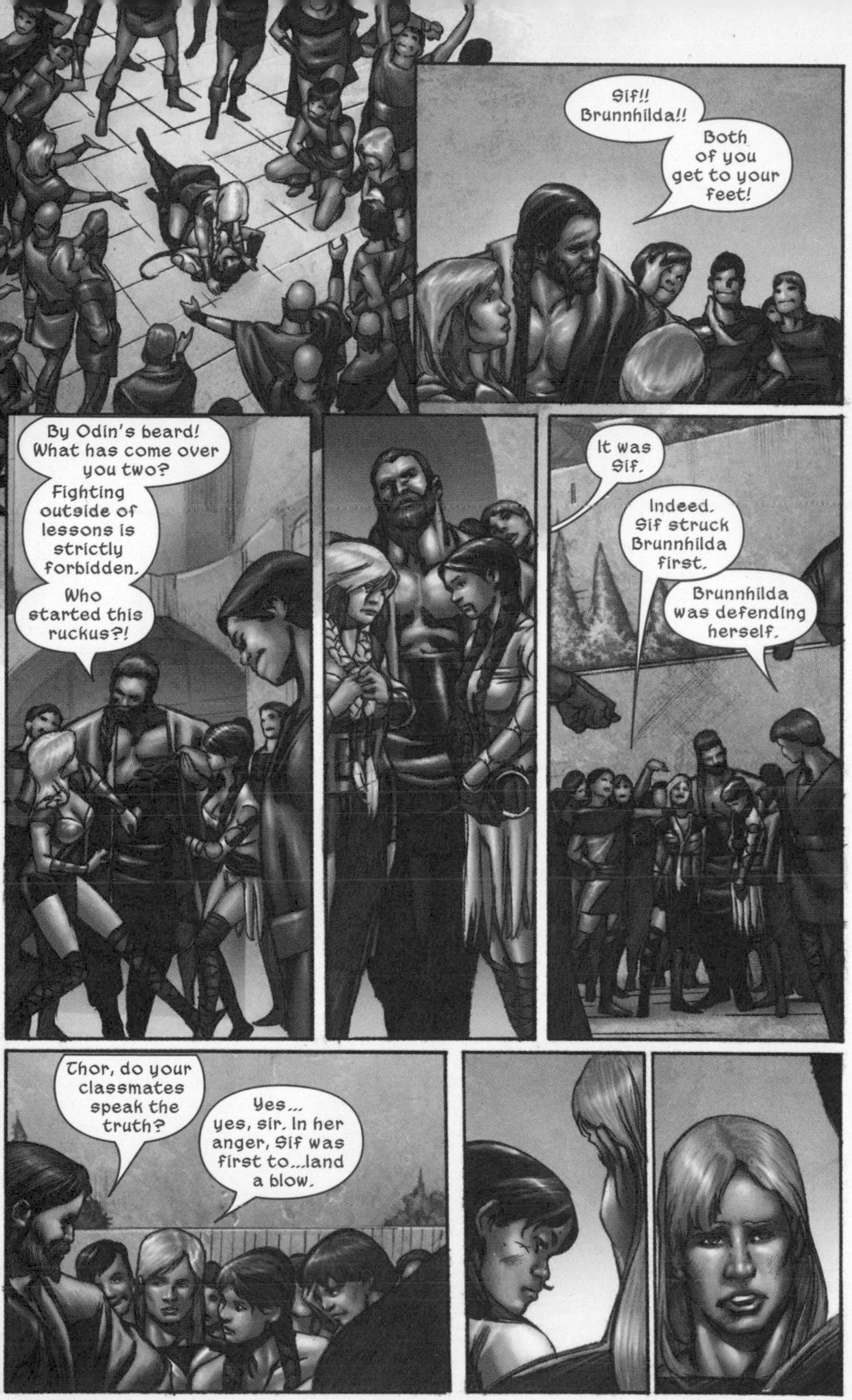
Sif!! Brunnhilda!!
Both of you get to your feet!
By Odin's beard! What has come over you two?
Fighting outside of lessons is strictly forbidden.
Who started this ruckus?!
It was Sif.
Indeed. Sif struck Brunnhilda first.
Brunnhilda was defending herself.
Thor, do your classmates speak the truth?
Yes... yes, sir. In her anger, Sif was first to...land a blow.

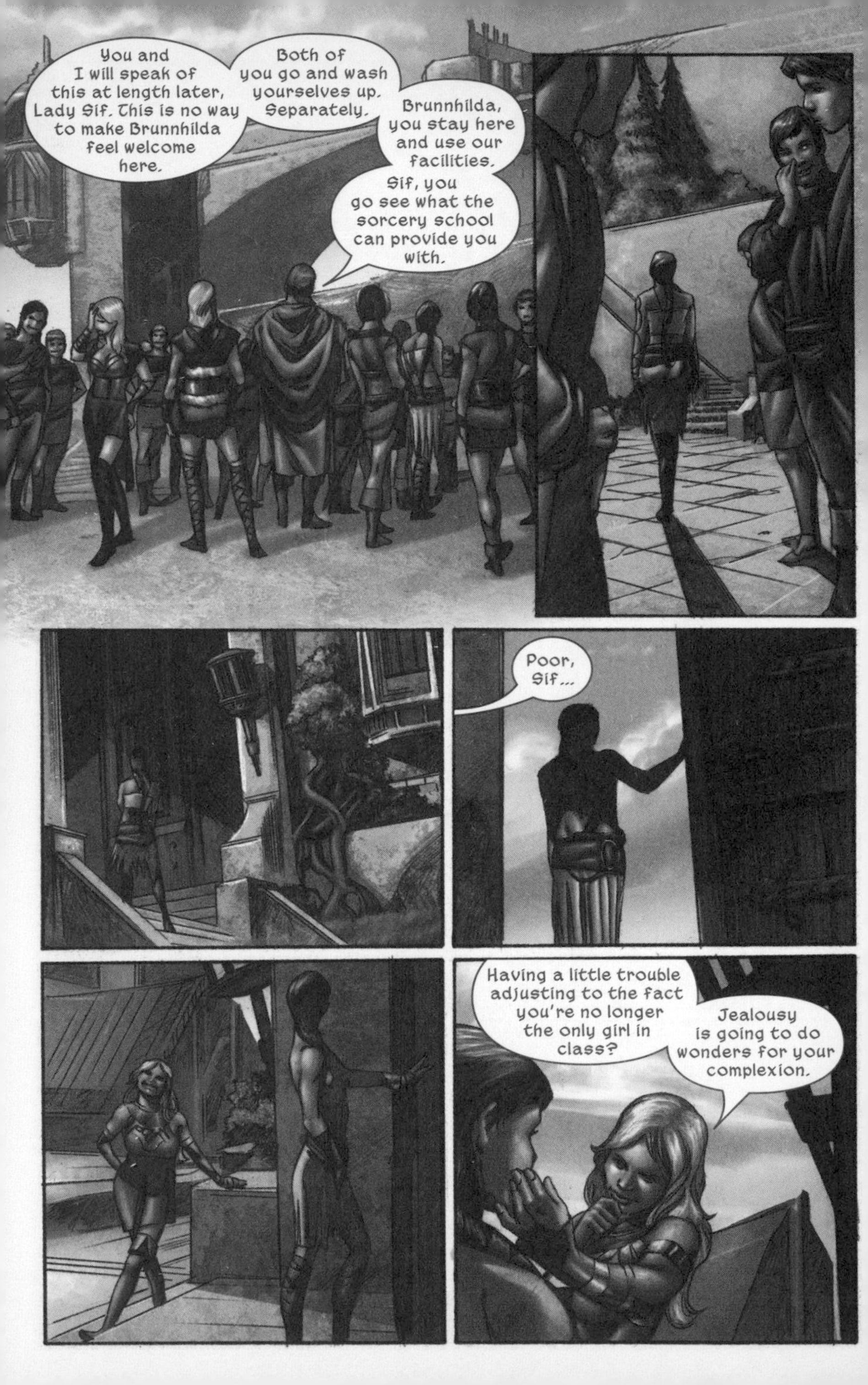
You and I will speak of this at length later, Lady Sif. This is no way to make Brunnhilda feel welcome here.
Both of you go and wash yourselves up. Separately.
Brunnhilda, you stay here and use our facilities.
Sif, you go see what the sorcery school can provide you with.
Poor, Sif...
Having a little trouble adjusting to the fact you're no longer the only girl in class?
Jealousy is going to do wonders for your complexion.

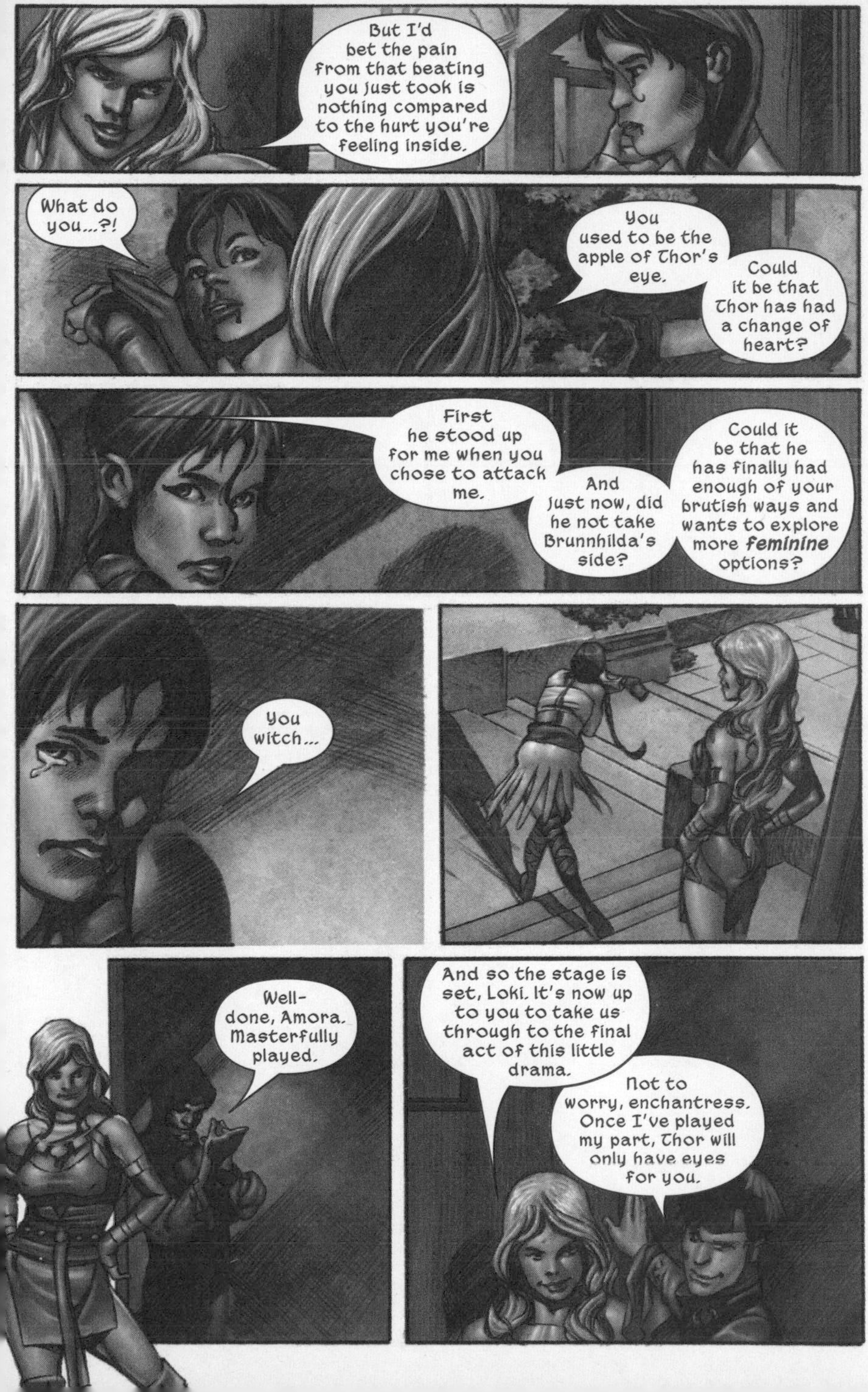
But I'd bet the pain from that beating you just took is nothing compared to the hurt you're feeling inside.
What do you...?!
You used to be the apple of Thor's eye.
Could it be that Thor has had a change of heart?
First he stood up for me when you chose to attack me.
And just now, did he not take Brunnhilda's side?
Could it be that he has finally had enough of your brutish ways and wants to explore more *feminine* options?
You witch...
Well-done, Amora. Masterfully played.
And so the stage is set, Loki. It's now up to you to take us through to the final act of this little drama.
Not to worry, enchantress. Once I've played my part, Thor will only have eyes for you.

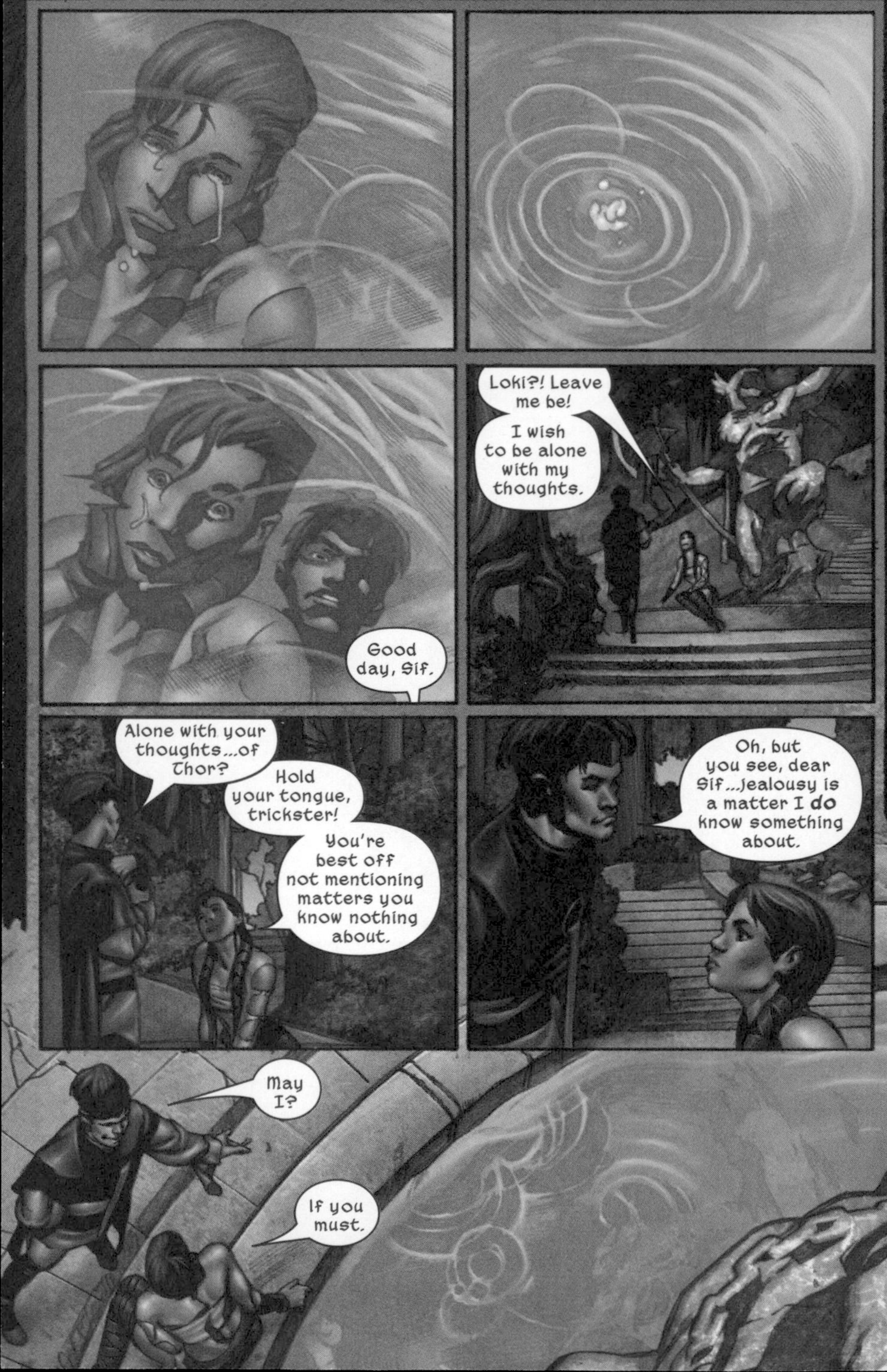
Good day, Sif.
Loki?! Leave me be!
I wish to be alone with my thoughts.
Alone with your thoughts...of Thor?
Hold your tongue, trickster!
You're best off not mentioning matters you know nothing about.
Oh, but you see, dear Sif...jealousy is a matter I do know something about.
May I?
If you must.

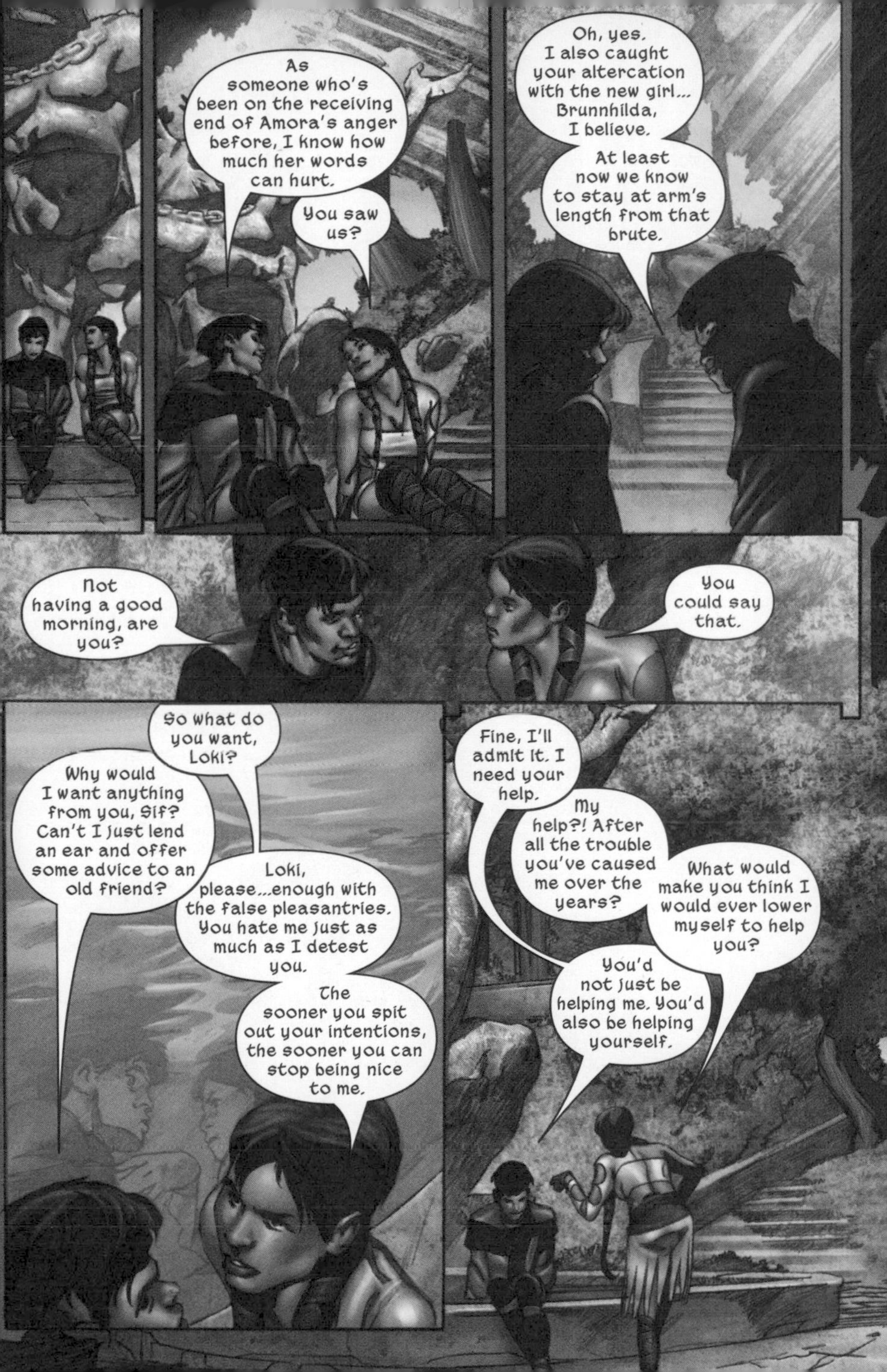
As someone who's been on the receiving end of Amora's anger before, I know how much her words can hurt.
You saw us?
Oh, yes. I also caught your altercation with the new girl... Brunnhilda, I believe.
At least now we know to stay at arm's length from that brute.
Not having a good morning, are you?
You could say that.
So what do you want, Loki?
Why would I want anything from you, Sif? Can't I just lend an ear and offer some advice to an old friend?
Loki, please...enough with the false pleasantries. You hate me just as much as I detest you.
The sooner you spit out your intentions, the sooner you can stop being nice to me.
Fine, I'll admit it. I need your help.
My help?! After all the trouble you've caused me over the years?
What would make you think I would ever lower myself to help you?
You'd not just be helping me. You'd also be helping yourself.

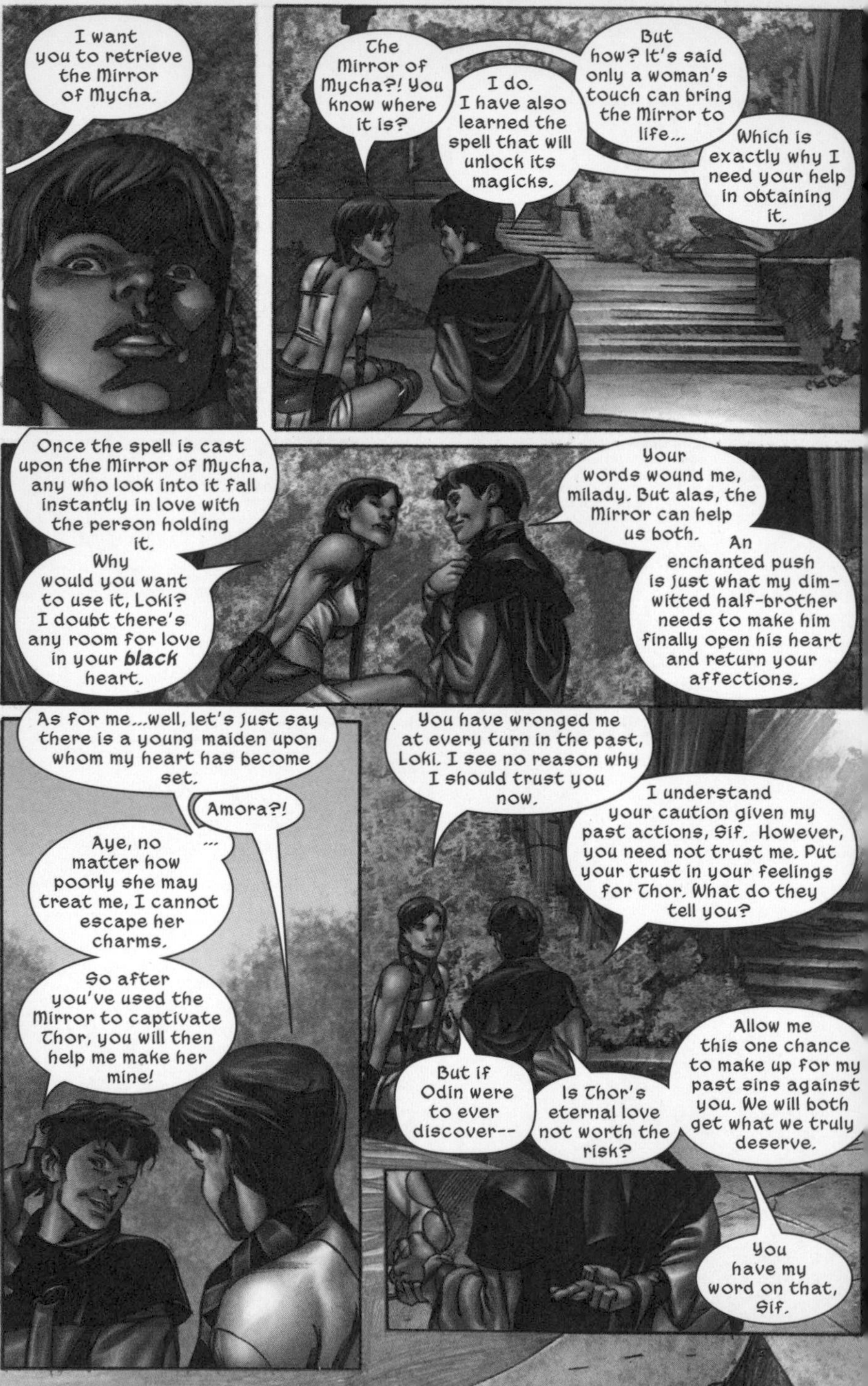

I want you to retrieve the Mirror of Mycha.
The Mirror of Mycha?! You know where it is?
I do. I have also learned the spell that will unlock its magicks.
But how? It's said only a woman's touch can bring the Mirror to life...
Which is exactly why I need your help in obtaining it.
Once the spell is cast upon the Mirror of Mycha, any who look into it fall instantly in love with the person holding it.
Why would you want to use it, Loki? I doubt there's any room for love in your black heart.
Your words wound me, milady. But alas, the Mirror can help us both.
An enchanted push is just what my dim-witted half-brother needs to make him finally open his heart and return your affections.
As for me...well, let's just say there is a young maiden upon whom my heart has become set.
Amora?!
...
Aye, no matter how poorly she may treat me, I cannot escape her charms.
So after you've used the Mirror to captivate Thor, you will then help me make her mine!
You have wronged me at every turn in the past, Loki. I see no reason why I should trust you now.
I understand your caution given my past actions, Sif. However, you need not trust me. Put your trust in your feelings for Thor. What do they tell you?
But if Odin were to ever discover--
Is Thor's eternal love not worth the risk?
Allow me this one chance to make up for my past sins against you. We will both get what we truly deserve.
You have my word on that, Sif.

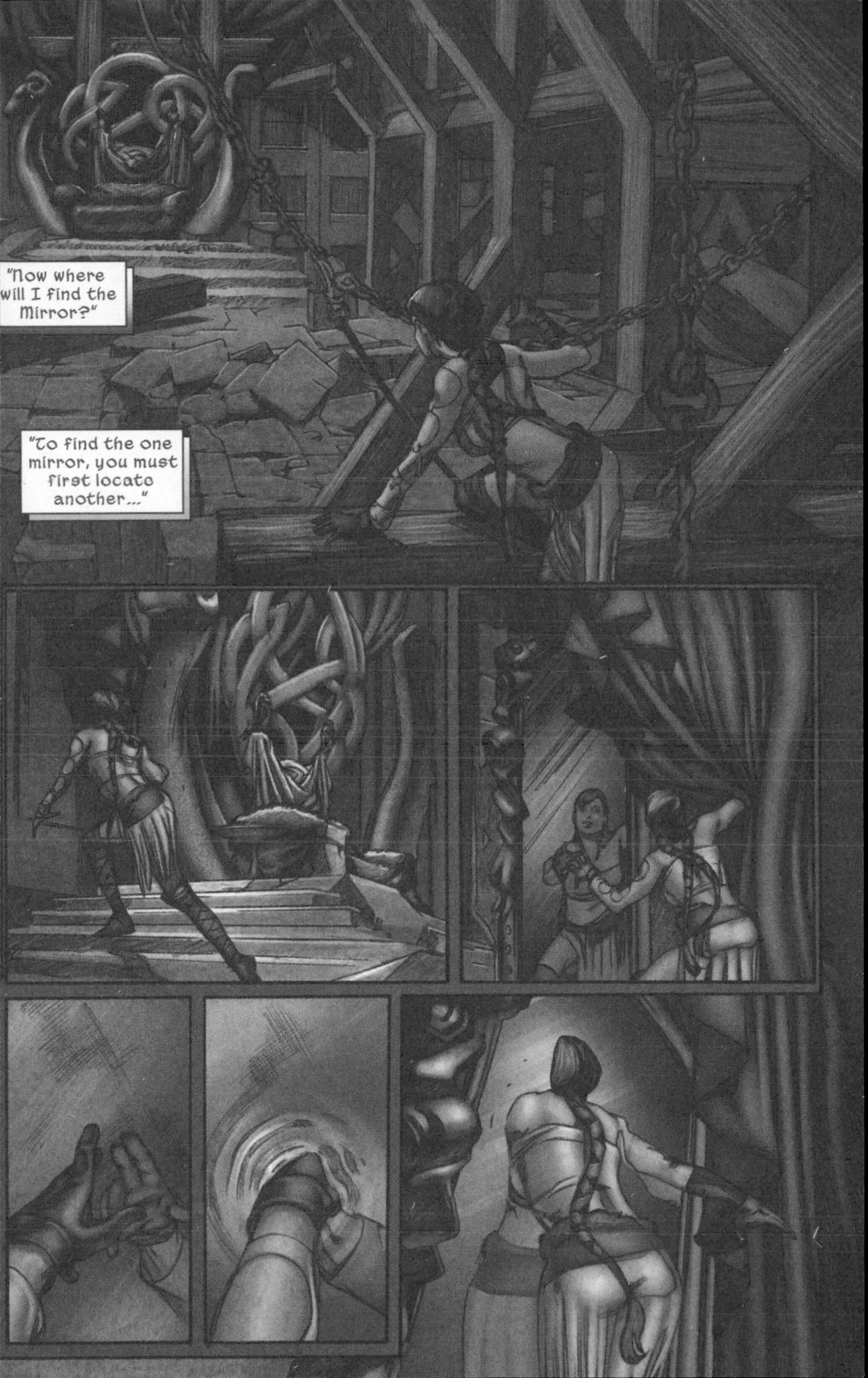
"Now where will I find the Mirror?"
"To find the one mirror, you must first locate another..."

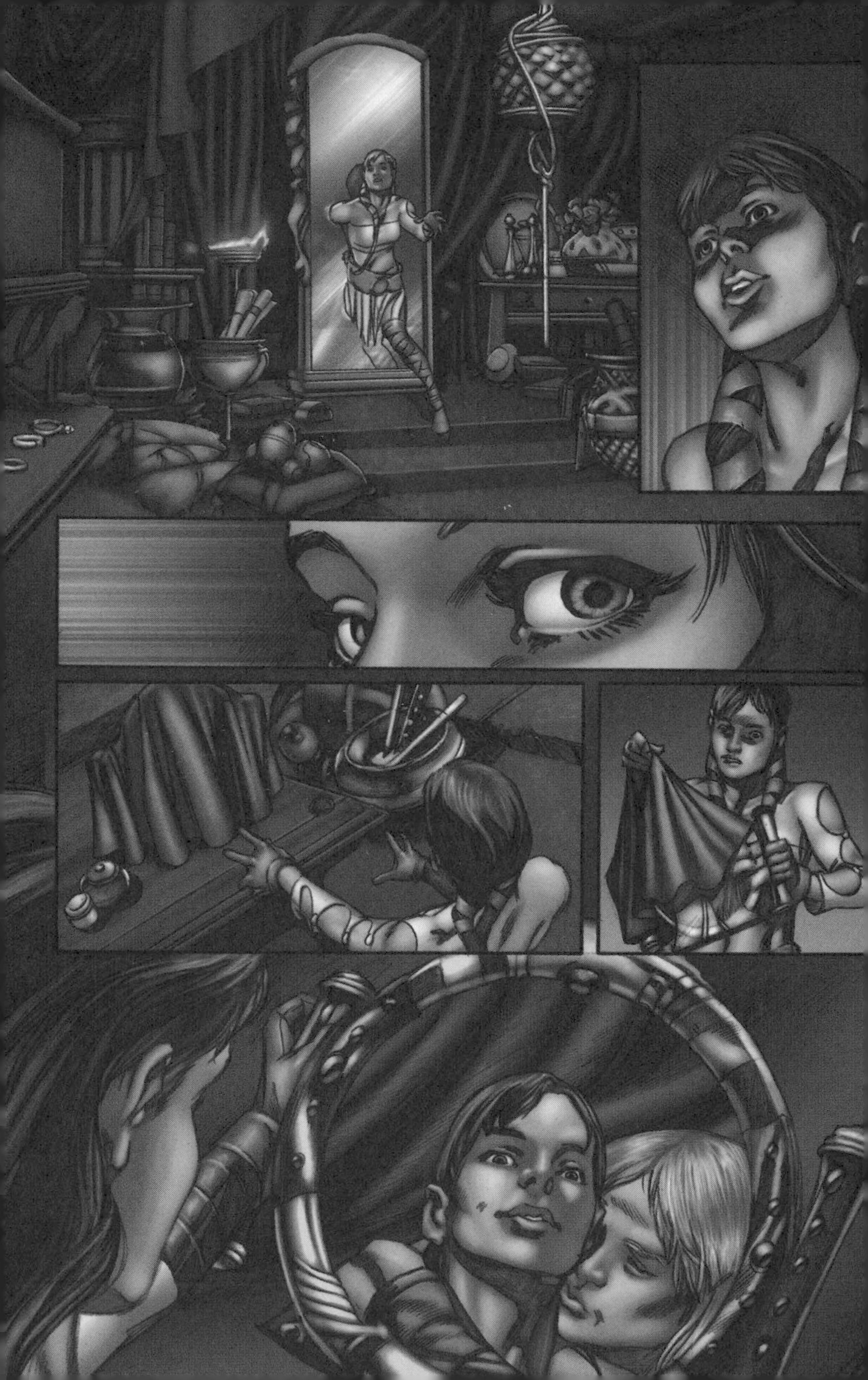

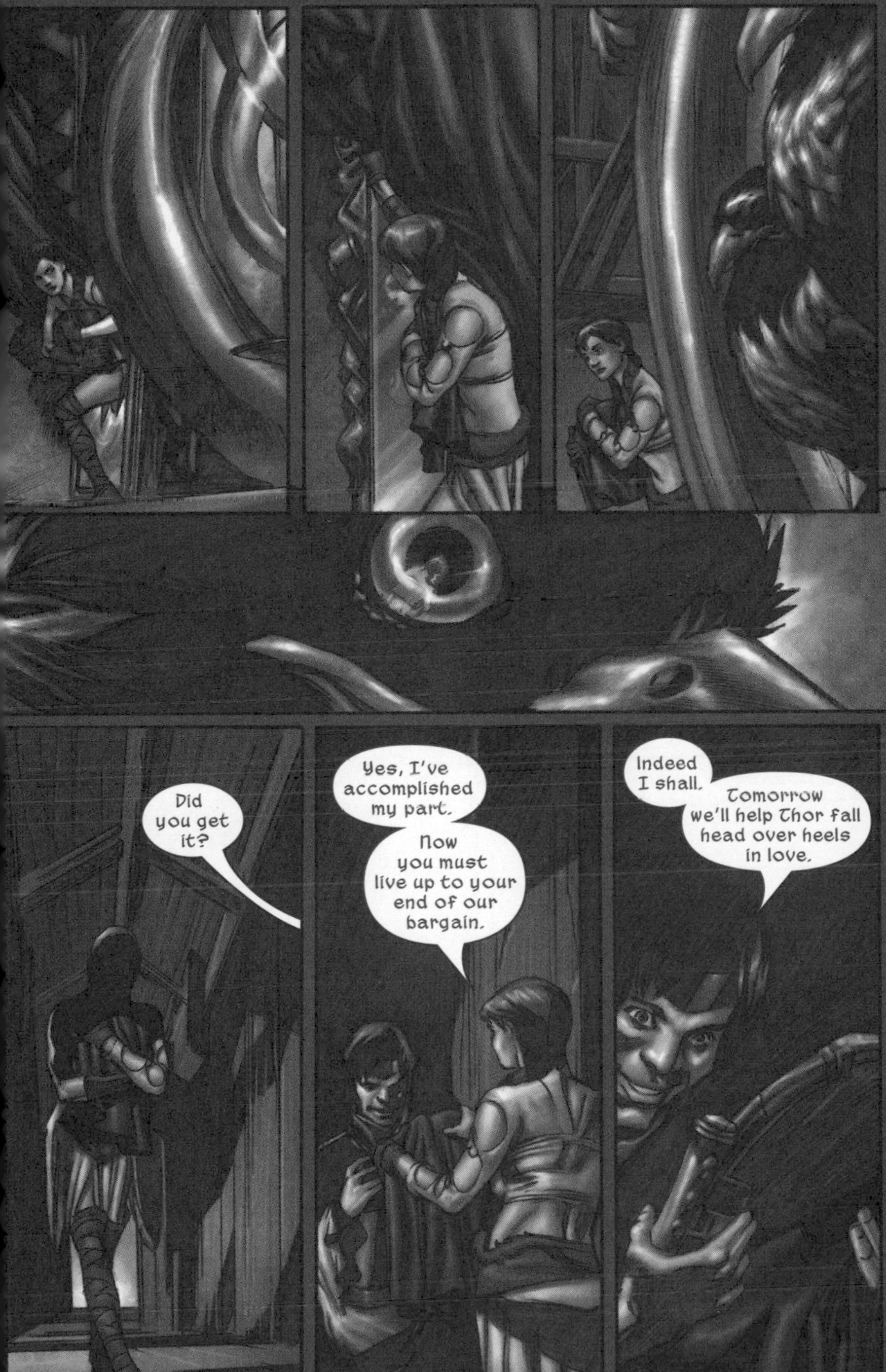
Did you get it?
Yes, I've accomplished my part.
Now you must live up to your end of our bargain.
Indeed I shall.
Tomorrow we'll help Thor fall head over heels in love.

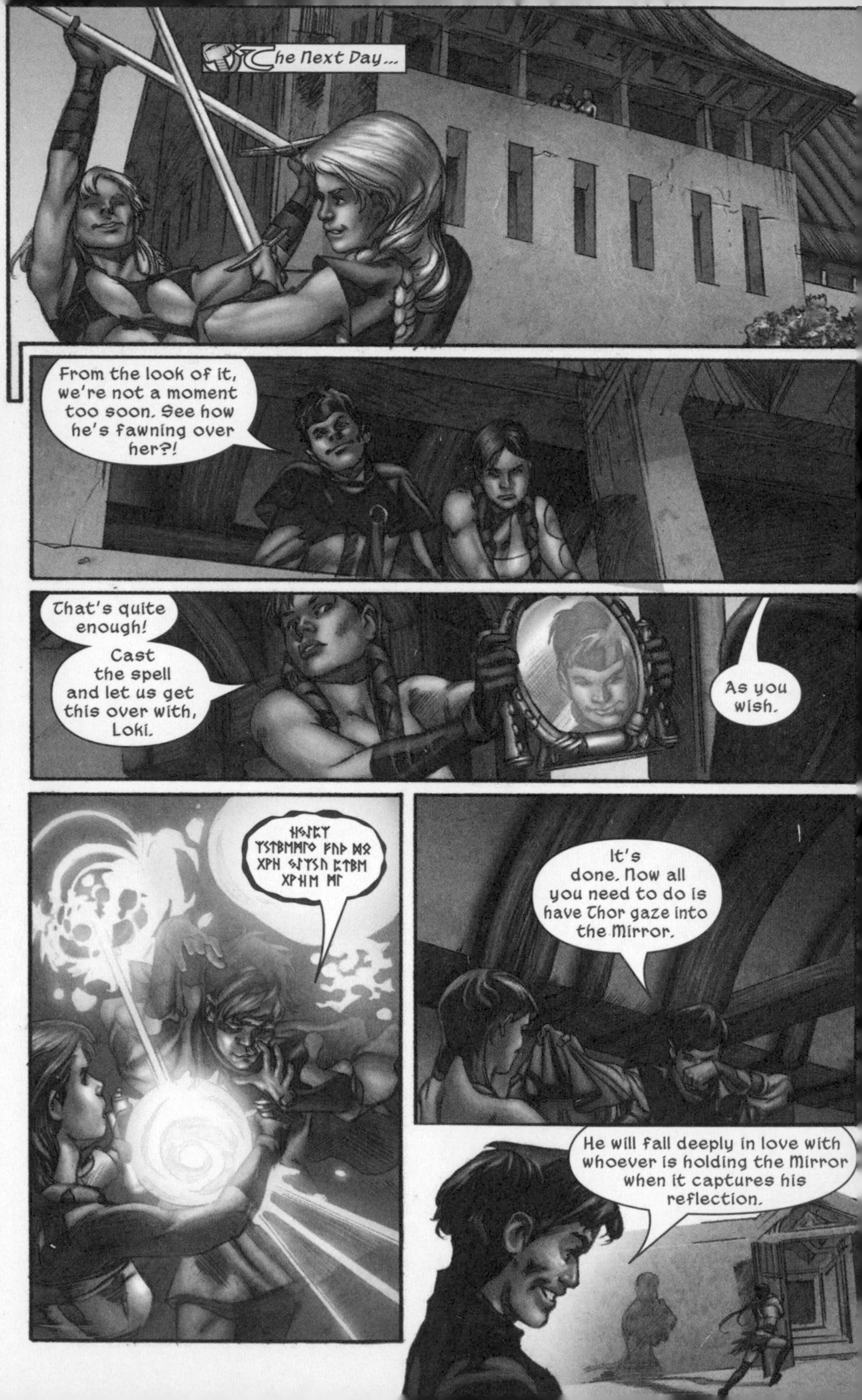
The Next Day...
From the look of it, we're not a moment too soon. See how he's fawning over her?!
That's quite enough!
Cast the spell and let us get this over with, Loki.
As you wish.
It's done. Now all you need to do is have Thor gaze into the Mirror.
He will fall deeply in love with whoever is holding the Mirror when it captures his reflection.

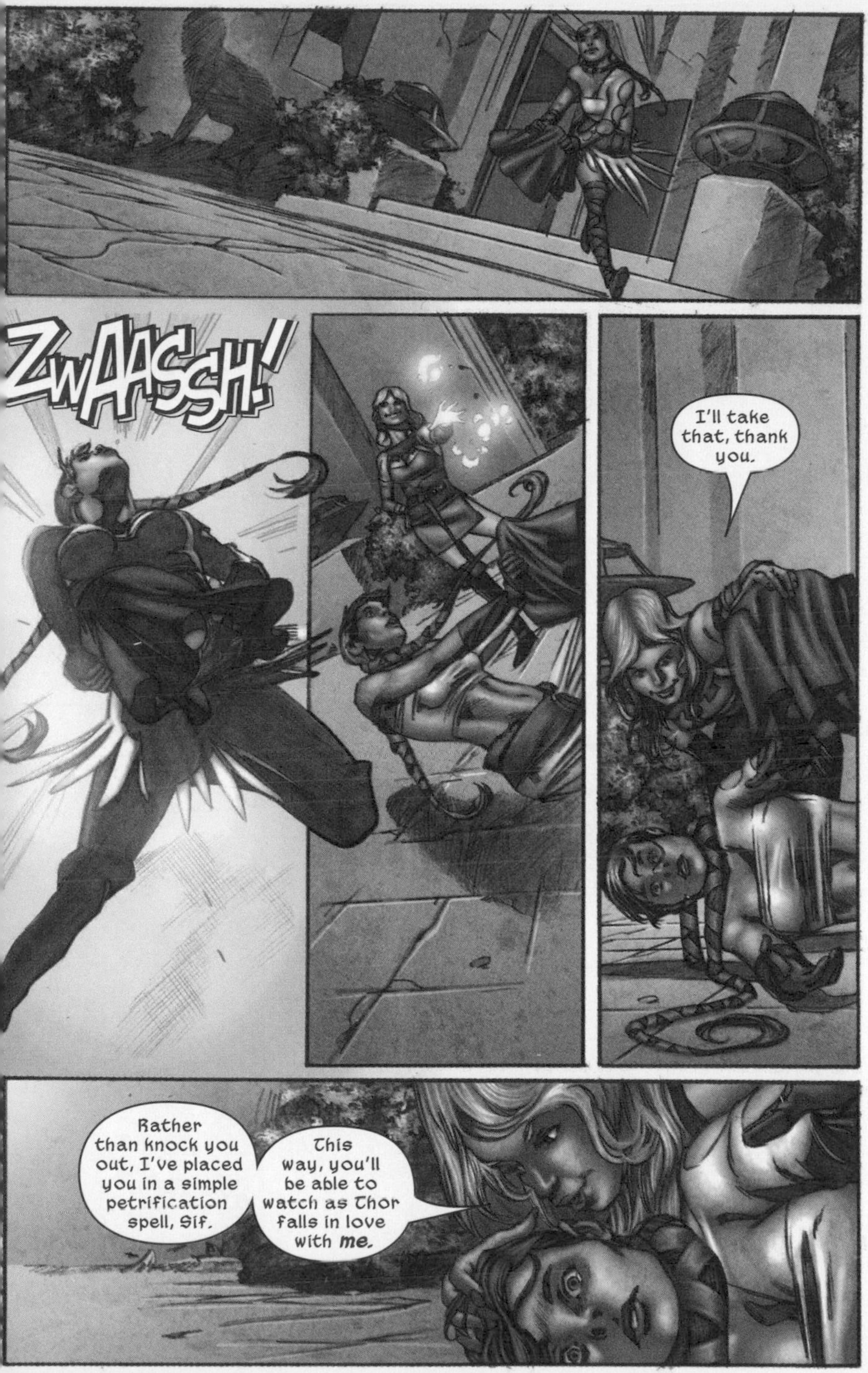

ZWAASSH!
I'll take that, thank you.
Rather than knock you out, I've placed you in a simple petrification spell, Sif.
This way, you'll be able to watch as Thor falls in love with *me.*

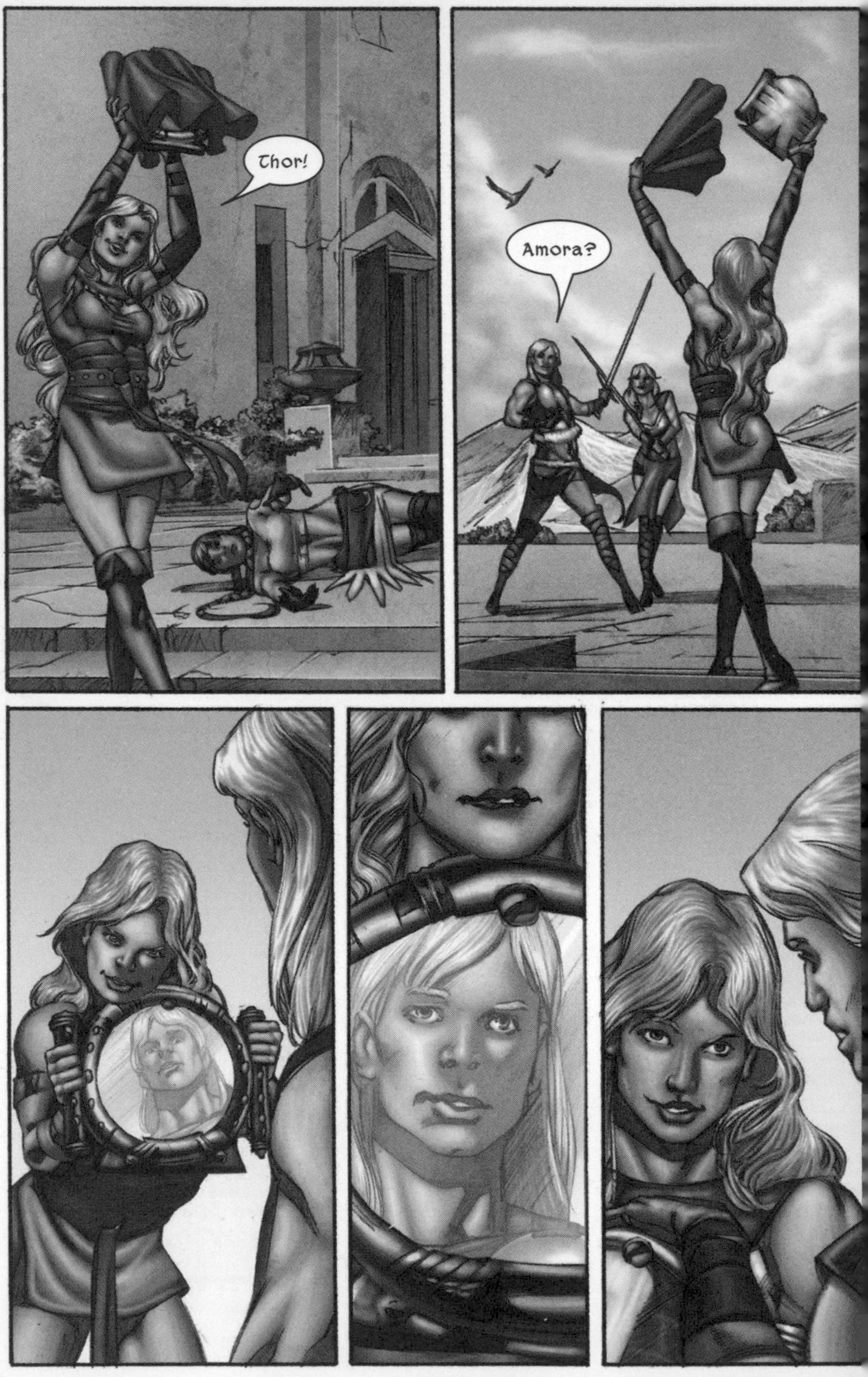
Thor!
Amora?

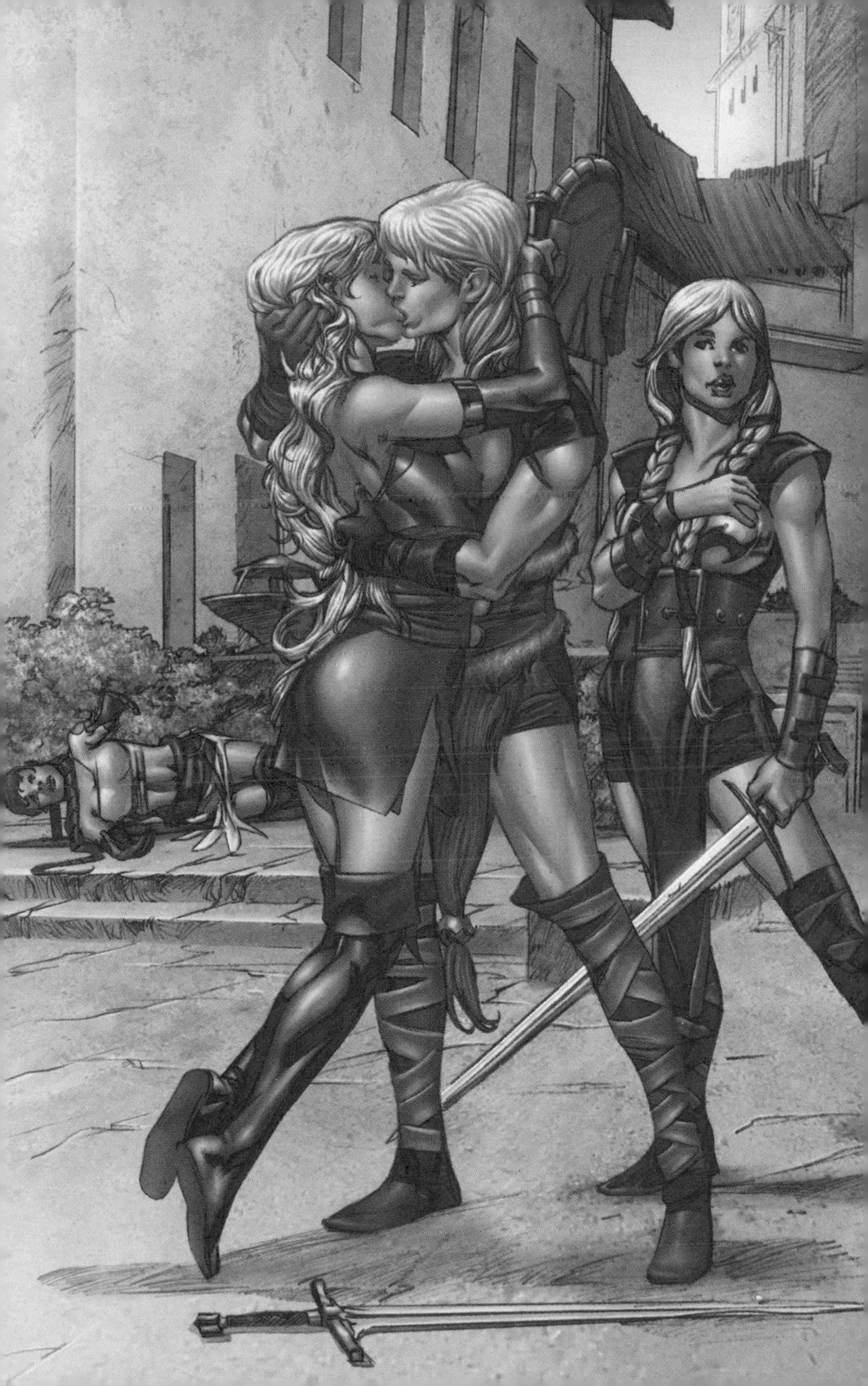

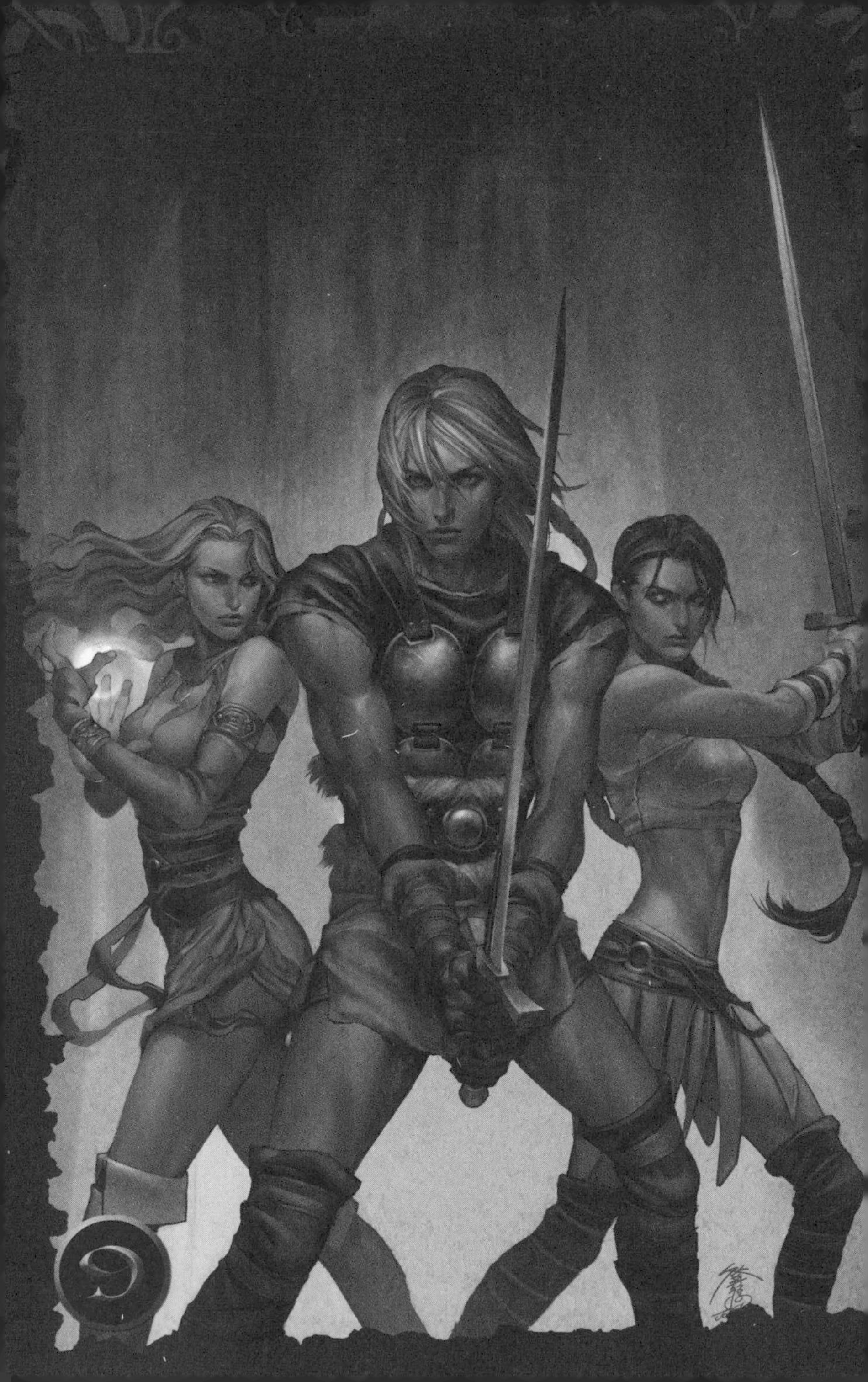

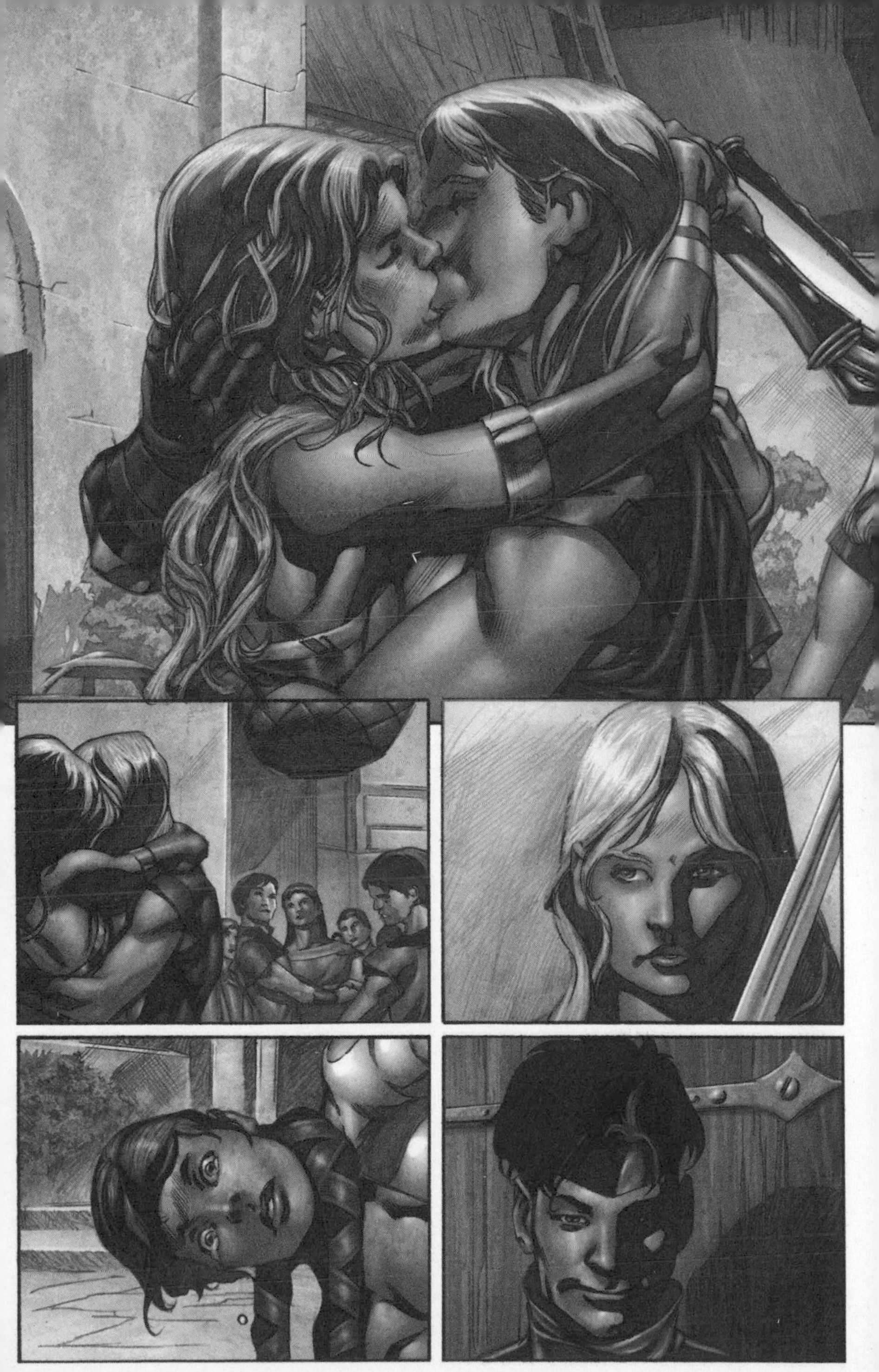

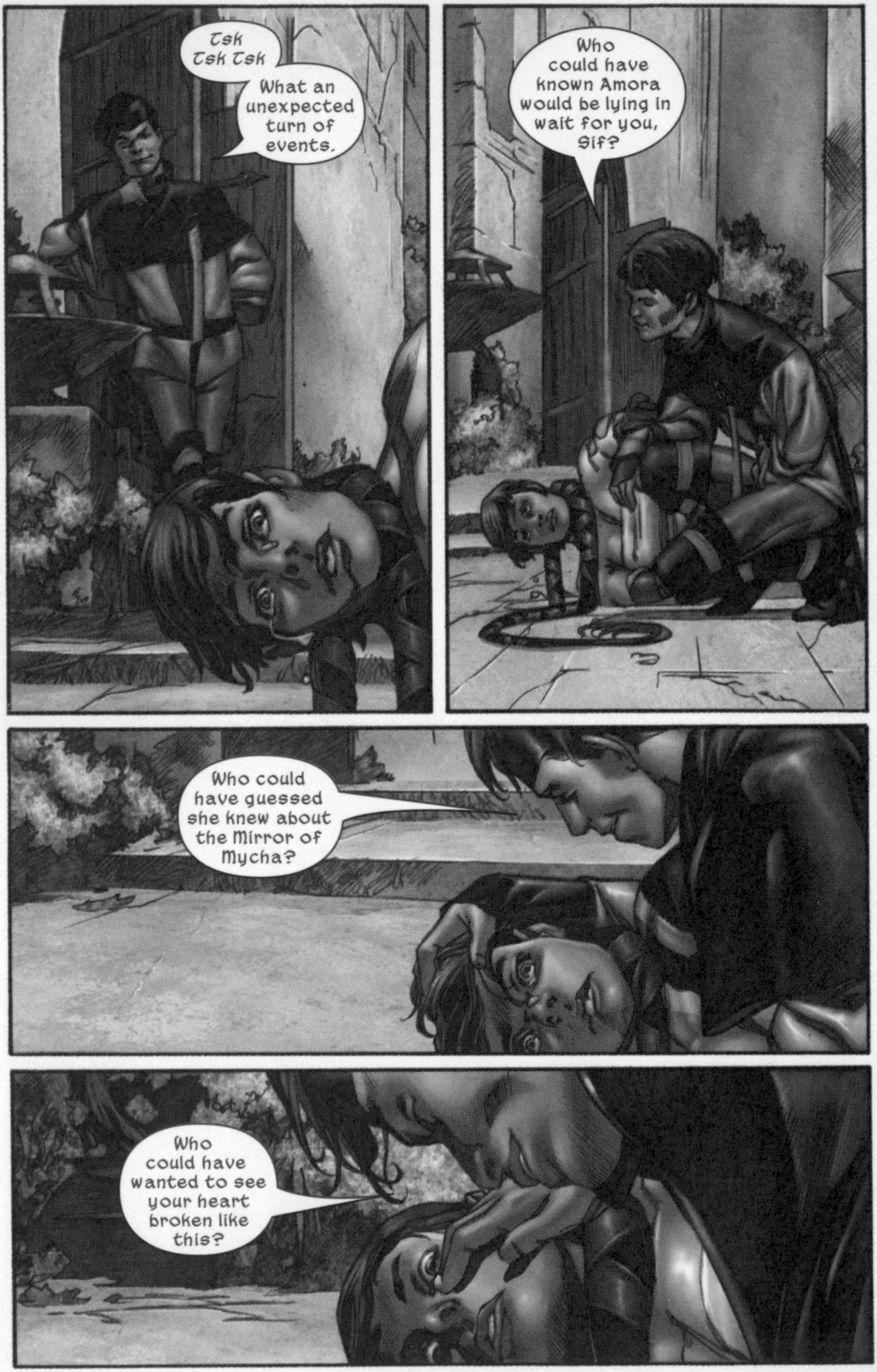
Tsk Tsk Tsk
What an unexpected turn of events.
Who could have known Amora would be lying in wait for you, Sif?
Who could have guessed she knew about the Mirror of Mycha?
Who could have wanted to see your heart broken like this?

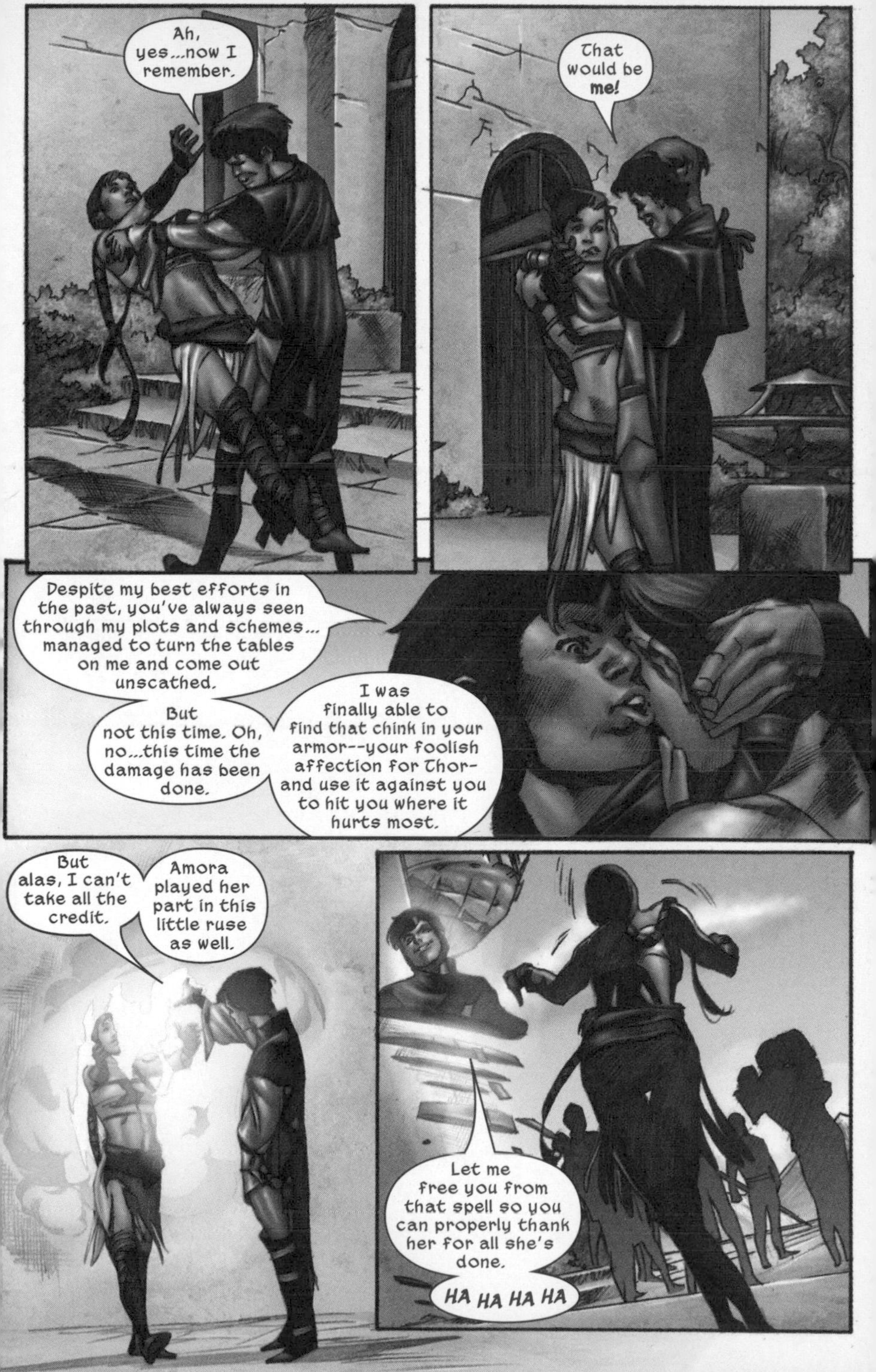
Ah, yes...now I remember.
That would be **me!**
Despite my best efforts in the past, you've always seen through my plots and schemes... managed to turn the tables on me and come out unscathed.
But not this time. Oh, no...this time the damage has been done.
I was finally able to find that chink in your armor--your foolish affection for Thor--and use it against you to hit you where it hurts most.
But alas, I can't take all the credit.
Amora played her part in this little ruse as well.
Let me free you from that spell so you can properly thank her for all she's done.
HA HA HA HA

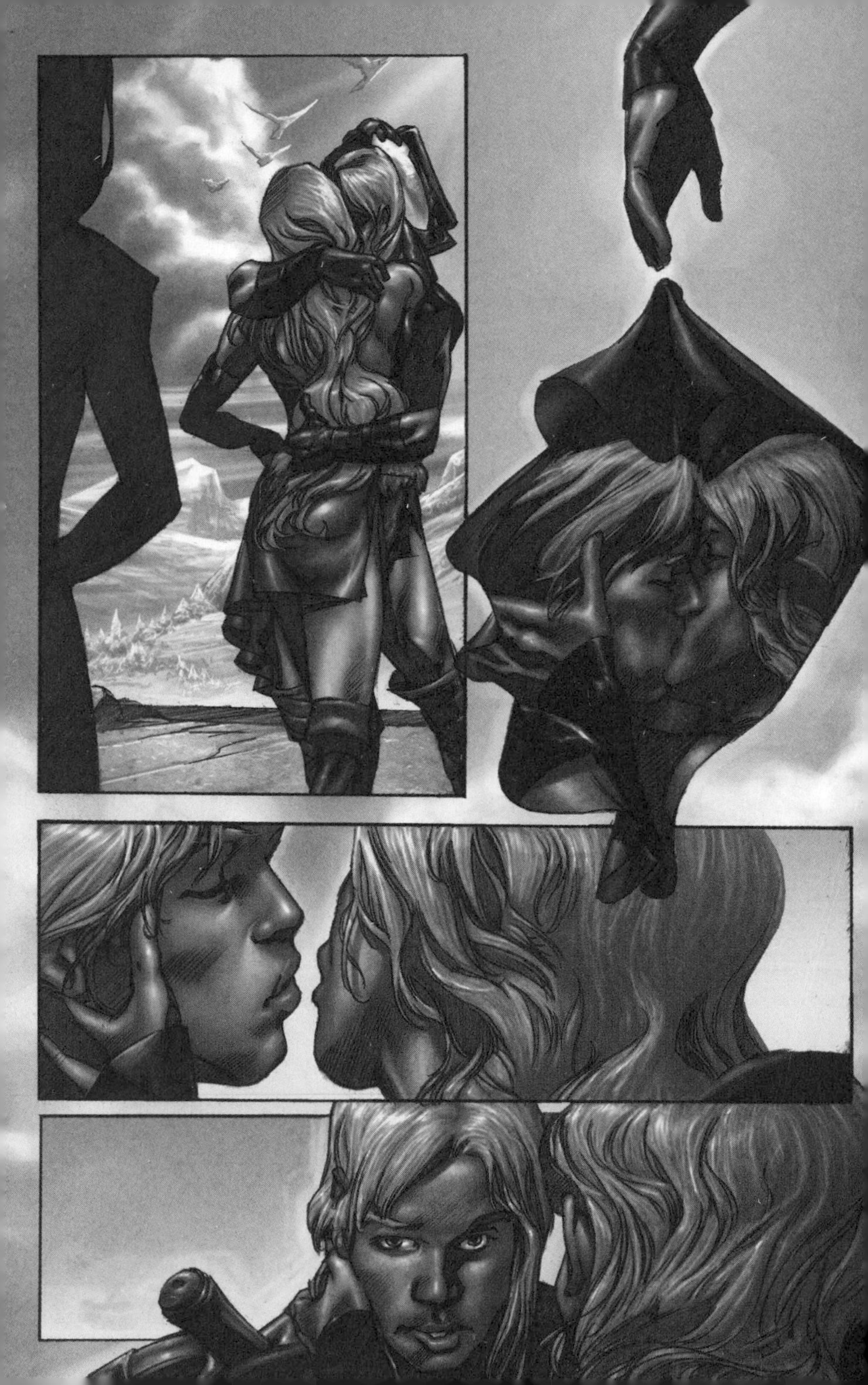

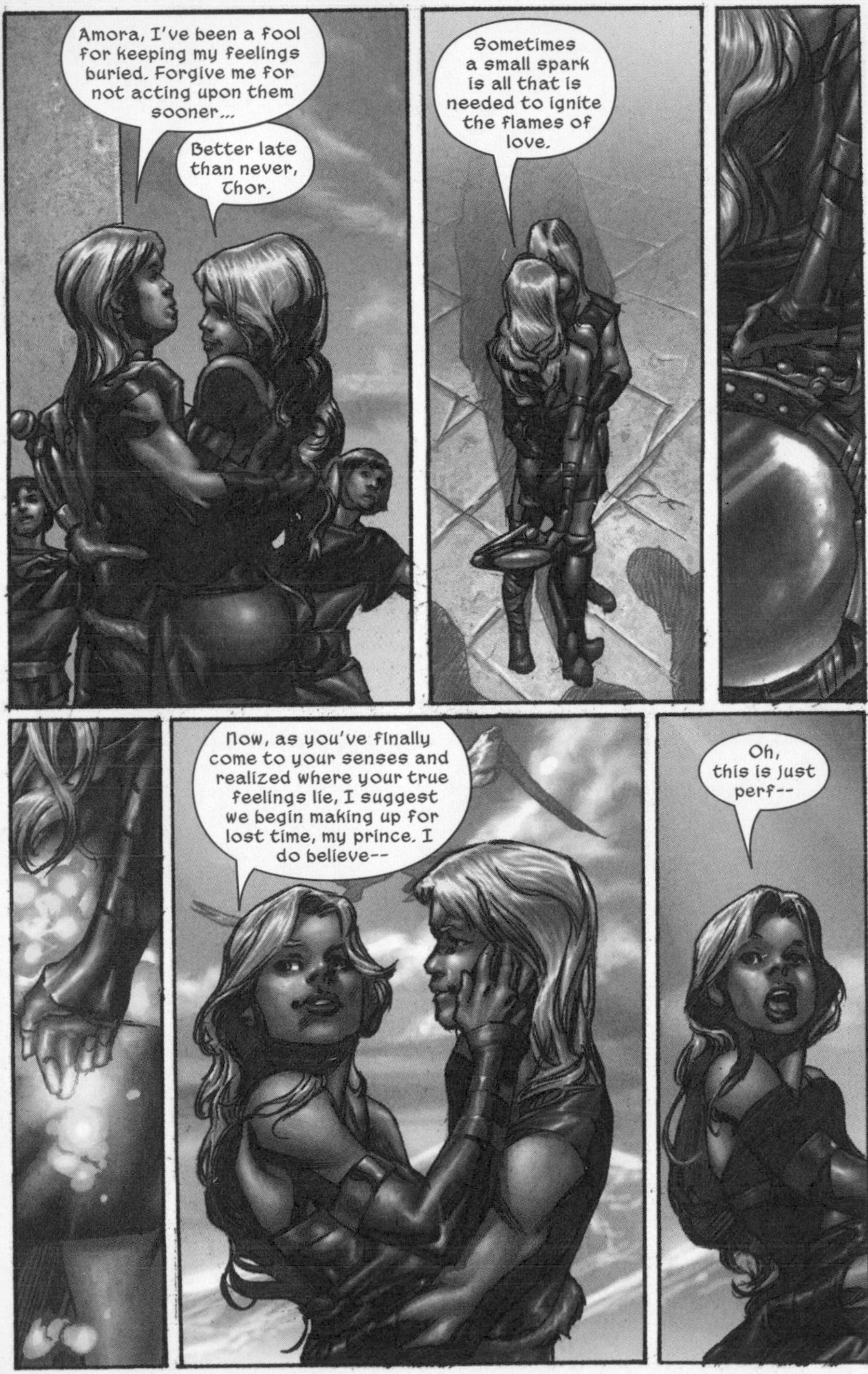
Amora, I've been a fool for keeping my feelings buried. Forgive me for not acting upon them sooner...
Better late than never, Thor.
Sometimes a small spark is all that is needed to ignite the flames of love.
Now, as you've finally come to your senses and realized where your true feelings lie, I suggest we begin making up for lost time, my prince. I do believe--
Oh, this is just perf--

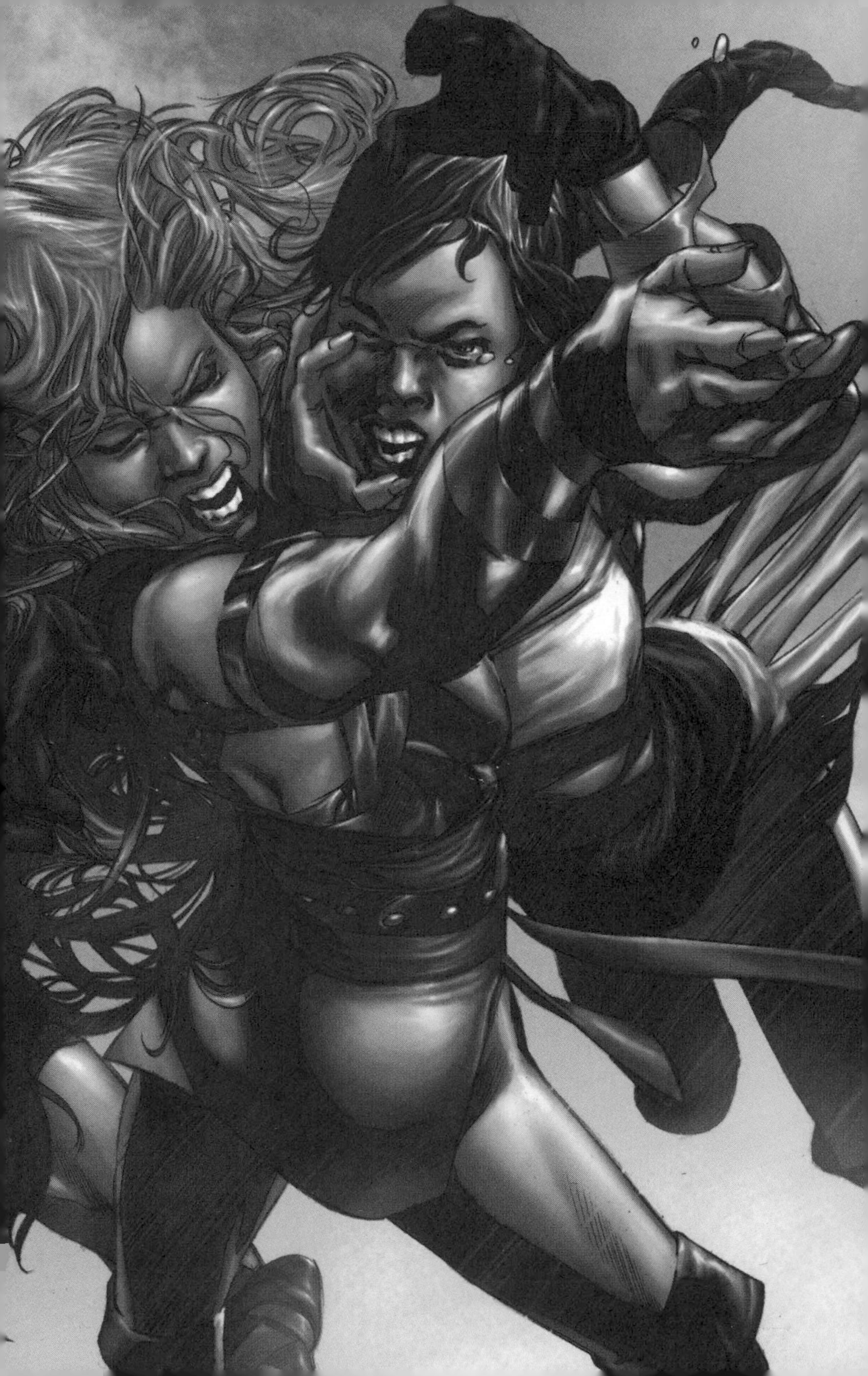

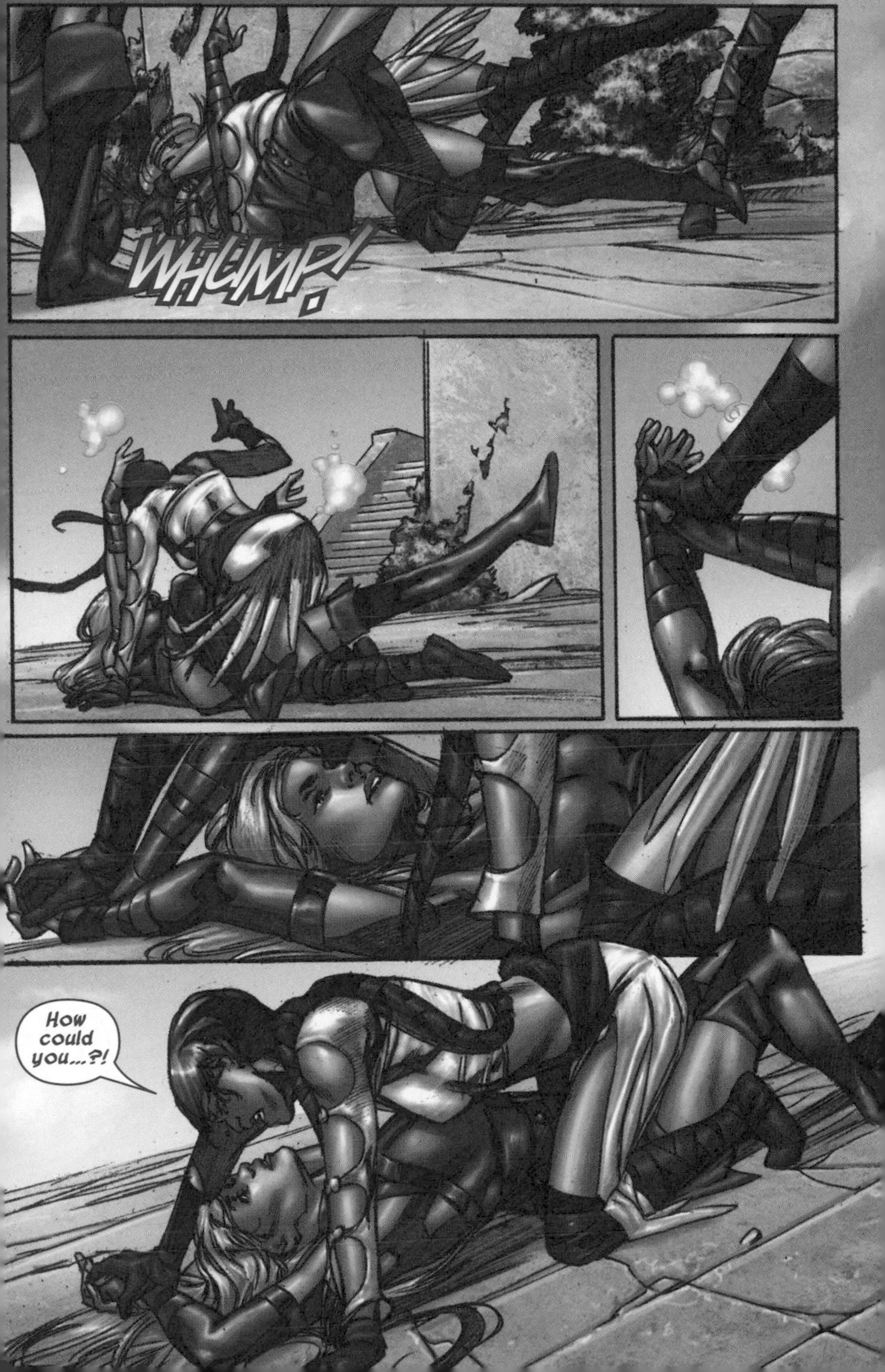
WHUMP!
How could you...?!

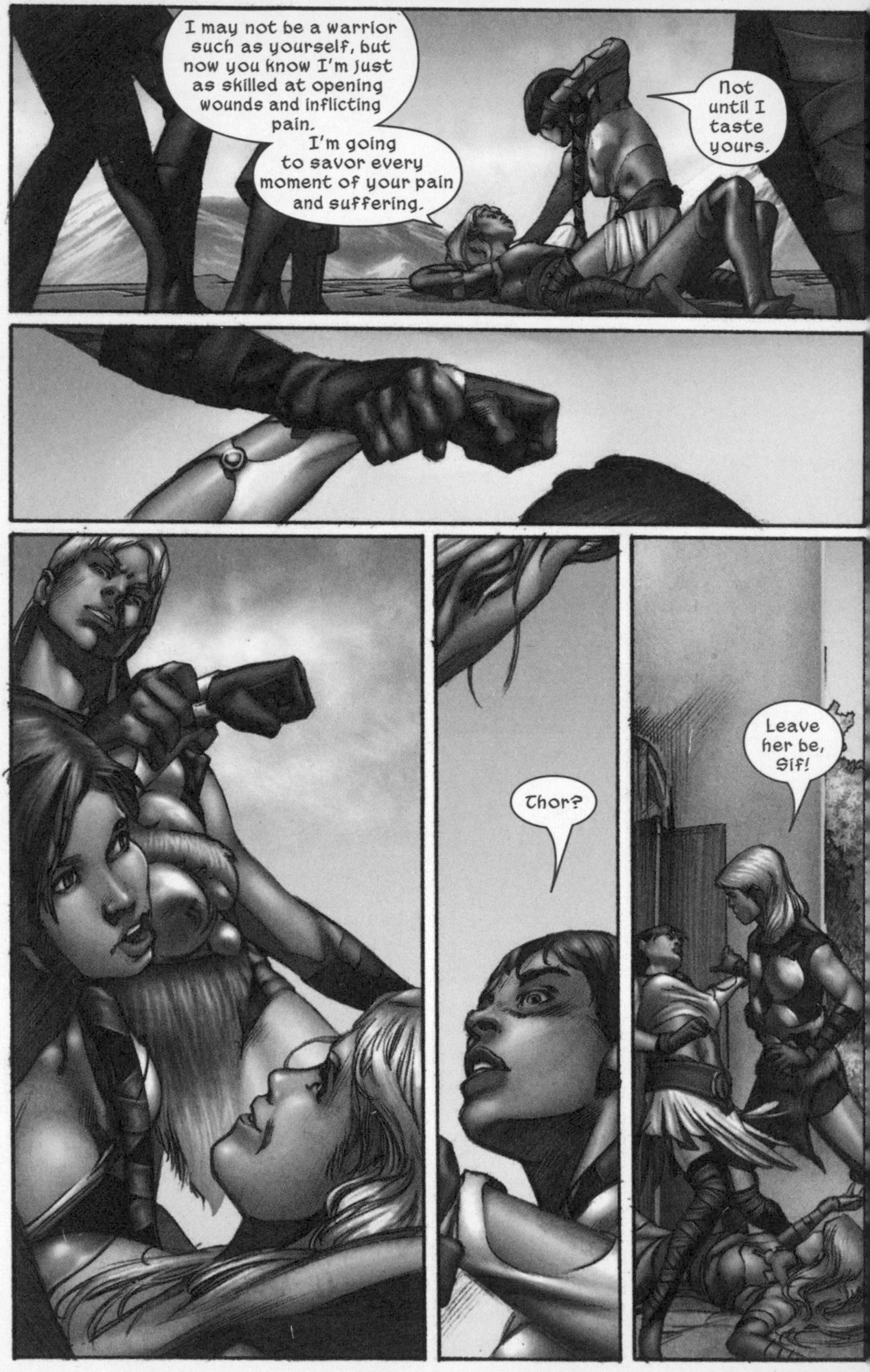
I may not be a warrior such as yourself, but now you know I'm just as skilled at opening wounds and inflicting pain.
I'm going to savor every moment of your pain and suffering.
Not until I taste yours.
Thor?
Leave her be, Sif!

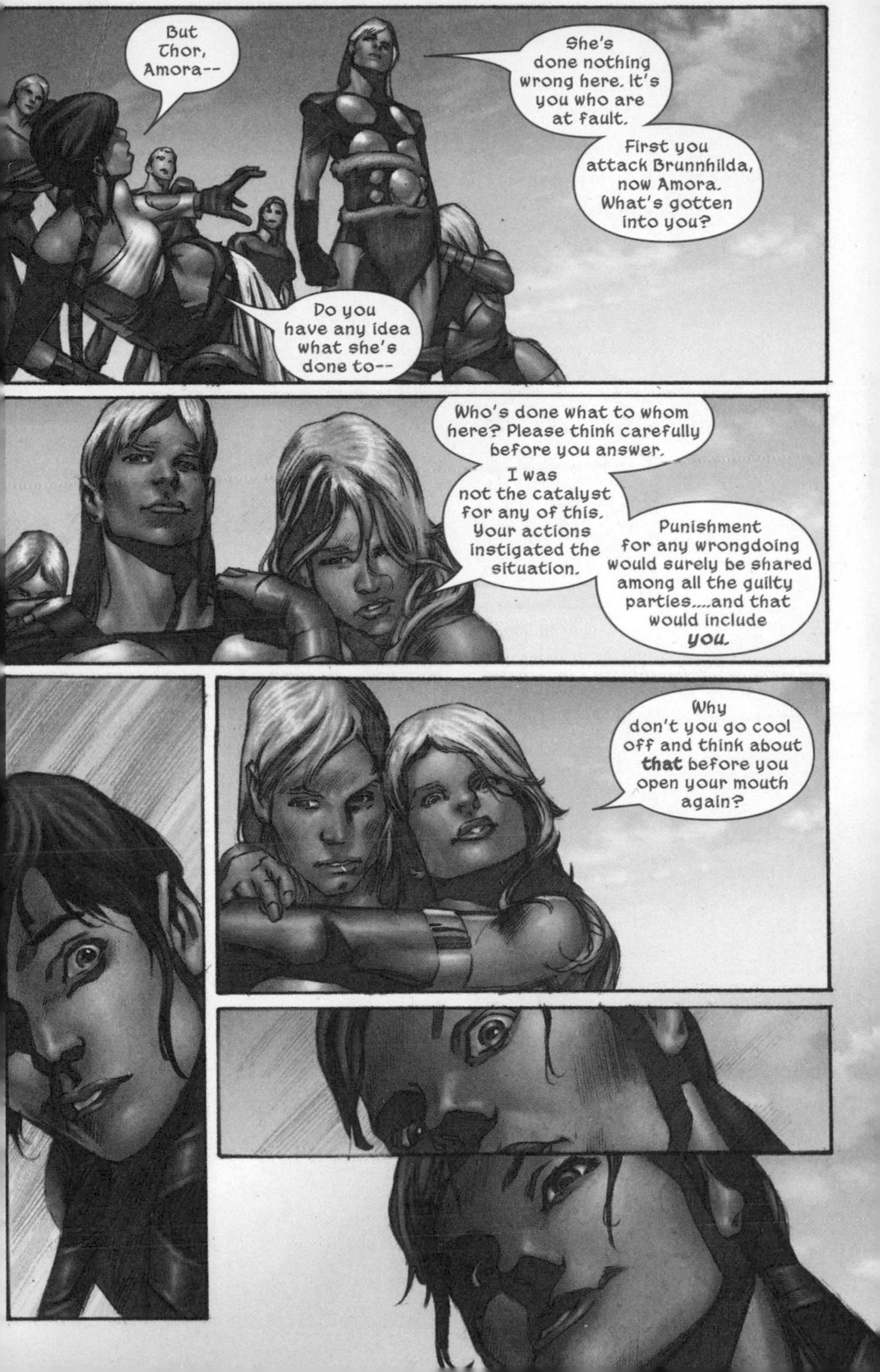
But Thor, Amora--
She's done nothing wrong here. It's you who are at fault.
First you attack Brunnhilda, now Amora. What's gotten into you?
Do you have any idea what she's done to--
Who's done what to whom here? Please think carefully before you answer.
I was not the catalyst for any of this. Your actions instigated the situation.
Punishment for any wrongdoing would surely be shared among all the guilty parties....and that would include **you.**
Why don't you go cool off and think about **that** before you open your mouth again?

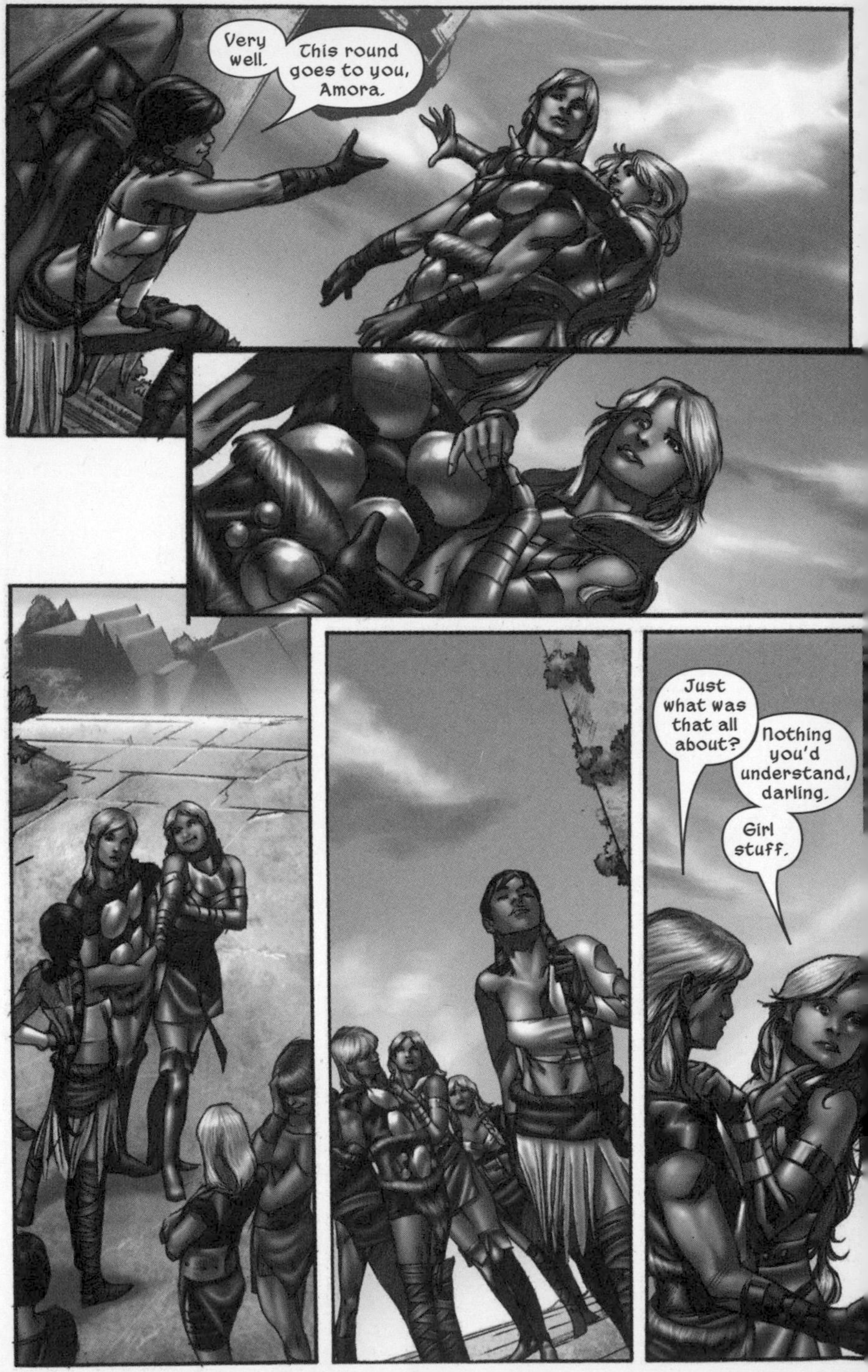
Very well.
This round goes to you, Amora.
Just what was that all about?
Nothing you'd understand, darling.
Girl stuff.

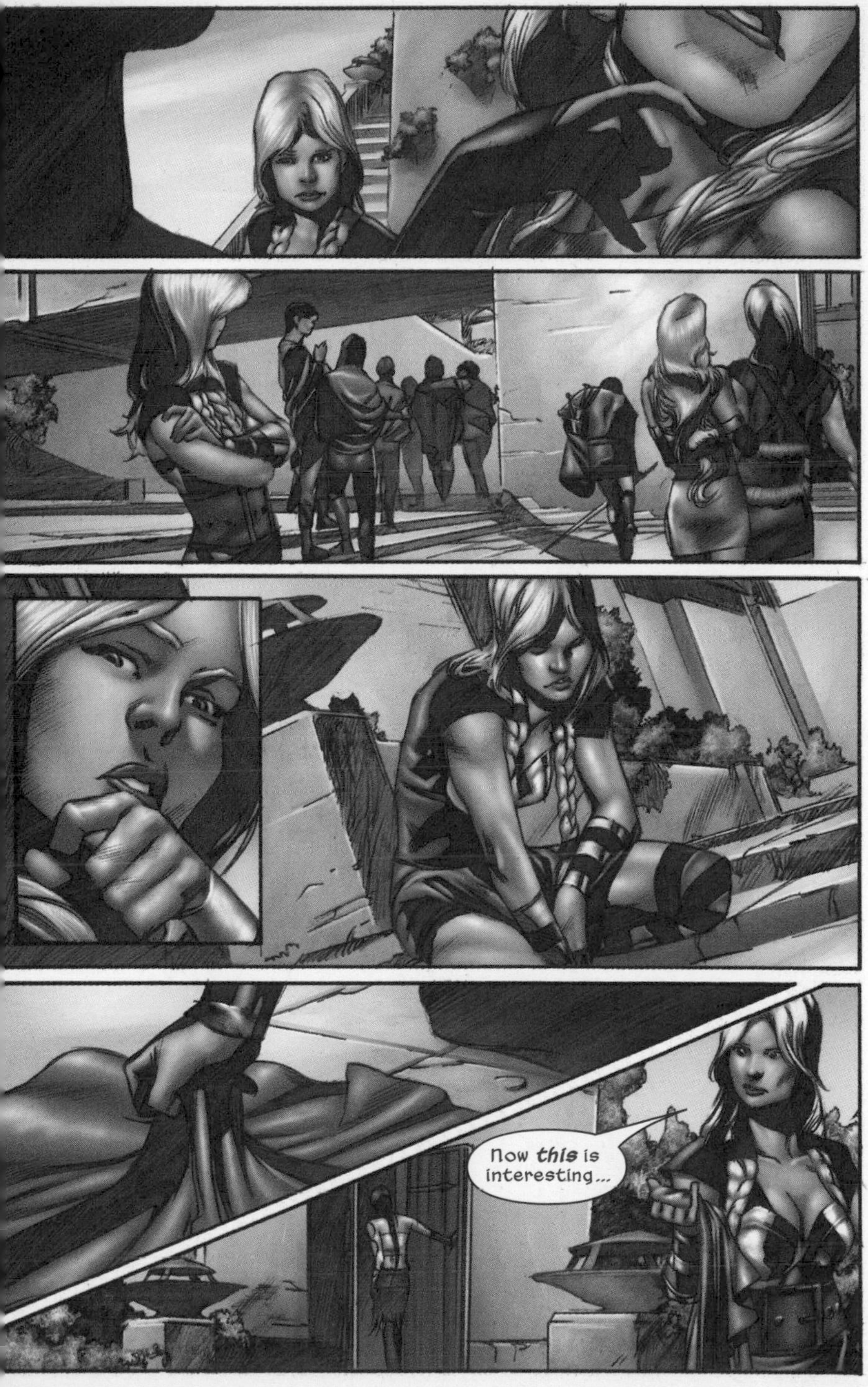
Now *this* is interesting...

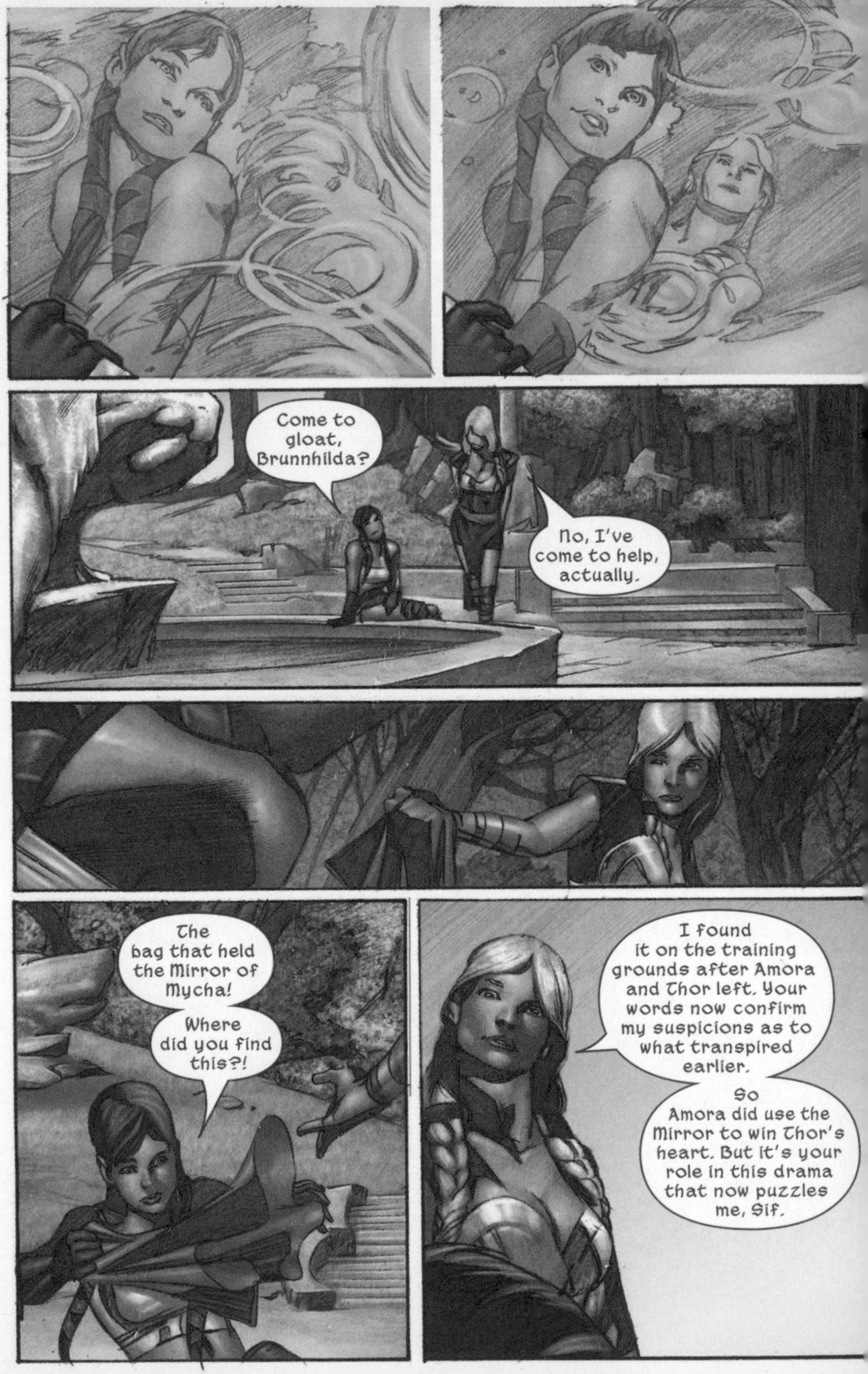

Come to gloat, Brunnhilda?
No, I've come to help, actually.
The bag that held the Mirror of Mycha!
Where did you find this?!
I found it on the training grounds after Amora and Thor left. Your words now confirm my suspicions as to what transpired earlier.
So Amora did use the Mirror to win Thor's heart. But it's your role in this drama that now puzzles me, Sif.

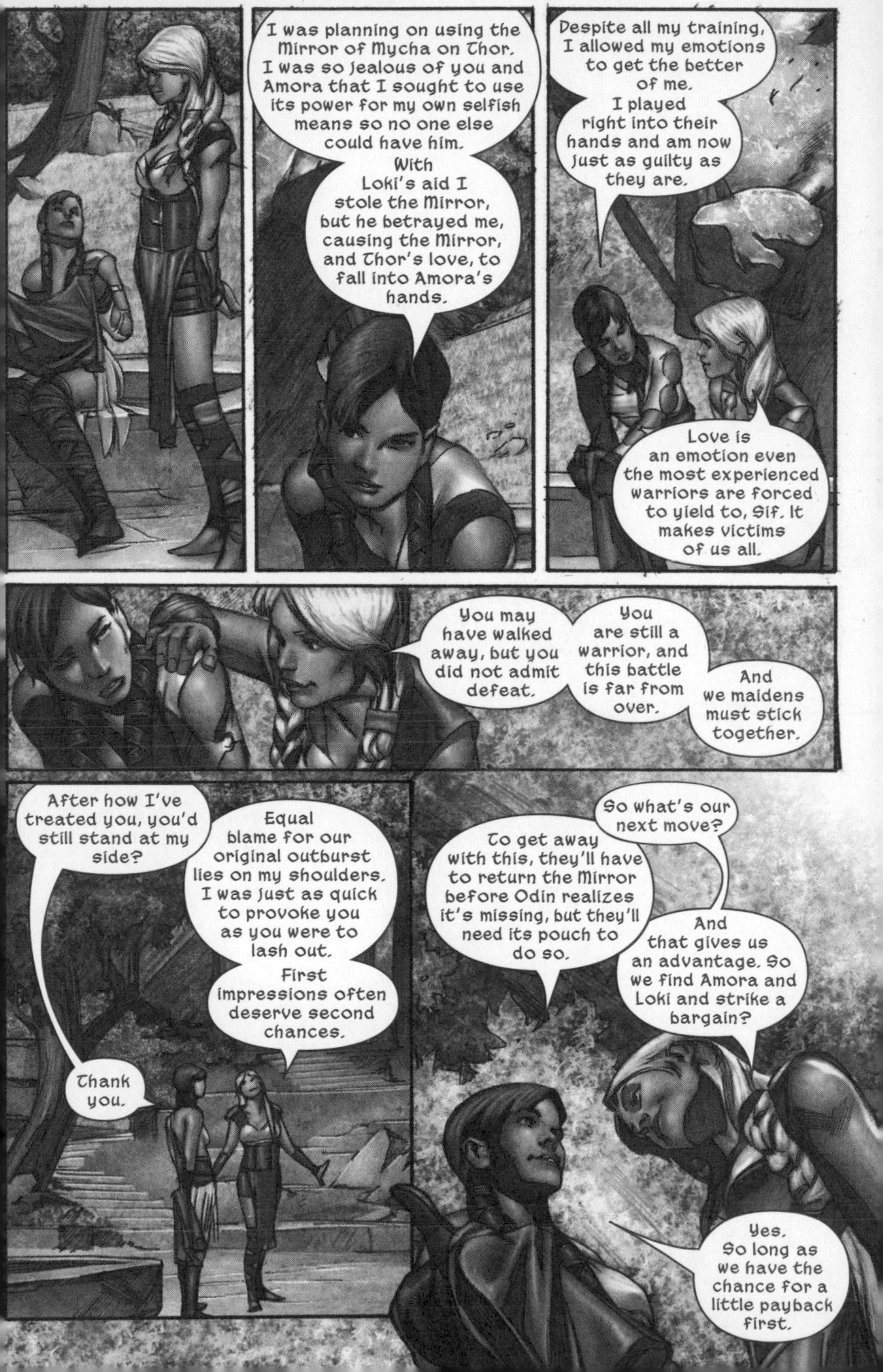
I was planning on using the Mirror of Mycha on Thor. I was so jealous of you and Amora that I sought to use its power for my own selfish means so no one else could have him.
With Loki's aid I stole the Mirror, but he betrayed me, causing the Mirror, and Thor's love, to fall into Amora's hands.
Despite all my training, I allowed my emotions to get the better of me.
I played right into their hands and am now just as guilty as they are.
Love is an emotion even the most experienced warriors are forced to yield to, Sif. It makes victims of us all.
You may have walked away, but you did not admit defeat.
You are still a warrior, and this battle is far from over.
And we maidens must stick together.
After how I've treated you, you'd still stand at my side?
Equal blame for our original outburst lies on my shoulders. I was just as quick to provoke you as you were to lash out.
First impressions often deserve second chances.
Thank you.
So what's our next move?
To get away with this, they'll have to return the Mirror before Odin realizes it's missing, but they'll need its pouch to do so.
And that gives us an advantage. So we find Amora and Loki and strike a bargain?
Yes. So long as we have the chance for a little payback first.

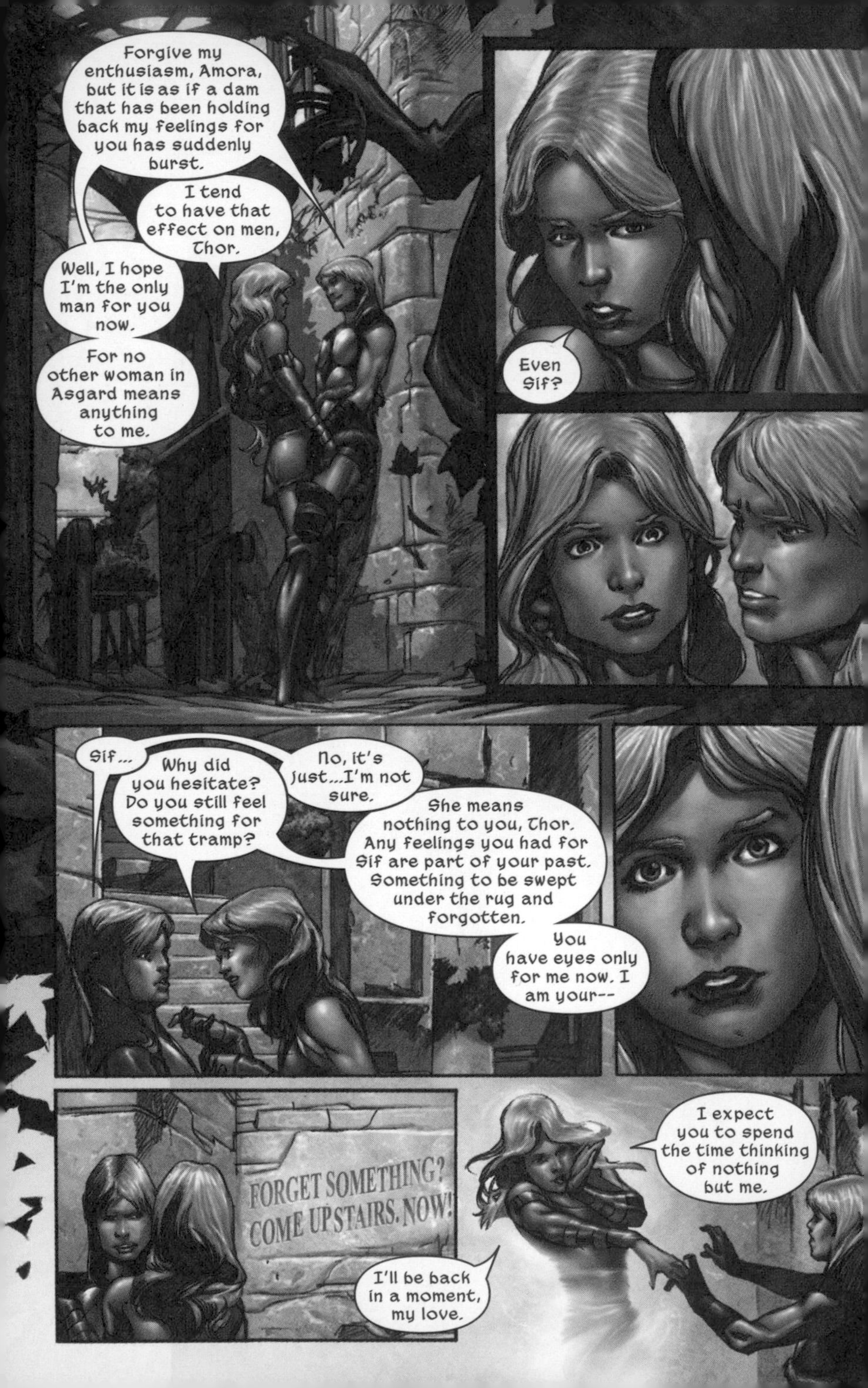
Forgive my enthusiasm, Amora, but it is as if a dam that has been holding back my feelings for you has suddenly burst.
I tend to have that effect on men, Thor.
Well, I hope I'm the only man for you now.
For no other woman in Asgard means anything to me.
Even Sif?
Sif...
Why did you hesitate? Do you still feel something for that tramp?
No, it's just...I'm not sure.
She means nothing to you, Thor. Any feelings you had for Sif are part of your past. Something to be swept under the rug and forgotten.
You have eyes only for me now. I am your--
FORGET SOMETHING? COME UPSTAIRS. NOW!
I'll be back in a moment, my love.
I expect you to spend the time thinking of nothing but me.

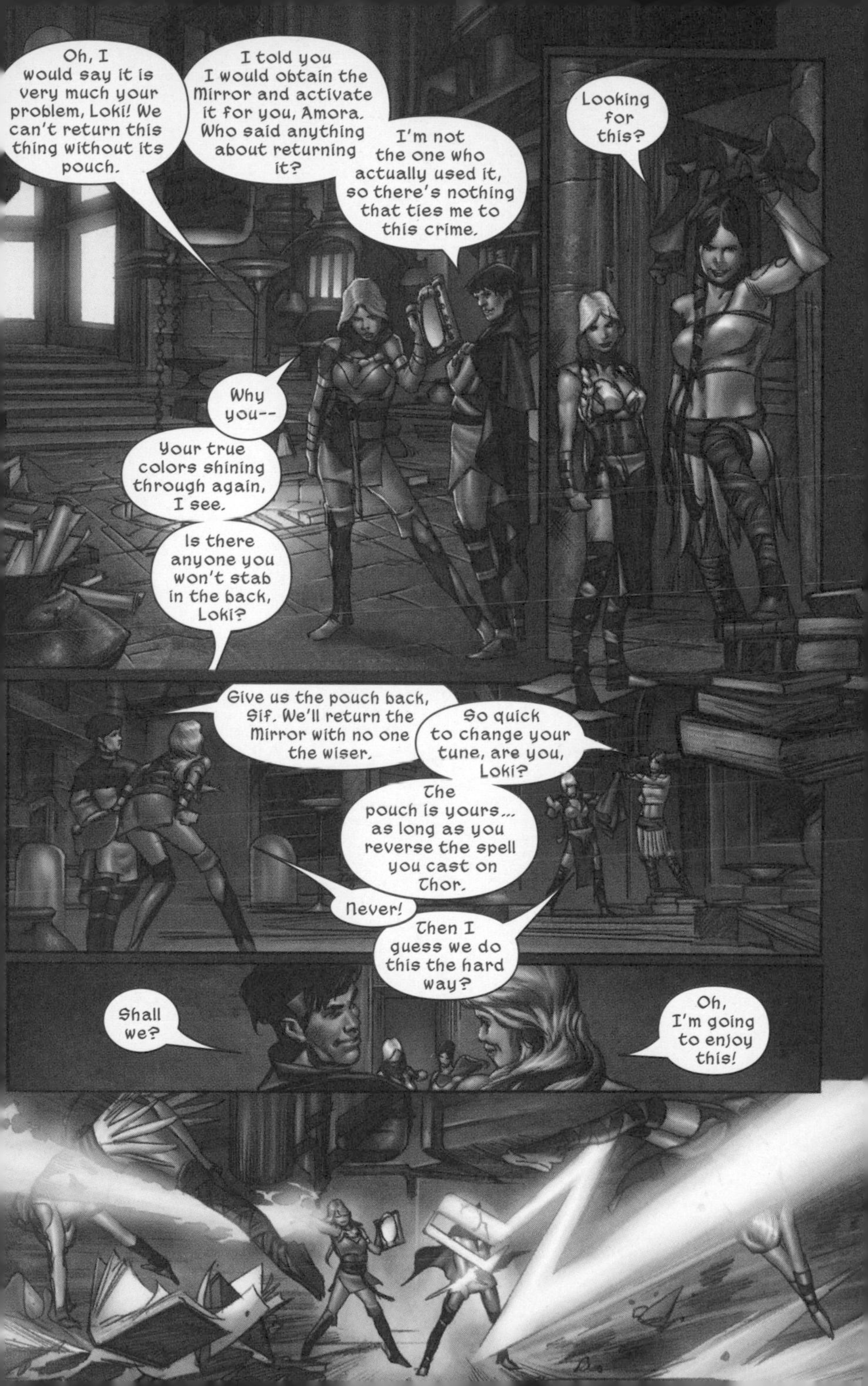
Oh, I would say it is very much your problem, Loki! We can't return this thing without its pouch.
I told you I would obtain the Mirror and activate it for you, Amora. Who said anything about returning it?
I'm not the one who actually used it, so there's nothing that ties me to this crime.
Looking for this?
Why you--
Your true colors shining through again, I see.
Is there anyone you won't stab in the back, Loki?
Give us the pouch back, Sif. We'll return the Mirror with no one the wiser.
So quick to change your tune, are you, Loki?
The pouch is yours... as long as you reverse the spell you cast on Thor.
Never!
Then I guess we do this the hard way?
Shall we?
Oh, I'm going to enjoy this!

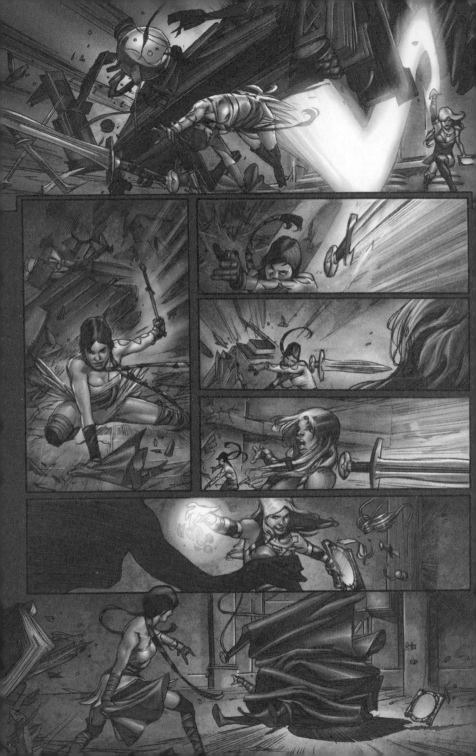

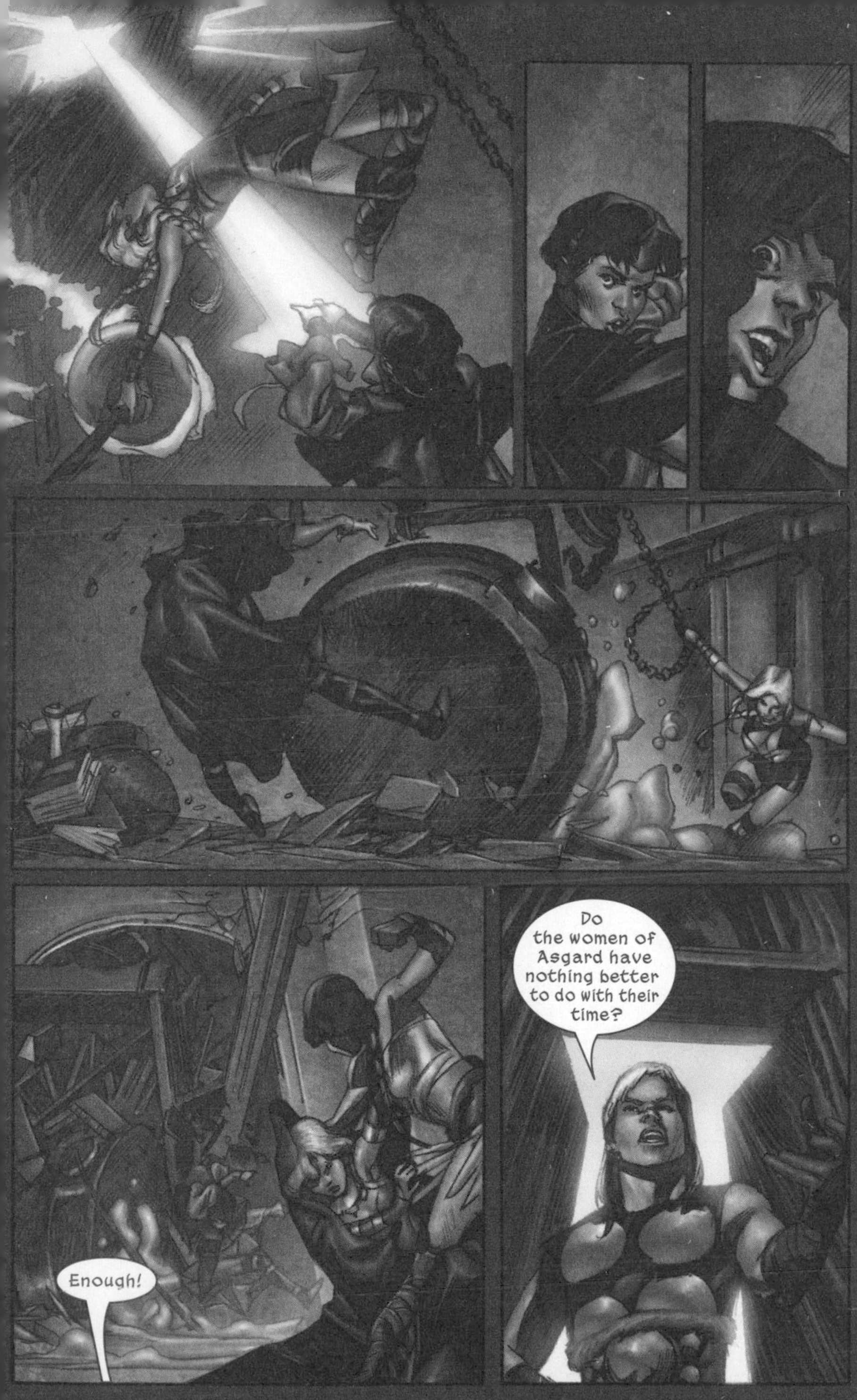
Enough!
Do the women of Asgard have nothing better to do with their time?

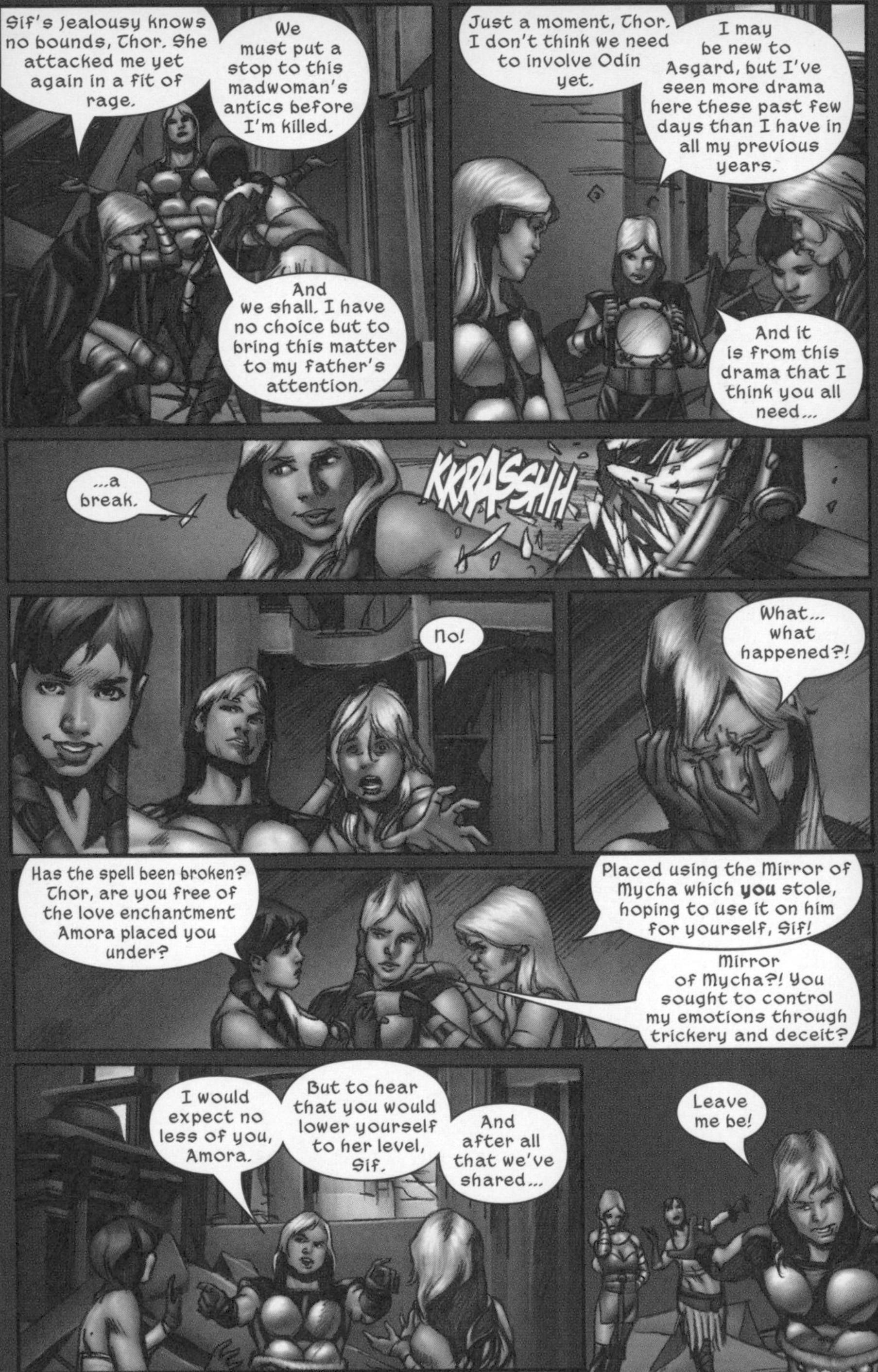
Sif's jealousy knows no bounds, Thor. She attacked me yet again in a fit of rage.
We must put a stop to this madwoman's antics before I'm killed.
And we shall. I have no choice but to bring this matter to my father's attention.
Just a moment, Thor. I don't think we need to involve Odin yet.
I may be new to Asgard, but I've seen more drama here these past few days than I have in all my previous years.
And it is from this drama that I think you all need...
...a break.
KKRASSHH
No!
What... what happened?!
Has the spell been broken? Thor, are you free of the love enchantment Amora placed you under?
Placed using the Mirror of Mycha which **you** stole, hoping to use it on him for yourself, Sif!
Mirror of Mycha?! You sought to control my emotions through trickery and deceit?
I would expect no less of you, Amora.
But to hear that you would lower yourself to her level, Sif.
And after all that we've shared...
Leave me be!

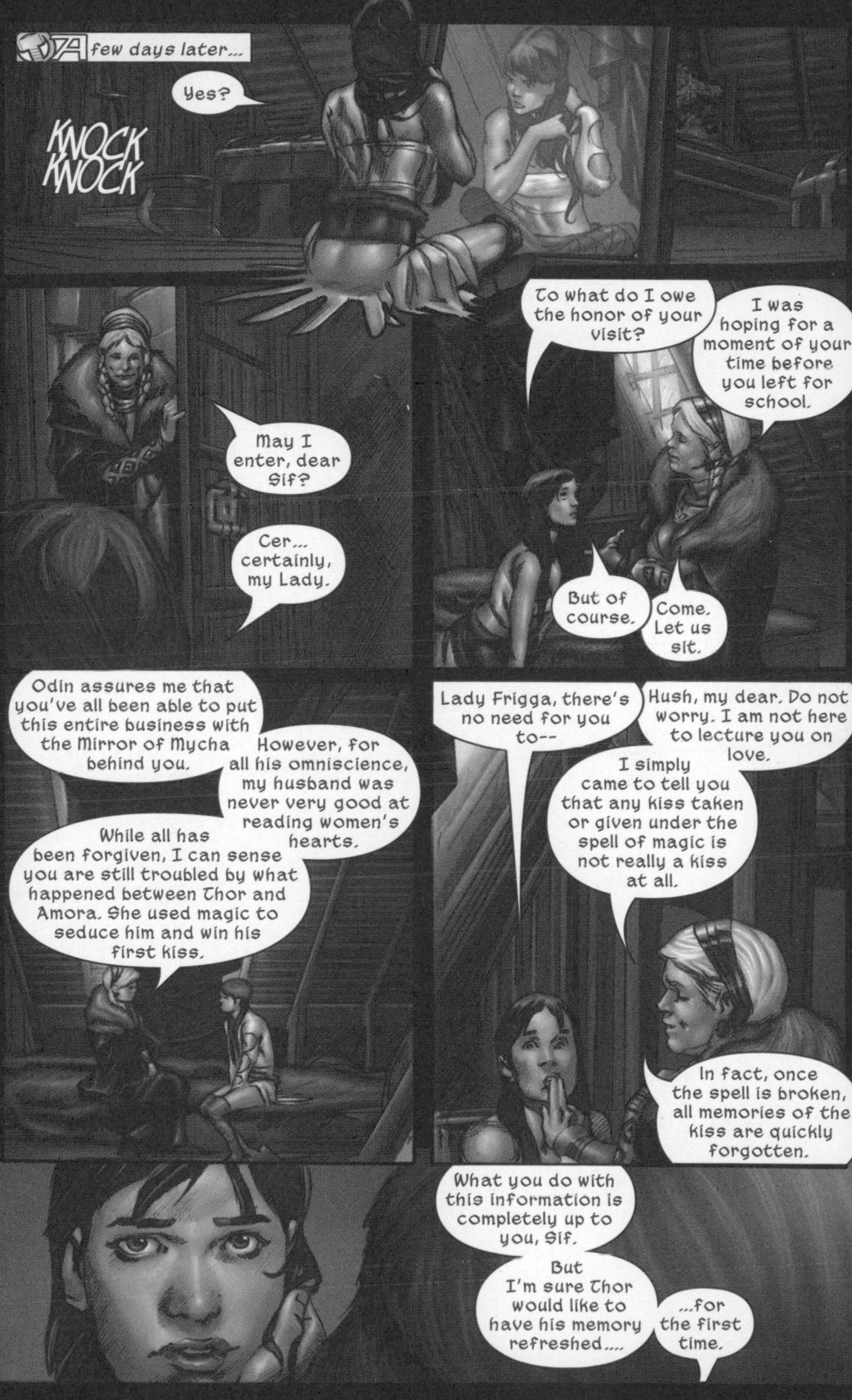
A few days later...
Yes?
KNOCK KNOCK
May I enter, dear Sif?
Cer... certainly, my Lady.
To what do I owe the honor of your visit?
I was hoping for a moment of your time before you left for school.
But of course.
Come. Let us sit.
Odin assures me that you've all been able to put this entire business with the Mirror of Mycha behind you.
However, for all his omniscience, my husband was never very good at reading women's hearts.
While all has been forgiven, I can sense you are still troubled by what happened between Thor and Amora. She used magic to seduce him and win his first kiss.
Lady Frigga, there's no need for you to--
Hush, my dear. Do not worry. I am not here to lecture you on love.
I simply came to tell you that any kiss taken or given under the spell of magic is not really a kiss at all.
In fact, once the spell is broken, all memories of the kiss are quickly forgotten.
What you do with this information is completely up to you, Sif.
But I'm sure Thor would like to have his memory refreshed....
...for the first time.

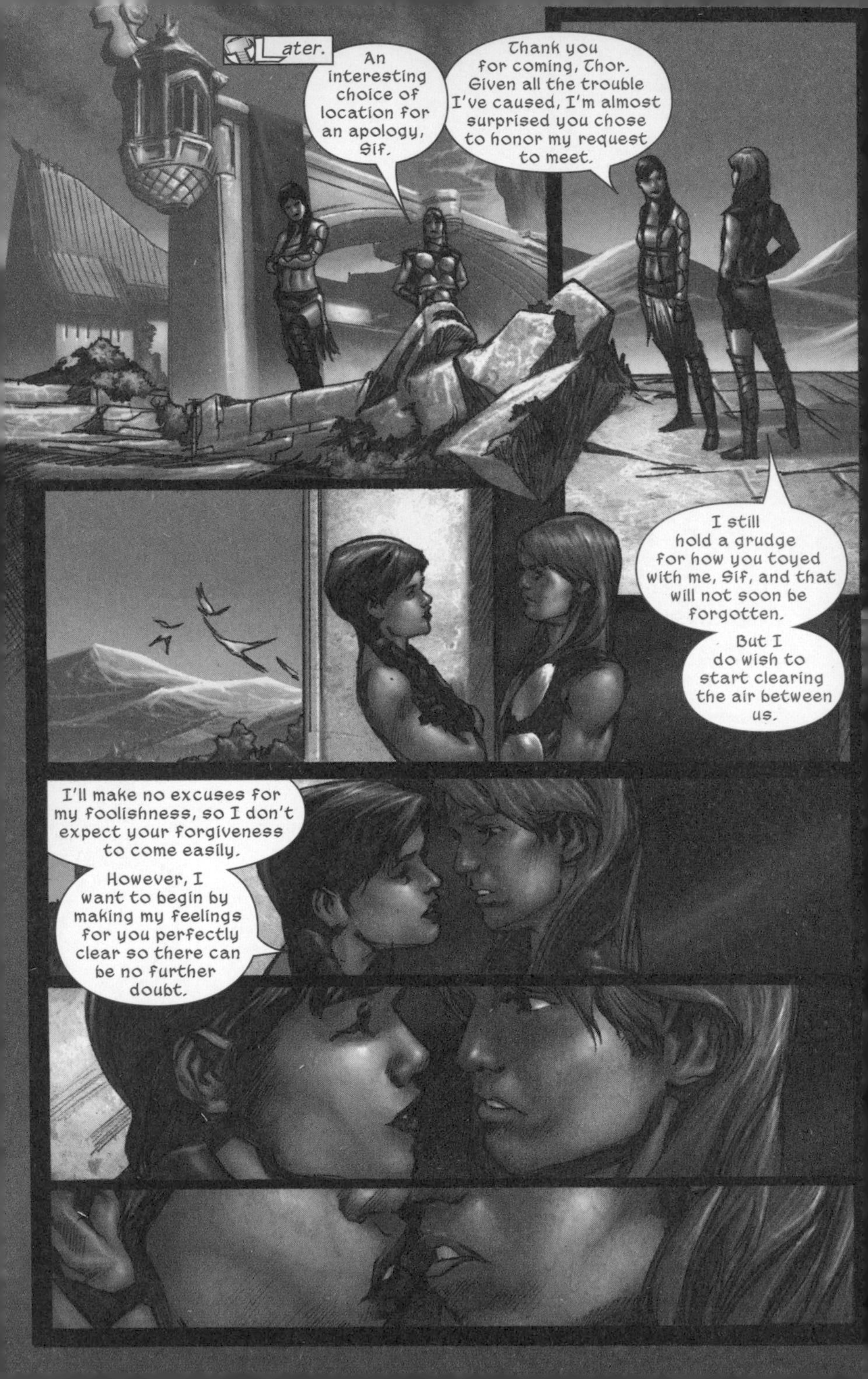
Later.
An interesting choice of location for an apology, Sif.
Thank you for coming, Thor. Given all the trouble I've caused, I'm almost surprised you chose to honor my request to meet.
I still hold a grudge for how you toyed with me, Sif, and that will not soon be forgotten.
But I do wish to start clearing the air between us.
I'll make no excuses for my foolishness, so I don't expect your forgiveness to come easily.
However, I want to begin by making my feelings for you perfectly clear so there can be no further doubt.

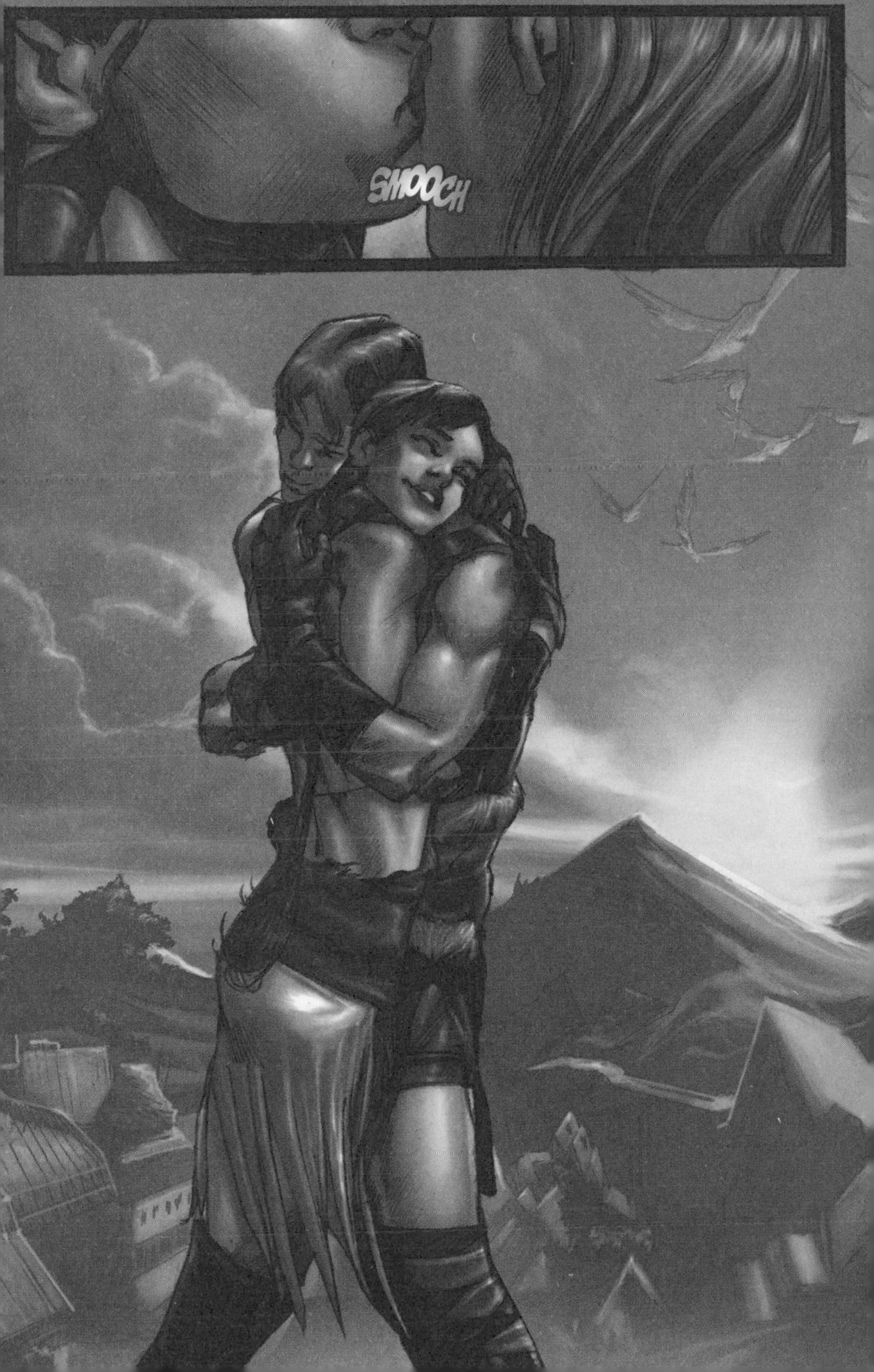
SMOOCH

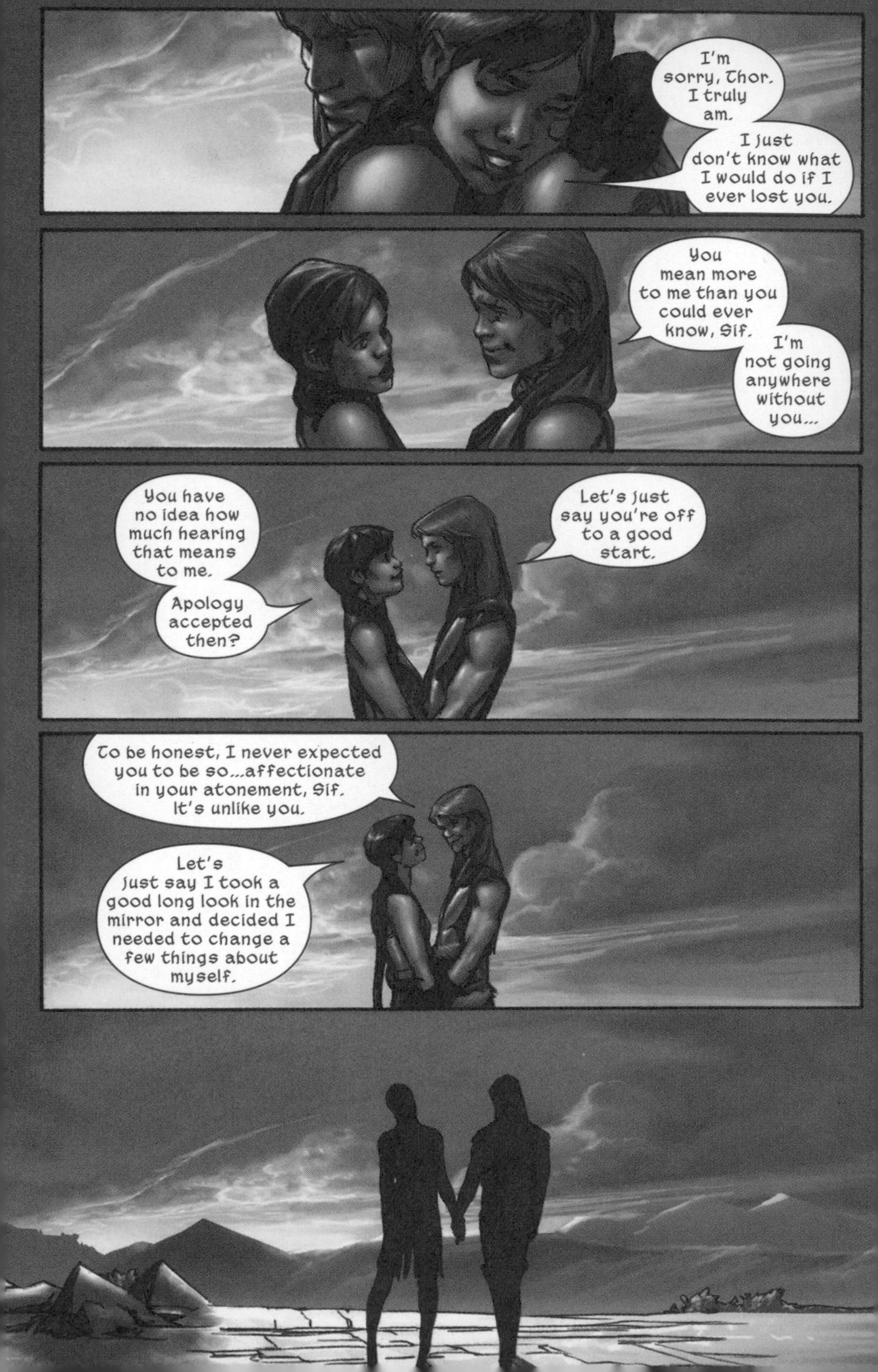
I'm sorry, Thor. I truly am.
I just don't know what I would do if I ever lost you.
You mean more to me than you could ever know, Sif.
I'm not going anywhere without you...
You have no idea how much hearing that means to me.
Apology accepted then?
Let's just say you're off to a good start.
To be honest, I never expected you to be so...affectionate in your atonement, Sif. It's unlike you.
Let's just say I took a good long look in the mirror and decided I needed to change a few things about myself.

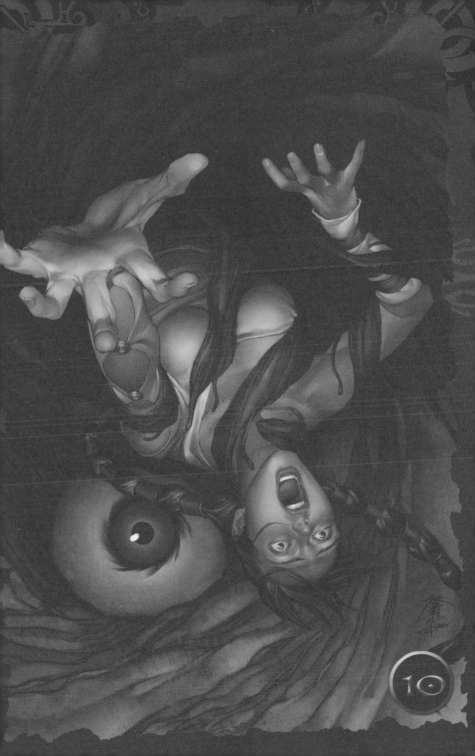

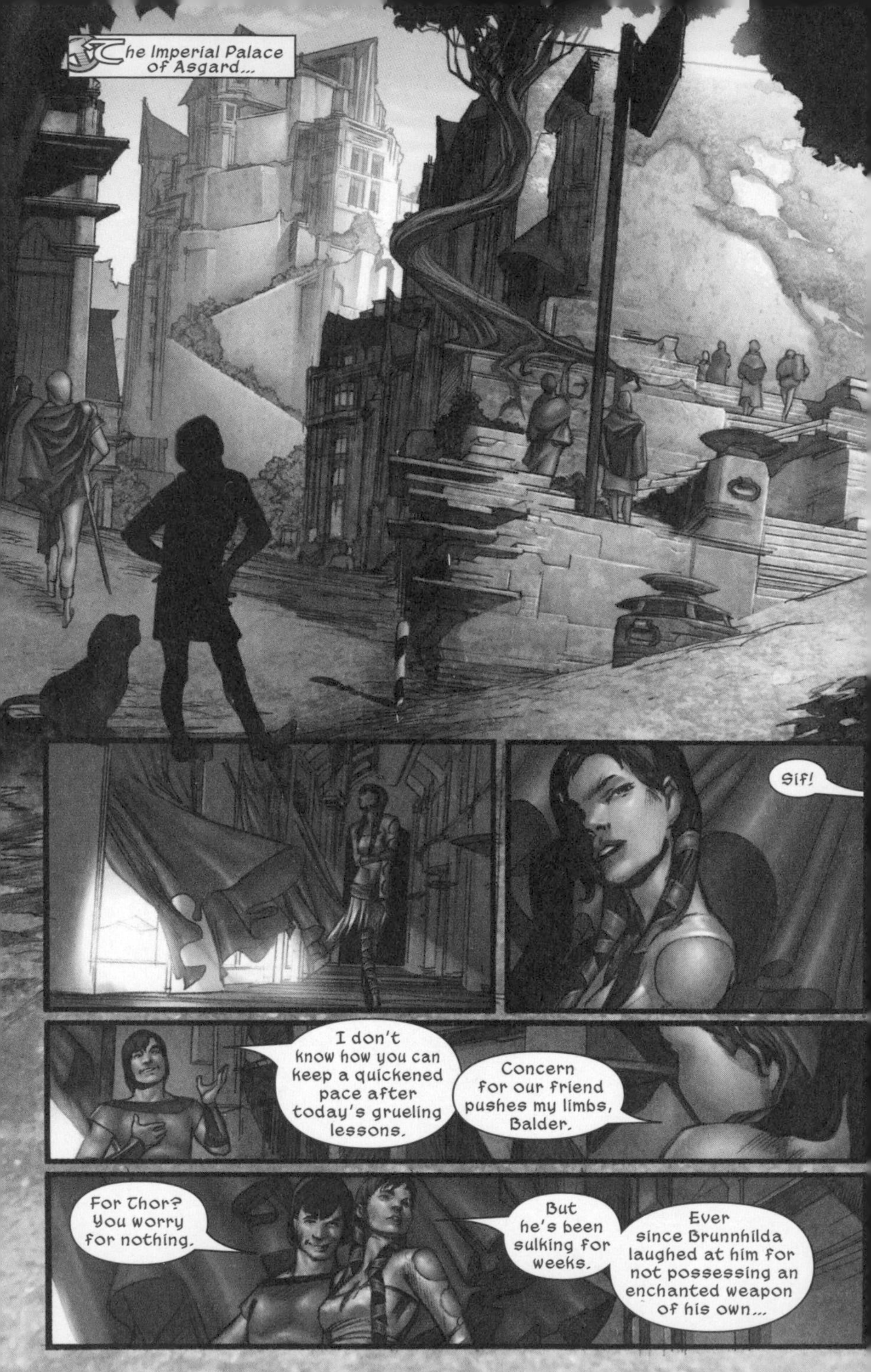
The Imperial Palace of Asgard...
Sif!
I don't know how you can keep a quickened pace after today's grueling lessons.
Concern for our friend pushes my limbs, Balder.
For Thor? You worry for nothing.
But he's been sulking for weeks.
Ever since Brunnhilda laughed at him for not possessing an enchanted weapon of his own...

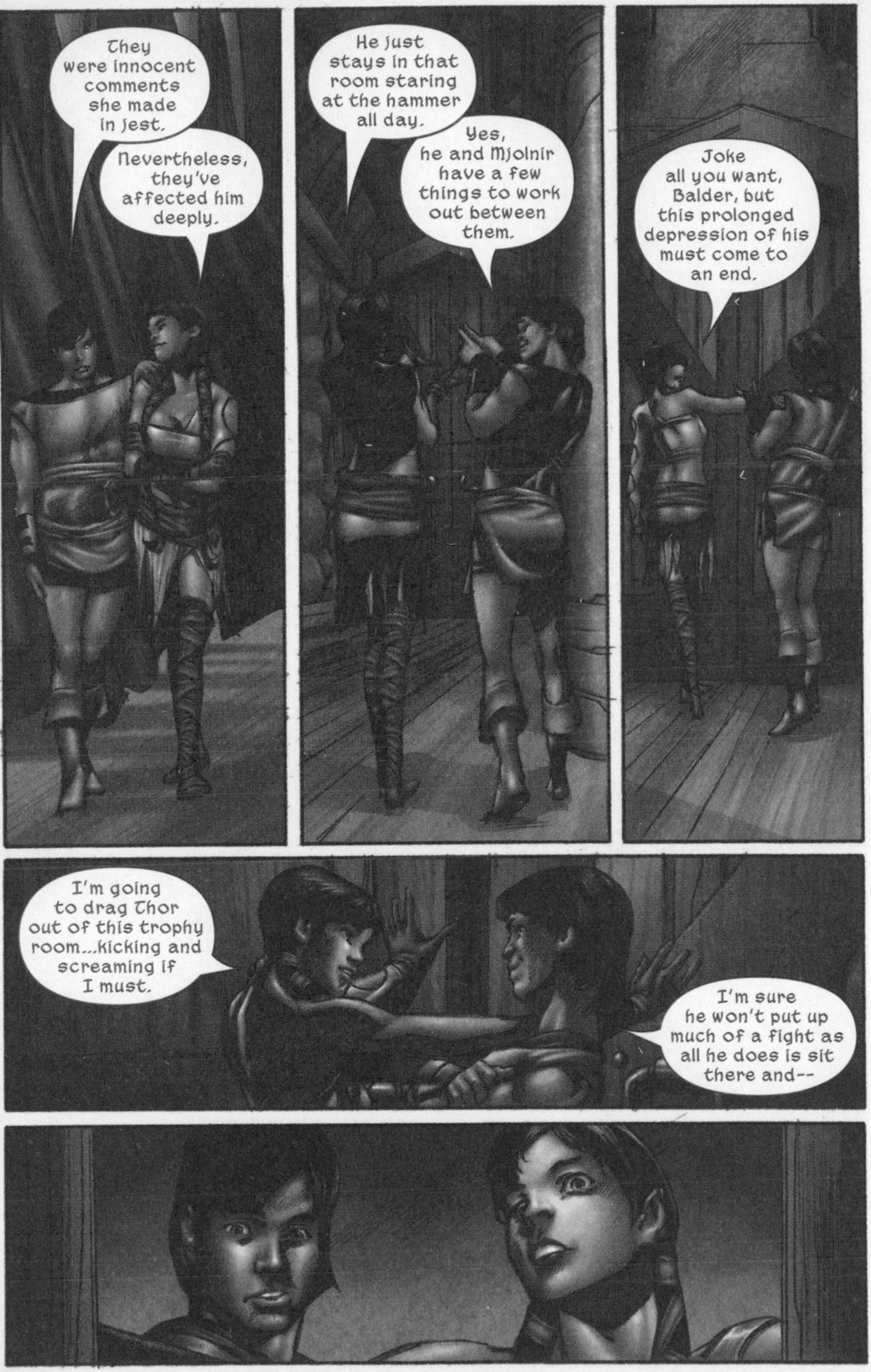
They were innocent comments she made in jest.
Nevertheless, they've affected him deeply.
He just stays in that room staring at the hammer all day.
Yes, he and Mjolnir have a few things to work out between them.
Joke all you want, Balder, but this prolonged depression of his must come to an end.
I'm going to drag Thor out of this trophy room...kicking and screaming if I must.
I'm sure he won't put up much of a fight as all he does is sit there and--

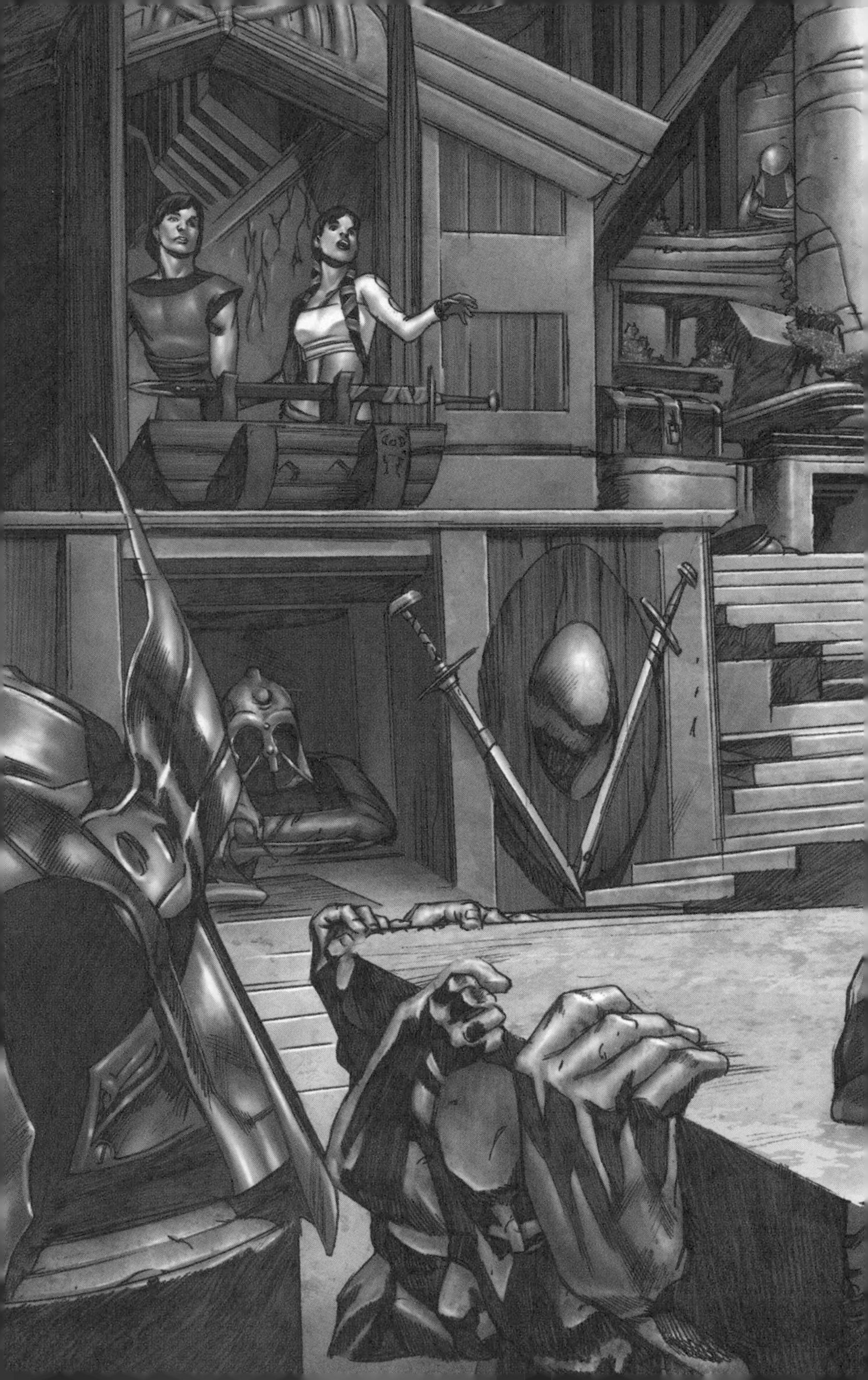

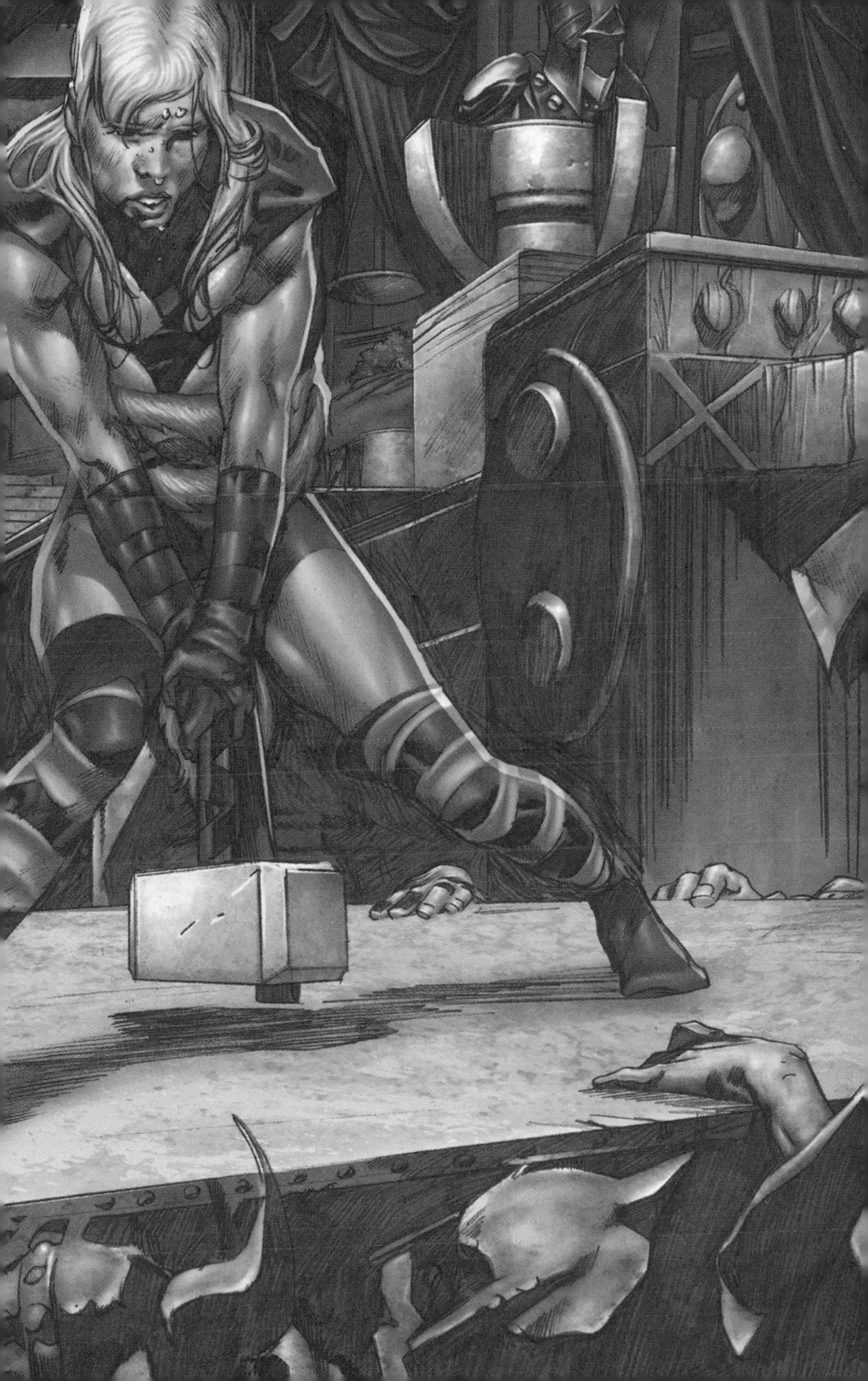

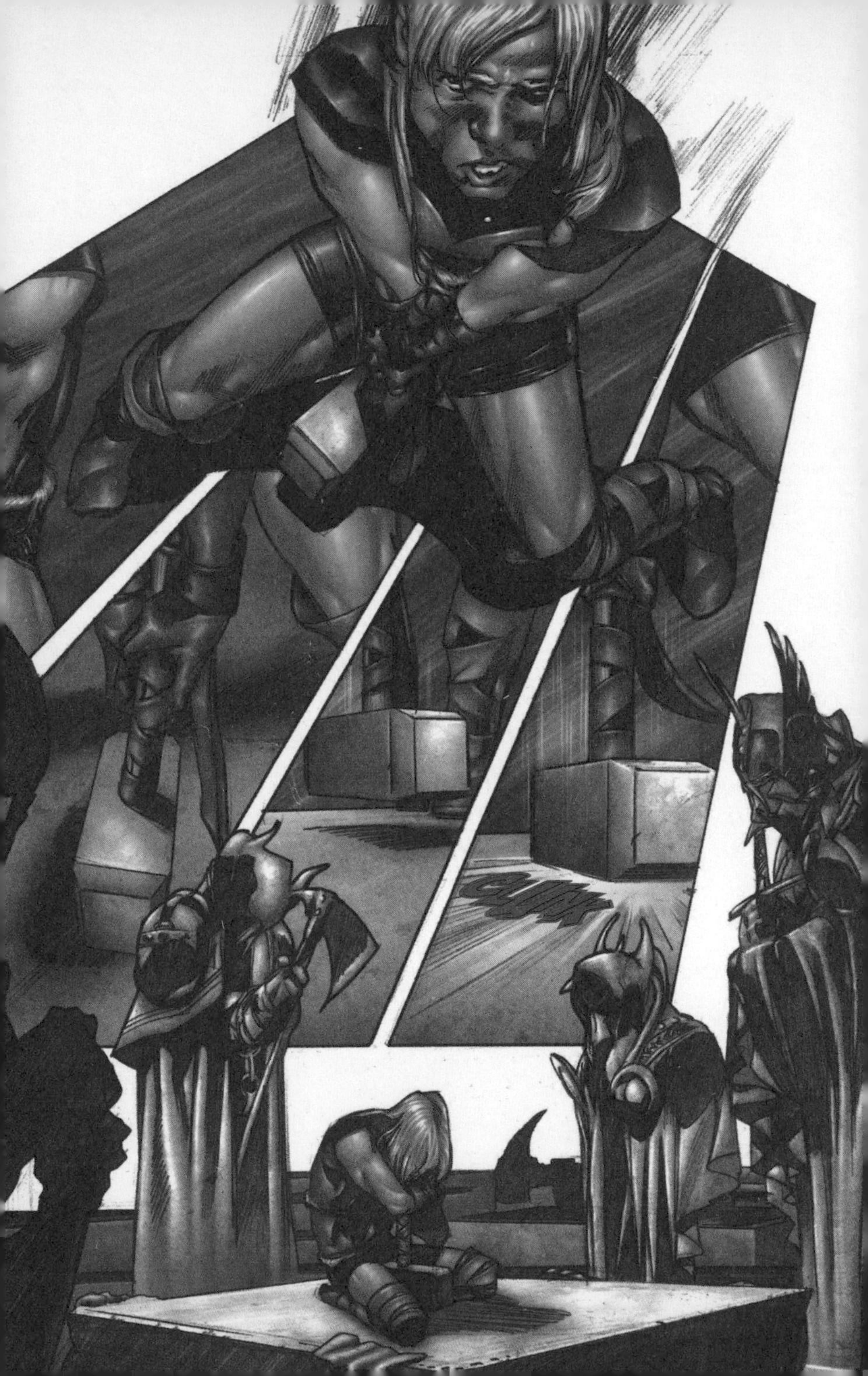
CLINK

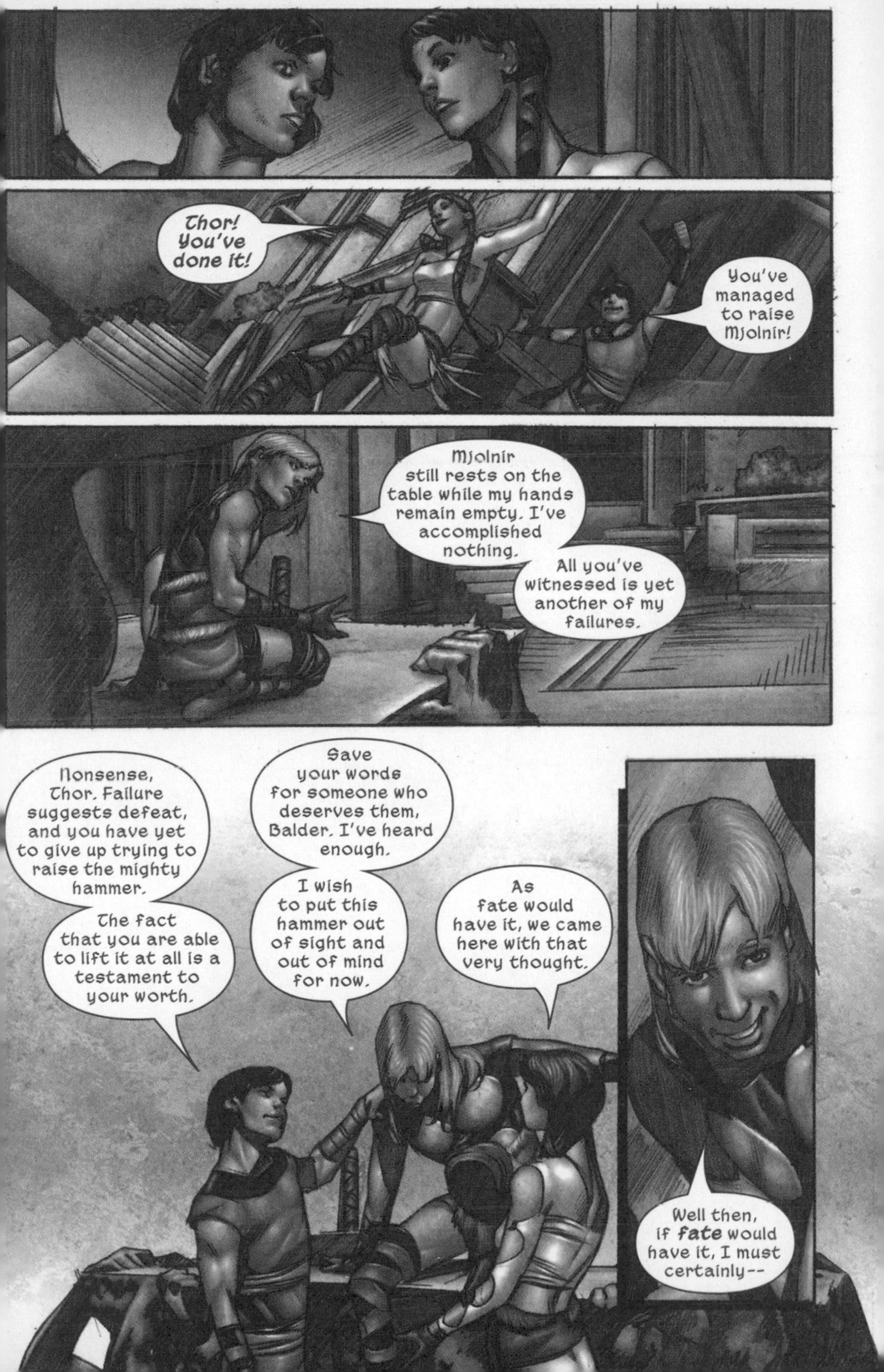
Thor! You've done it!
You've managed to raise Mjolnir!
Mjolnir still rests on the table while my hands remain empty. I've accomplished nothing.
All you've witnessed is yet another of my failures.
Nonsense, Thor. Failure suggests defeat, and you have yet to give up trying to raise the mighty hammer.
The fact that you are able to lift it at all is a testament to your worth.
Save your words for someone who deserves them, Balder. I've heard enough.
I wish to put this hammer out of sight and out of mind for now.
As fate would have it, we came here with that very thought.
Well then, if *fate* would have it, I must certainly--

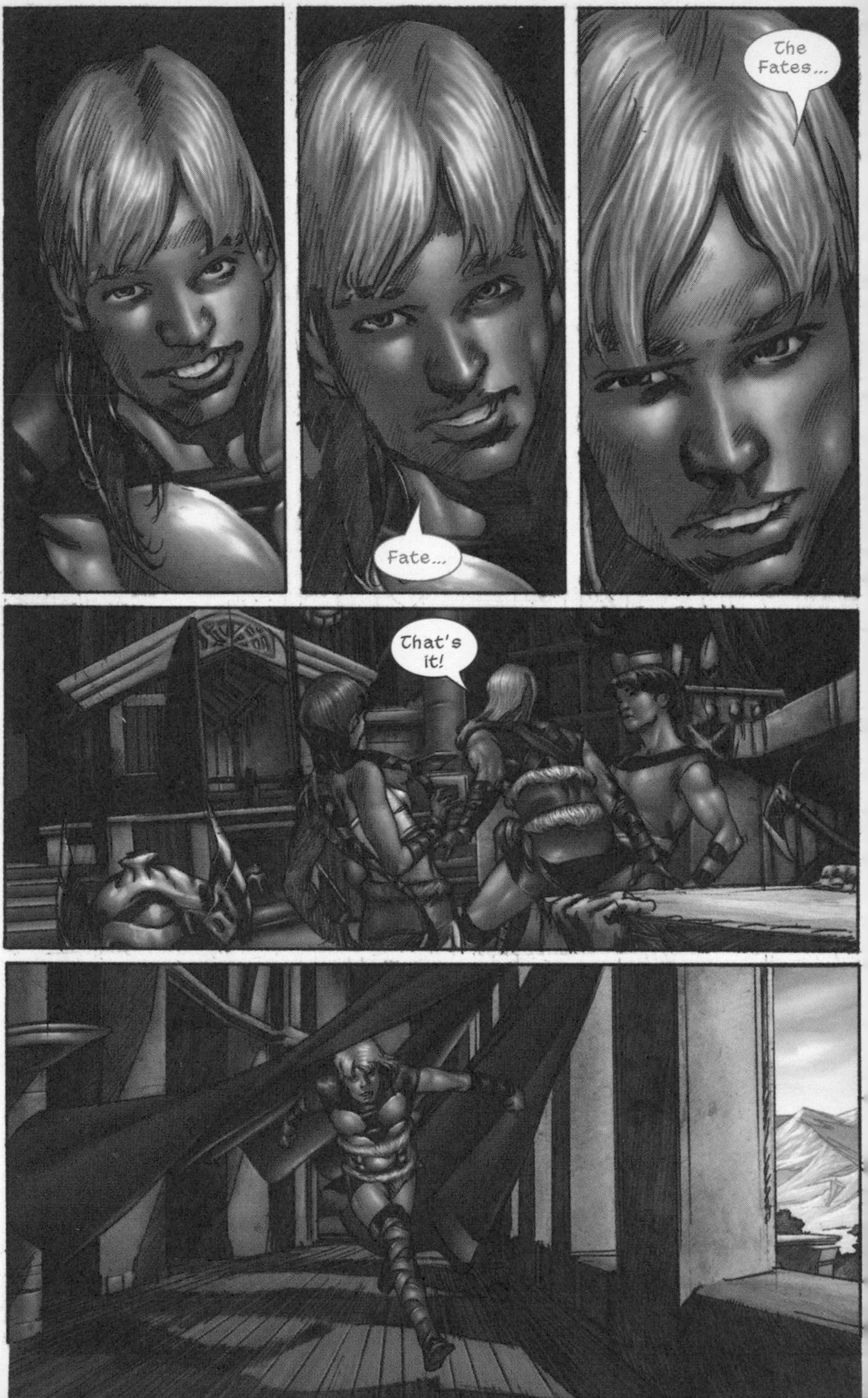
Fate...
The Fates...
That's it!

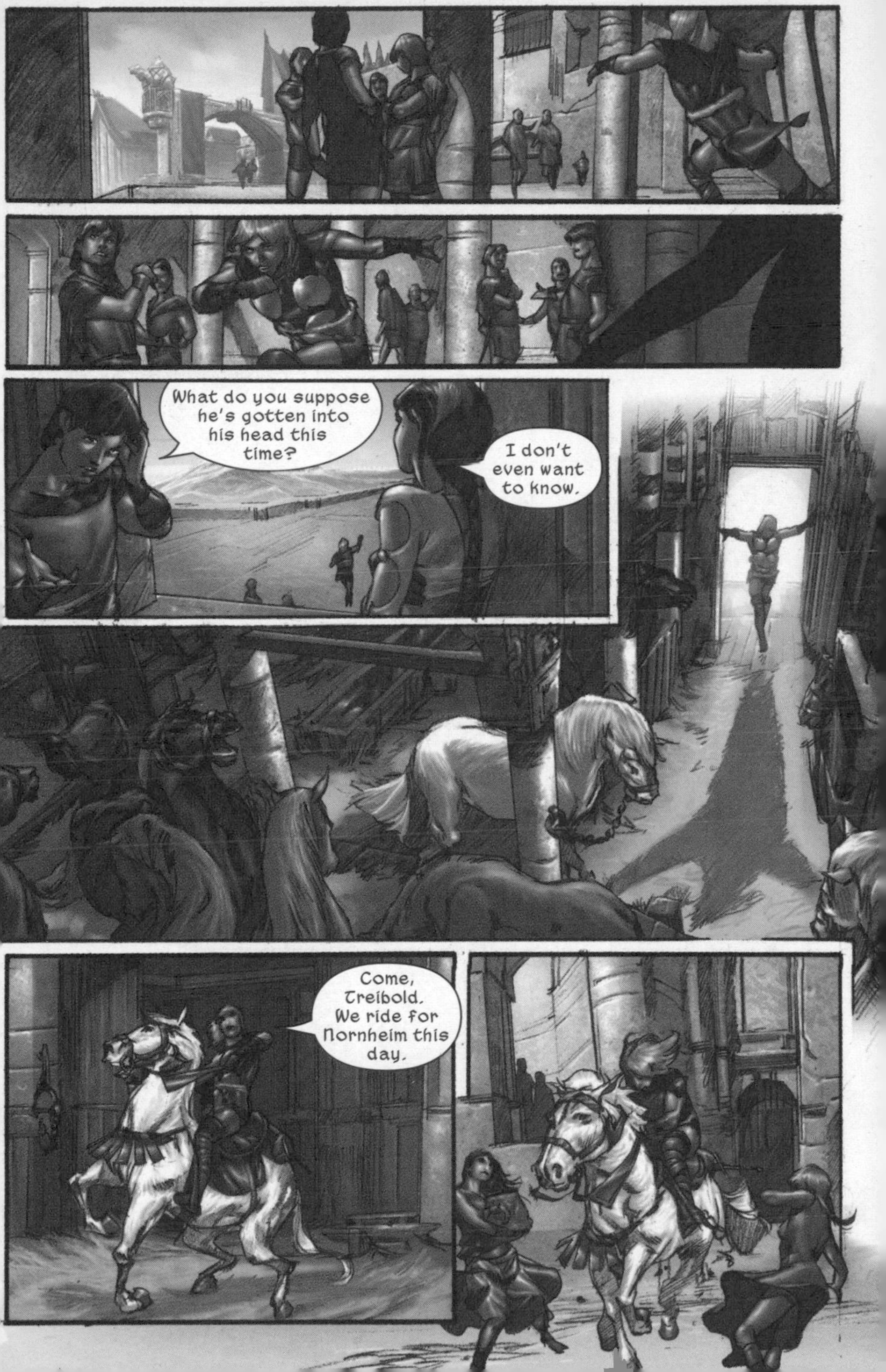
What do you suppose he's gotten into his head this time?
I don't even want to know.
Come, Treibold. We ride for Nornheim this day.

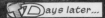

NEEIGGH

I might have to agree with you, my friend. Perhaps coming here was not the best of ideas.

But as they say, he who seeks fate, will by fate be found.

WE KNOW NOT WHO *THEY* BE, BUT THEY DO INDEED SPEAK THE TRUTH, THOR ODINSON.

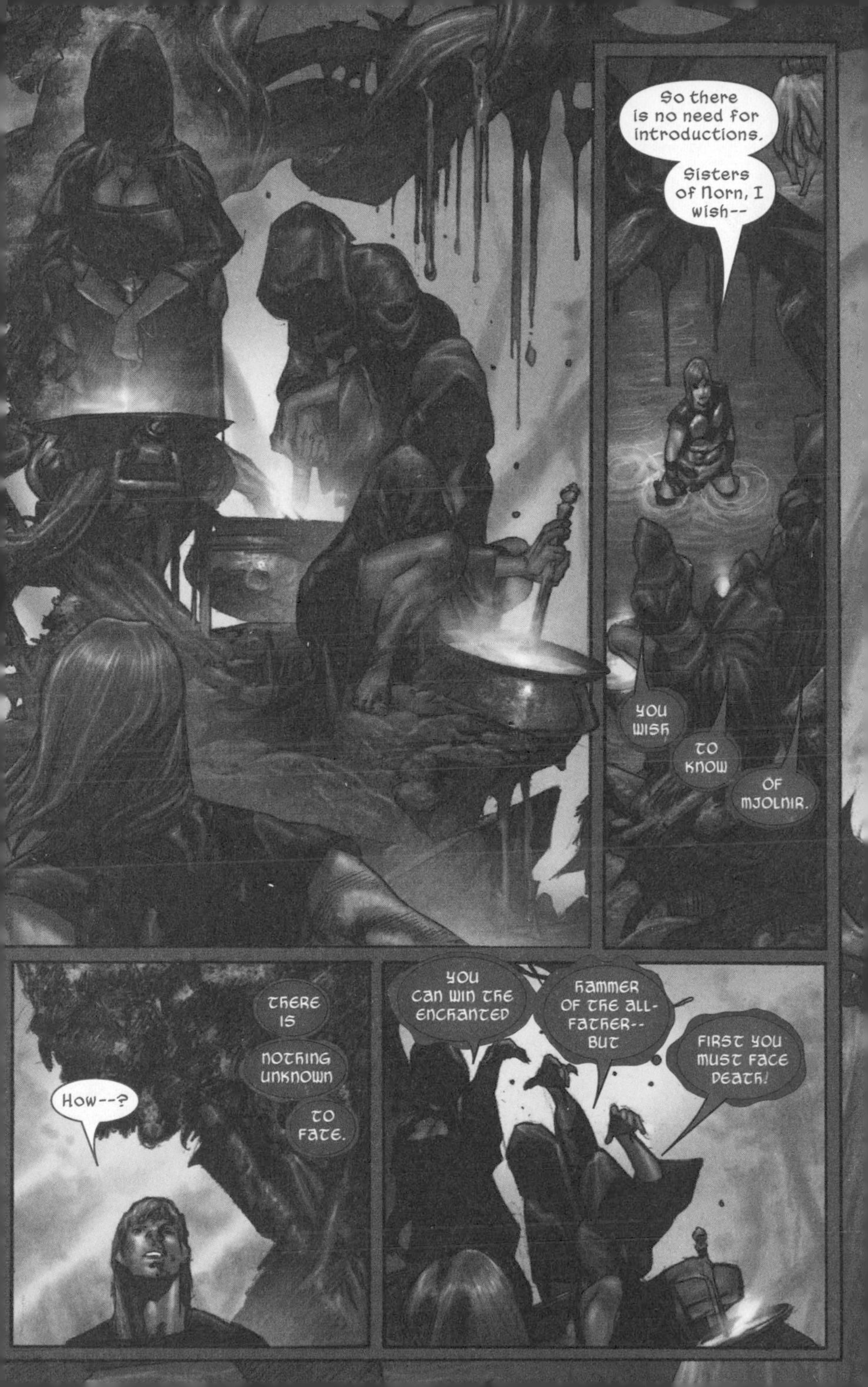
So there is no need for introductions.
Sisters of Norn, I wish--
YOU WISH
TO KNOW
OF MJOLNIR.
THERE IS
NOTHING UNKNOWN
TO FATE.
How--?
YOU CAN WIN THE ENCHANTED
HAMMER OF THE ALL-FATHER--BUT
FIRST YOU MUST FACE DEATH!

I must face death?! That is how I must prove my worth to bear Mjolnir?
But I have felt Hela's cold touch before! Was once not enough?
FWASSH
What was the meaning of their words? Must I die again in order to become worthy?
Surely this cannot mean I'm doomed?! But the Fates never lie!
So be it! Even if death stands between me and my destiny, I will not back down!
I must have the hammer!
Mjolnir will be mine!

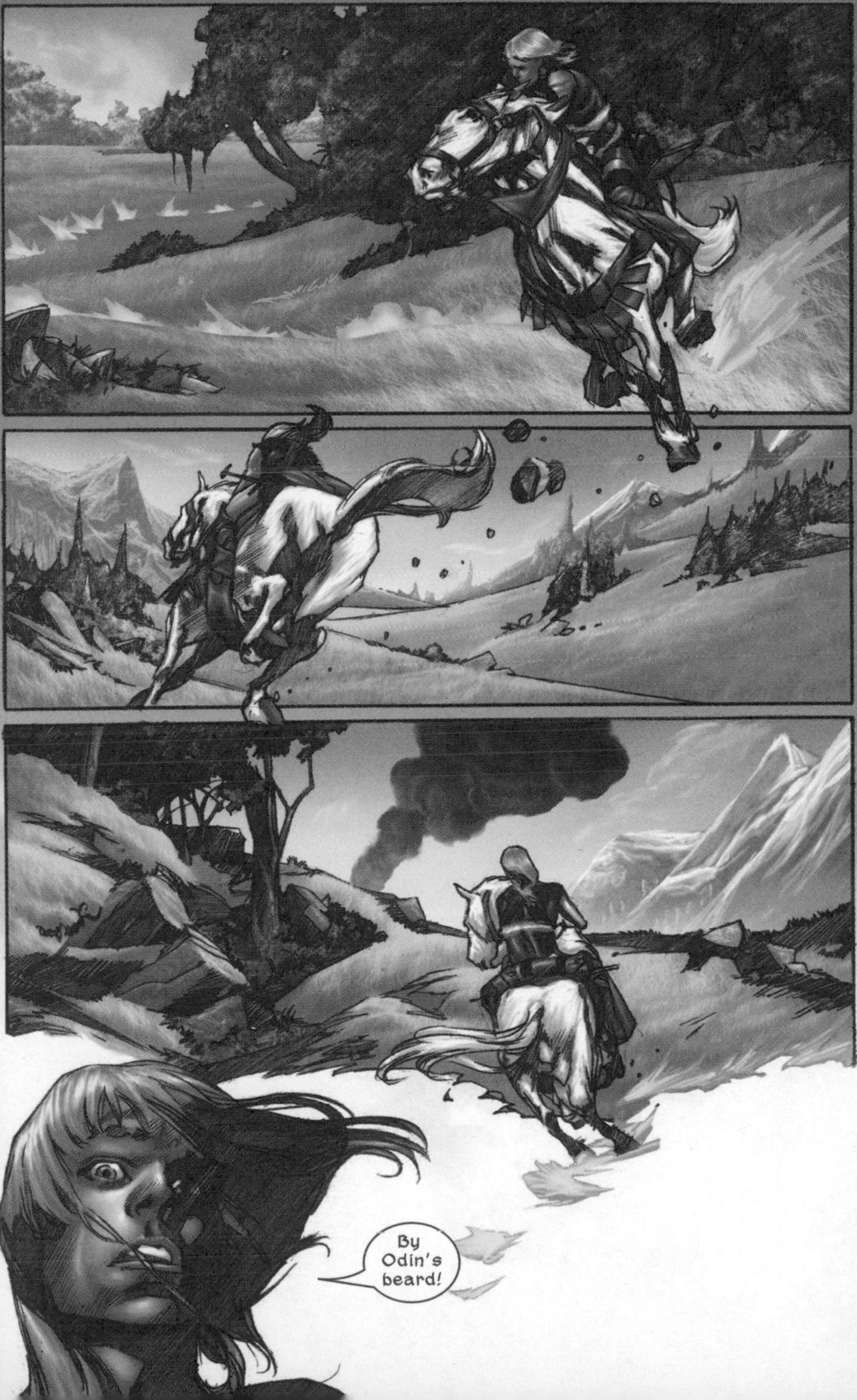
By Odin's beard!

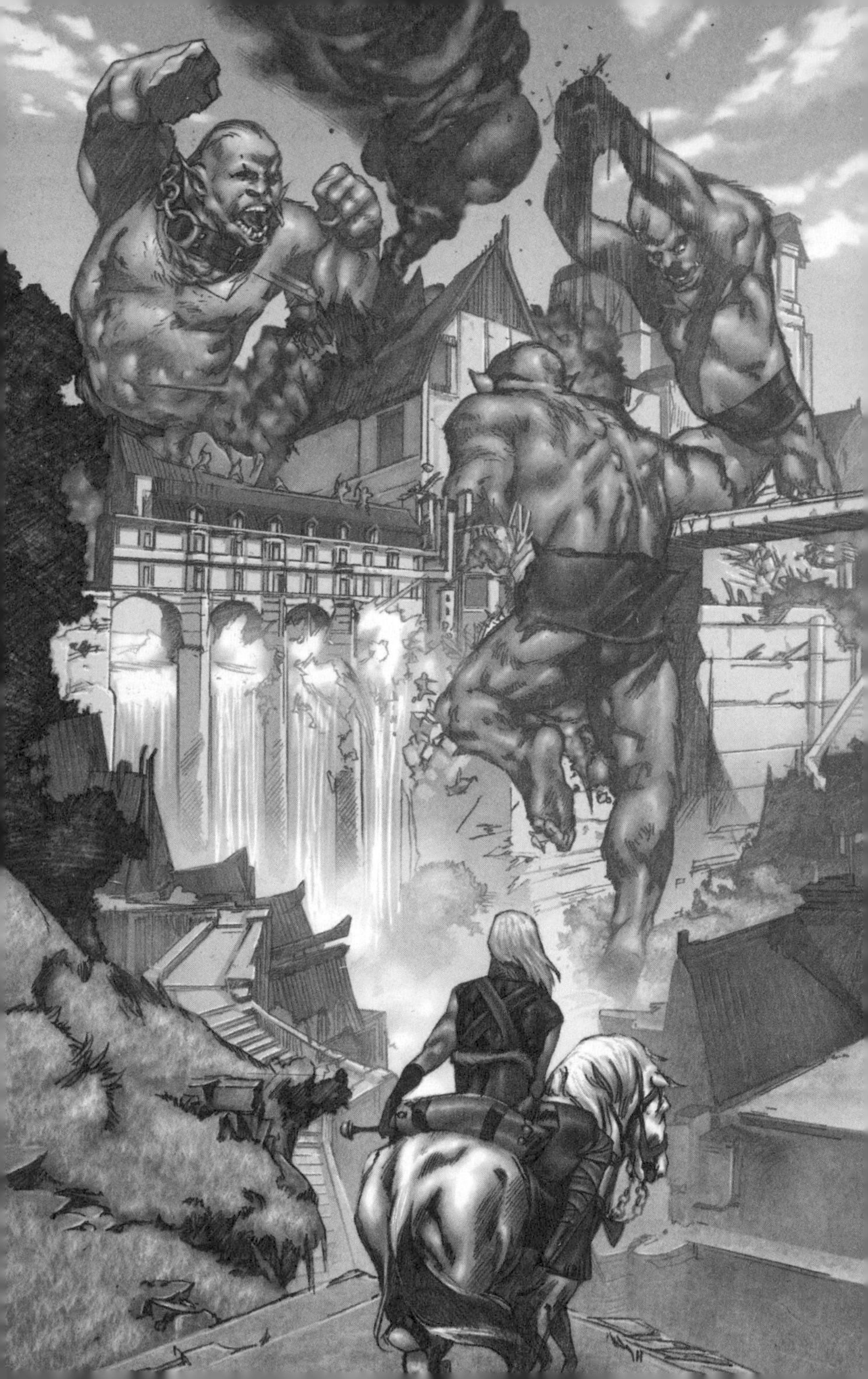

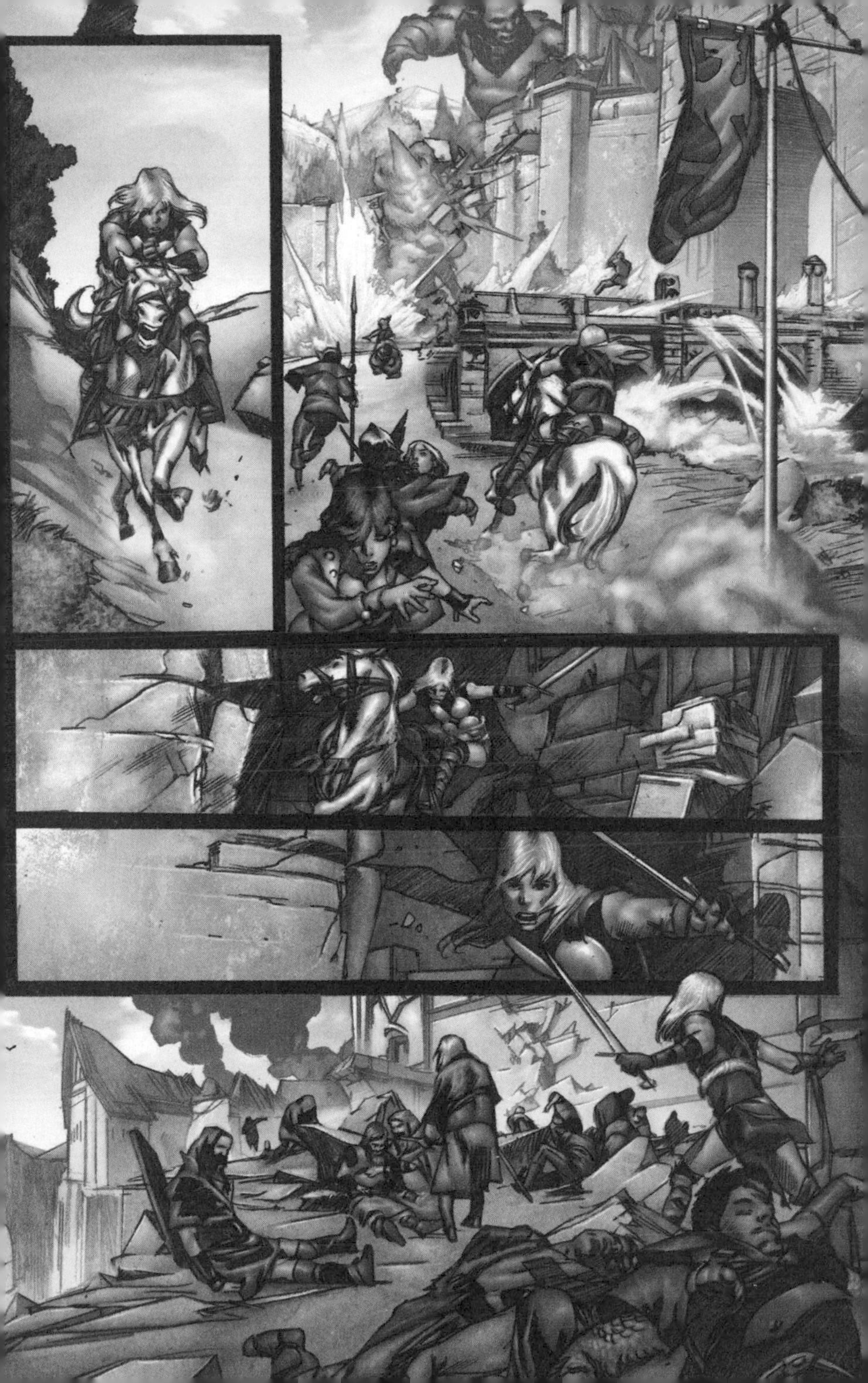

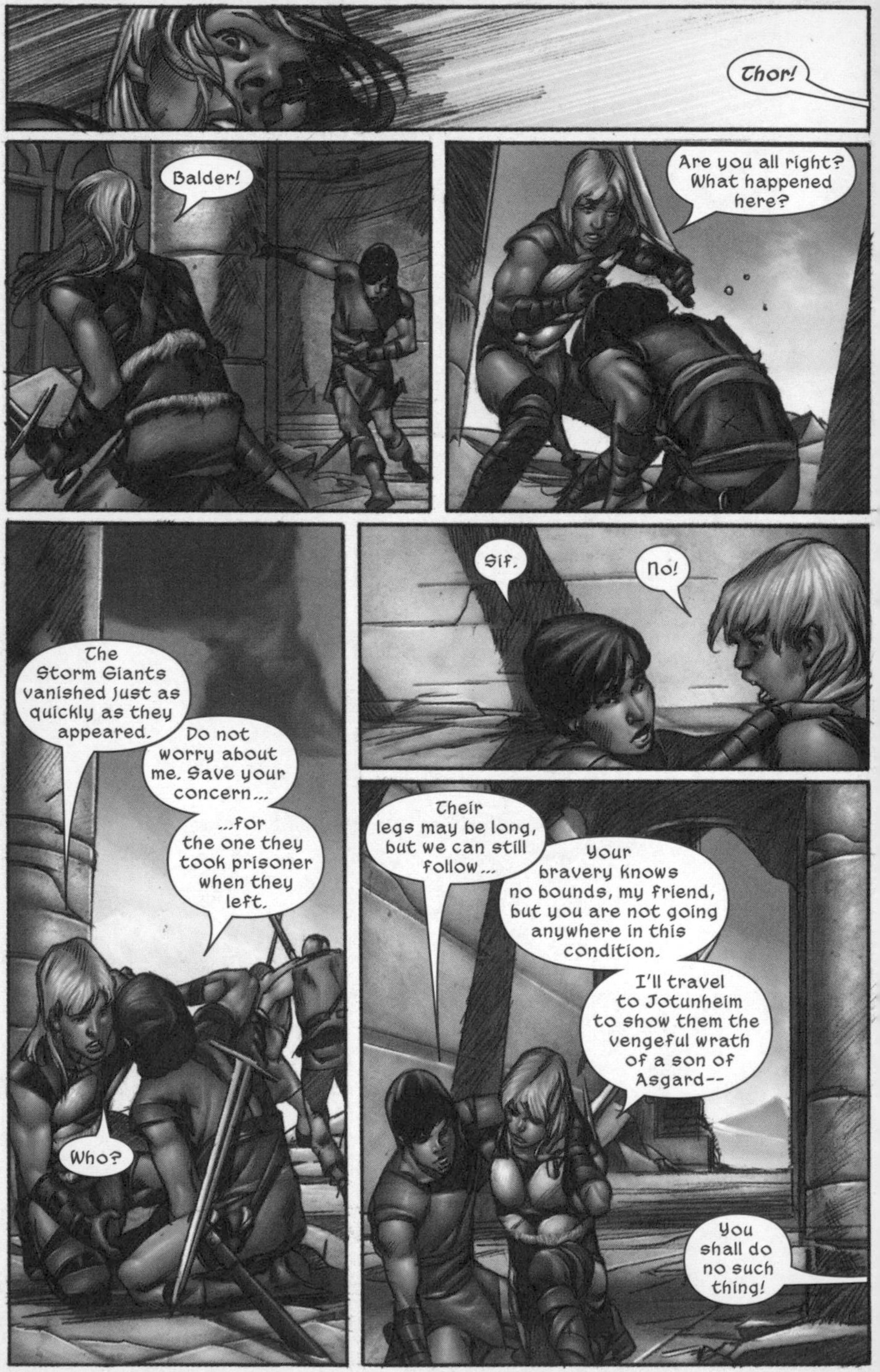
Thor!
Balder!
Are you all right? What happened here?
The Storm Giants vanished just as quickly as they appeared.
Do not worry about me. Save your concern...
...for the one they took prisoner when they left.
Who?
Sif.
No!
Their legs may be long, but we can still follow...
Your bravery knows no bounds, my friend, but you are not going anywhere in this condition.
I'll travel to Jotunheim to show them the vengeful wrath of a son of Asgard--
You shall do no such thing!

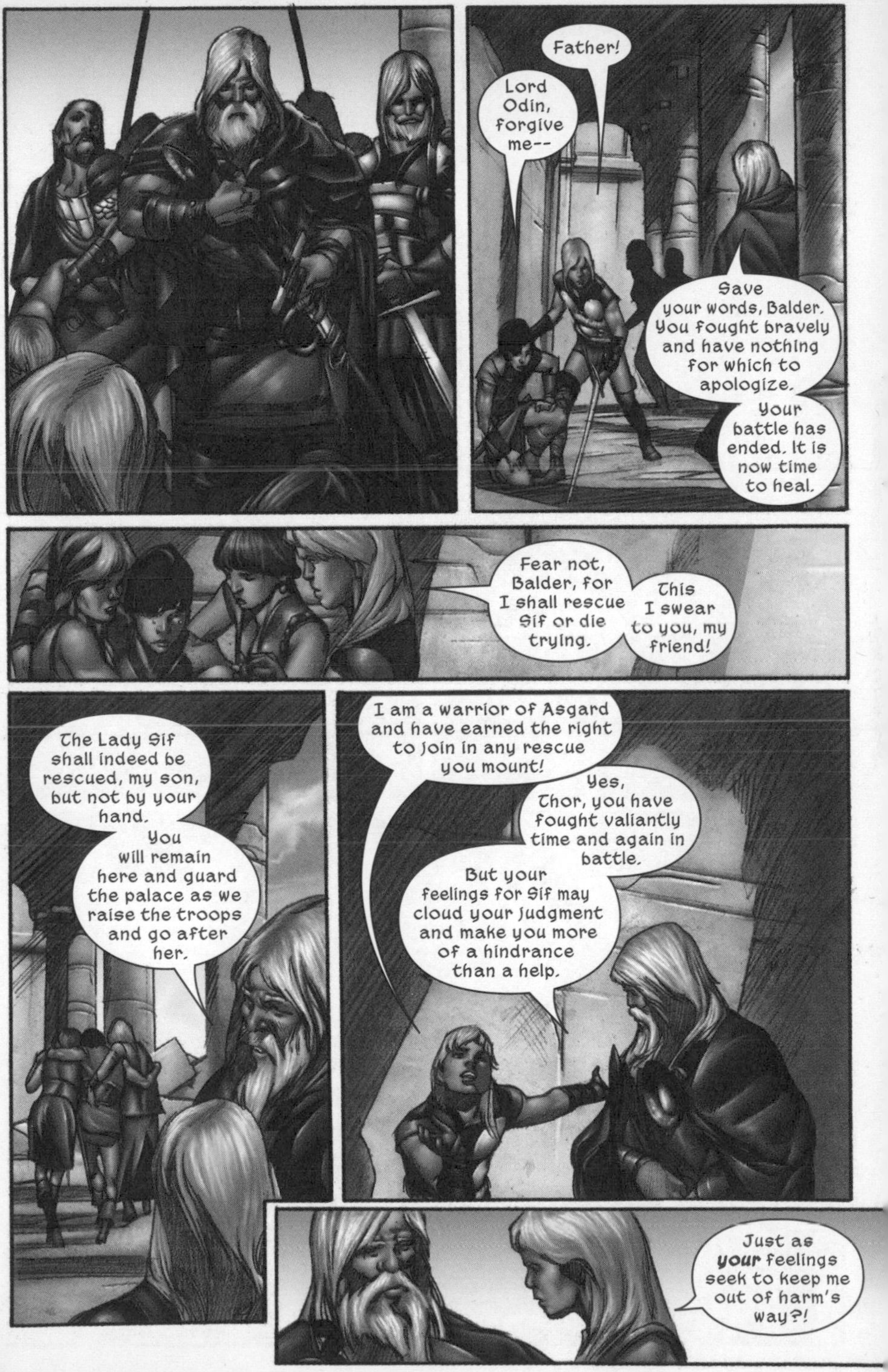
Lord Odin, forgive me--
Father!
Save your words, Balder. You fought bravely and have nothing for which to apologize.
Your battle has ended. It is now time to heal.
Fear not, Balder, for I shall rescue Sif or die trying.
This I swear to you, my friend!
The Lady Sif shall indeed be rescued, my son, but not by your hand.
You will remain here and guard the palace as we raise the troops and go after her.
I am a warrior of Asgard and have earned the right to join in any rescue you mount!
Yes, Thor, you have fought valiantly time and again in battle.
But your feelings for Sif may cloud your judgment and make you more of a hindrance than a help.
Just as **your** feelings seek to keep me out of harm's way?!

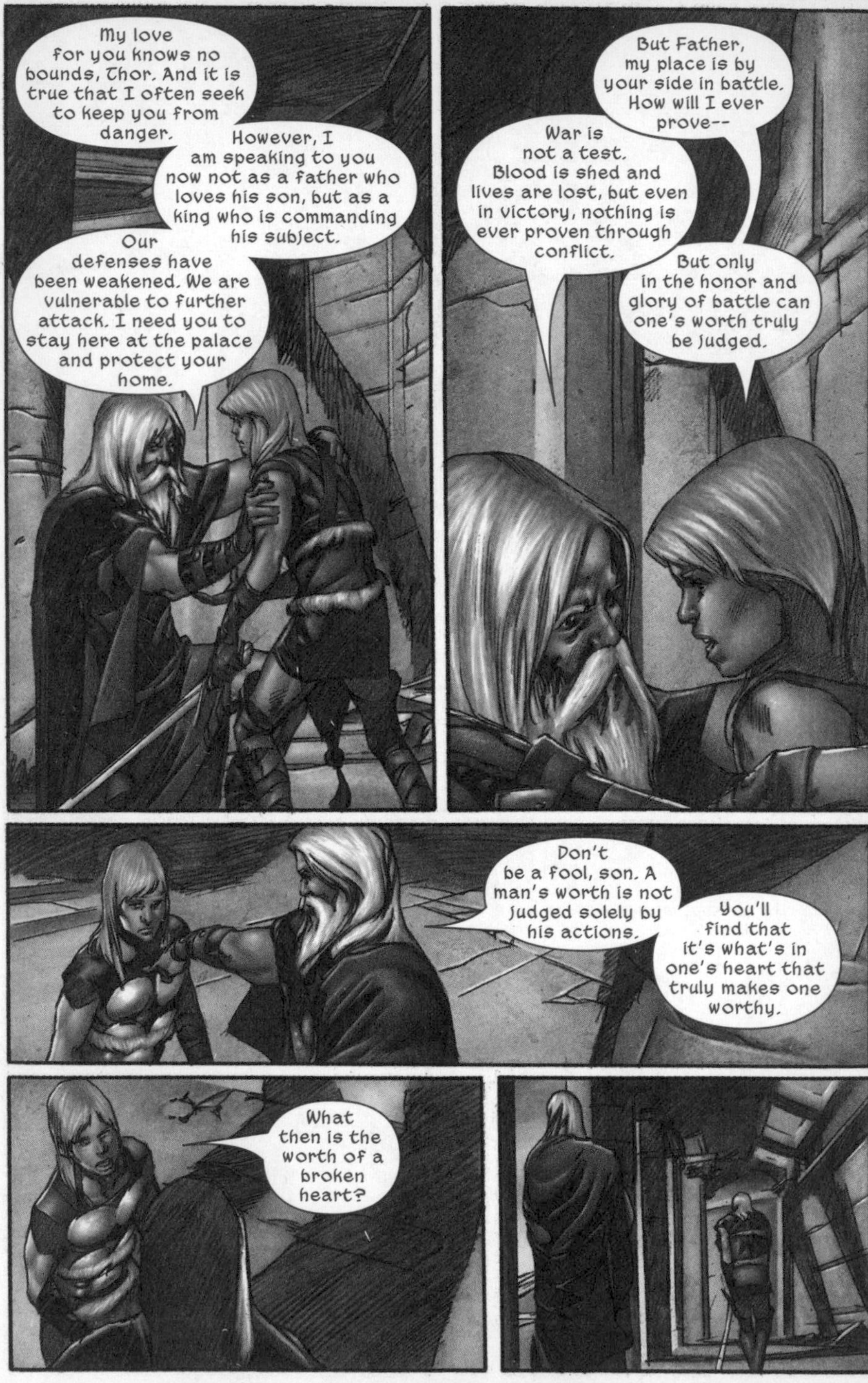
My love for you knows no bounds, Thor. And it is true that I often seek to keep you from danger.
However, I am speaking to you now not as a father who loves his son, but as a king who is commanding his subject.
Our defenses have been weakened. We are vulnerable to further attack. I need you to stay here at the palace and protect your home.
But Father, my place is by your side in battle. How will I ever prove--
War is not a test. Blood is shed and lives are lost, but even in victory, nothing is ever proven through conflict.
But only in the honor and glory of battle can one's worth truly be judged.
Don't be a fool, son. A man's worth is not judged solely by his actions.
You'll find that it's what's in one's heart that truly makes one worthy.
What then is the worth of a broken heart?

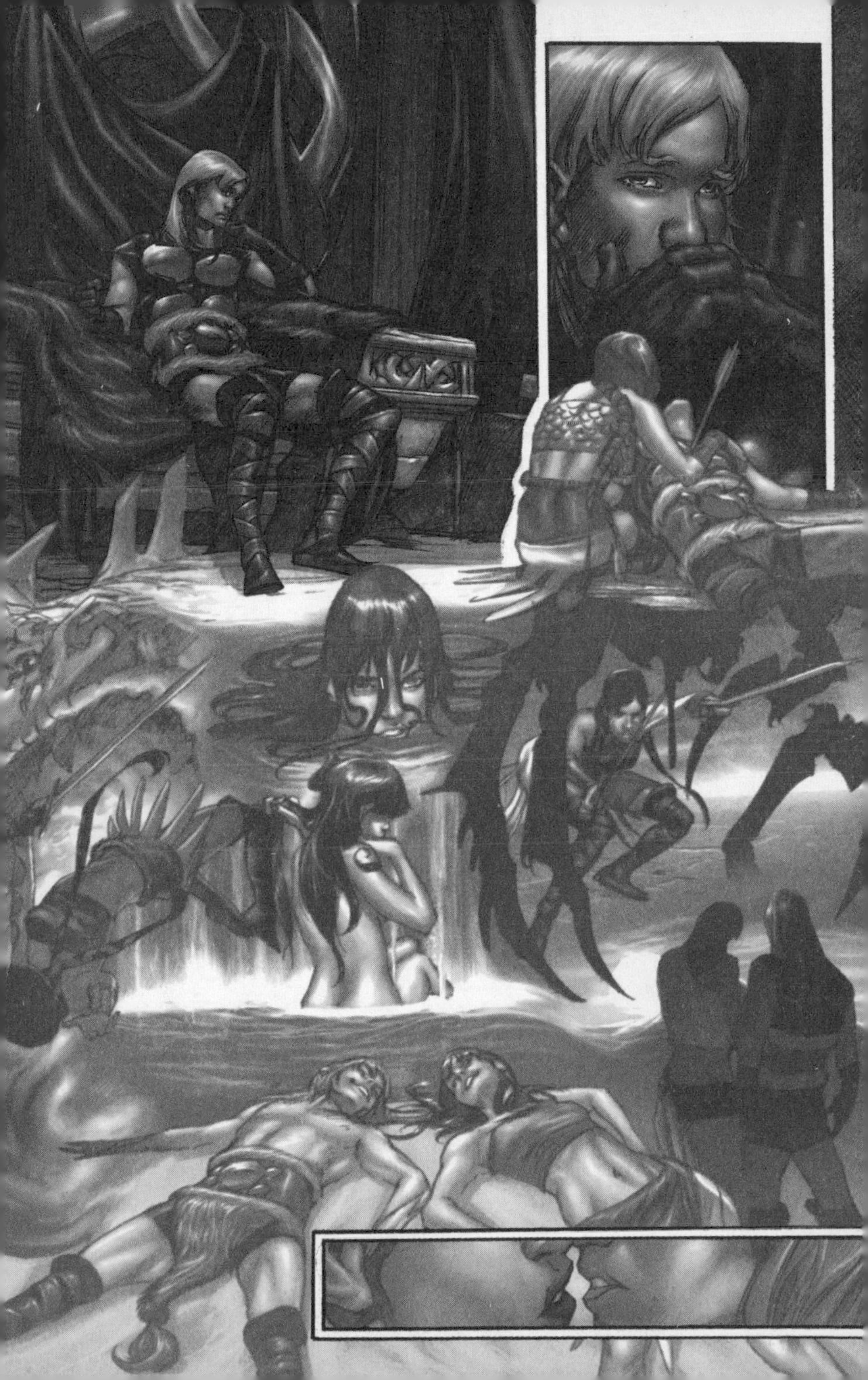

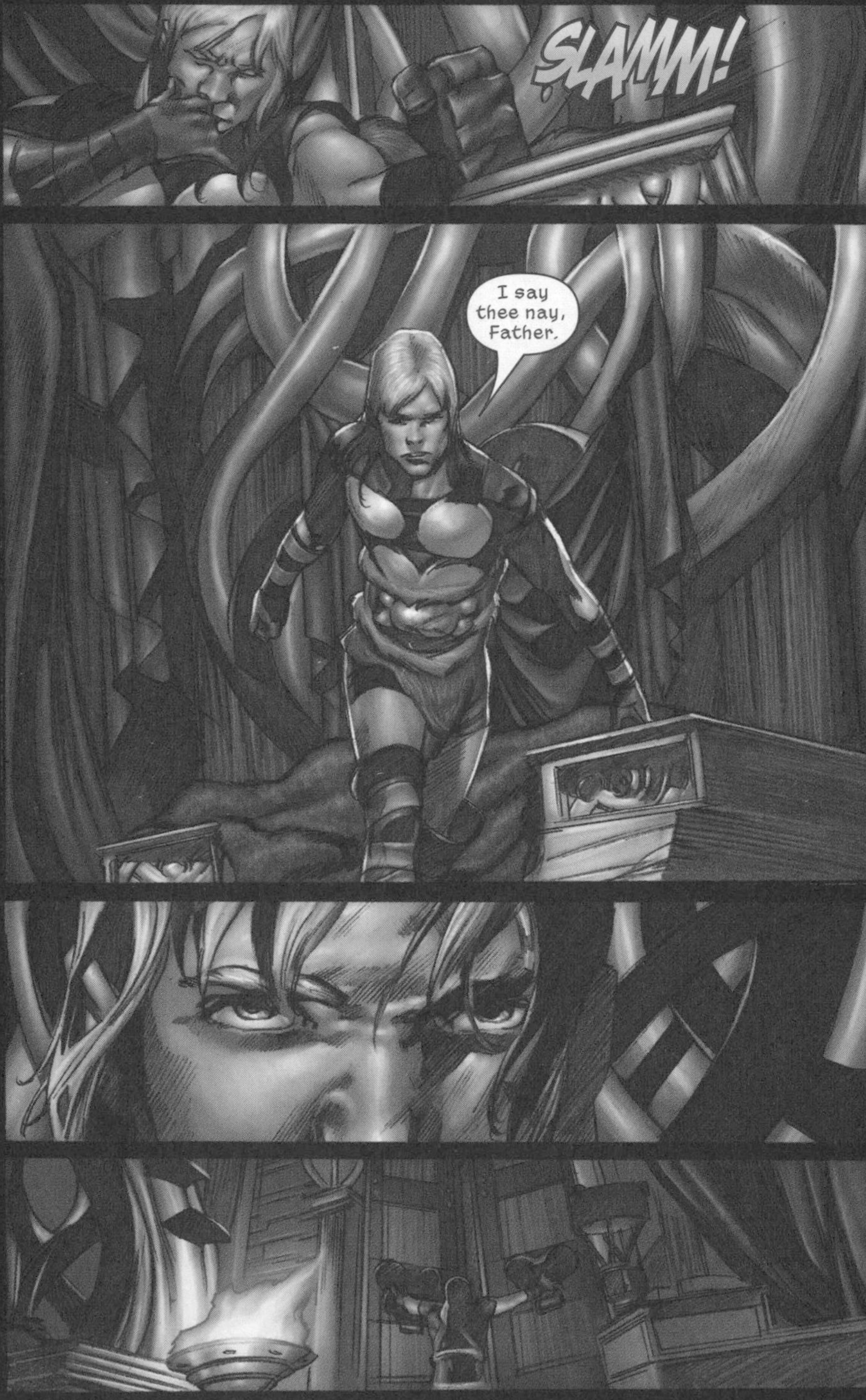
SLAMM!
I say thee nay, Father.

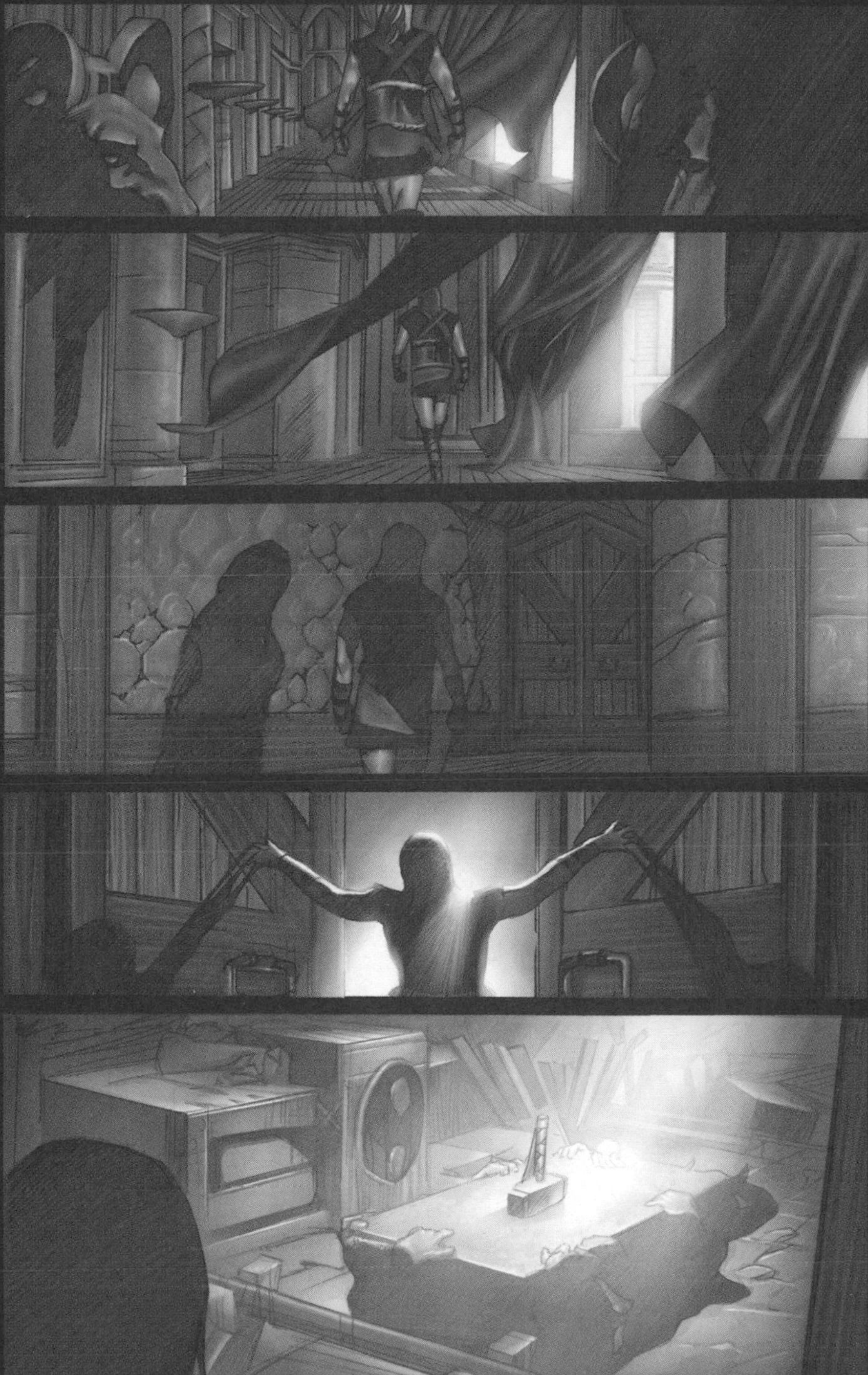

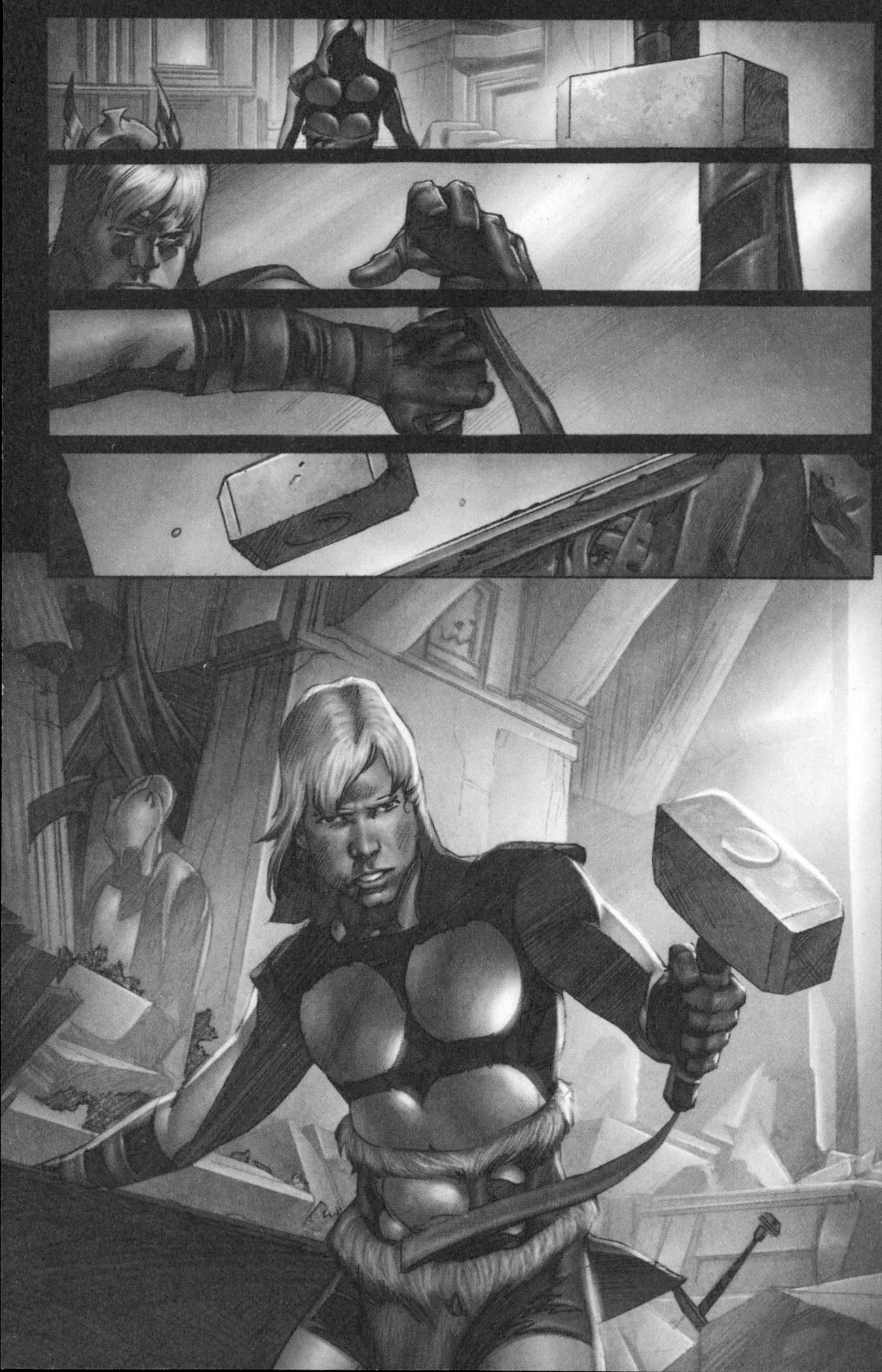

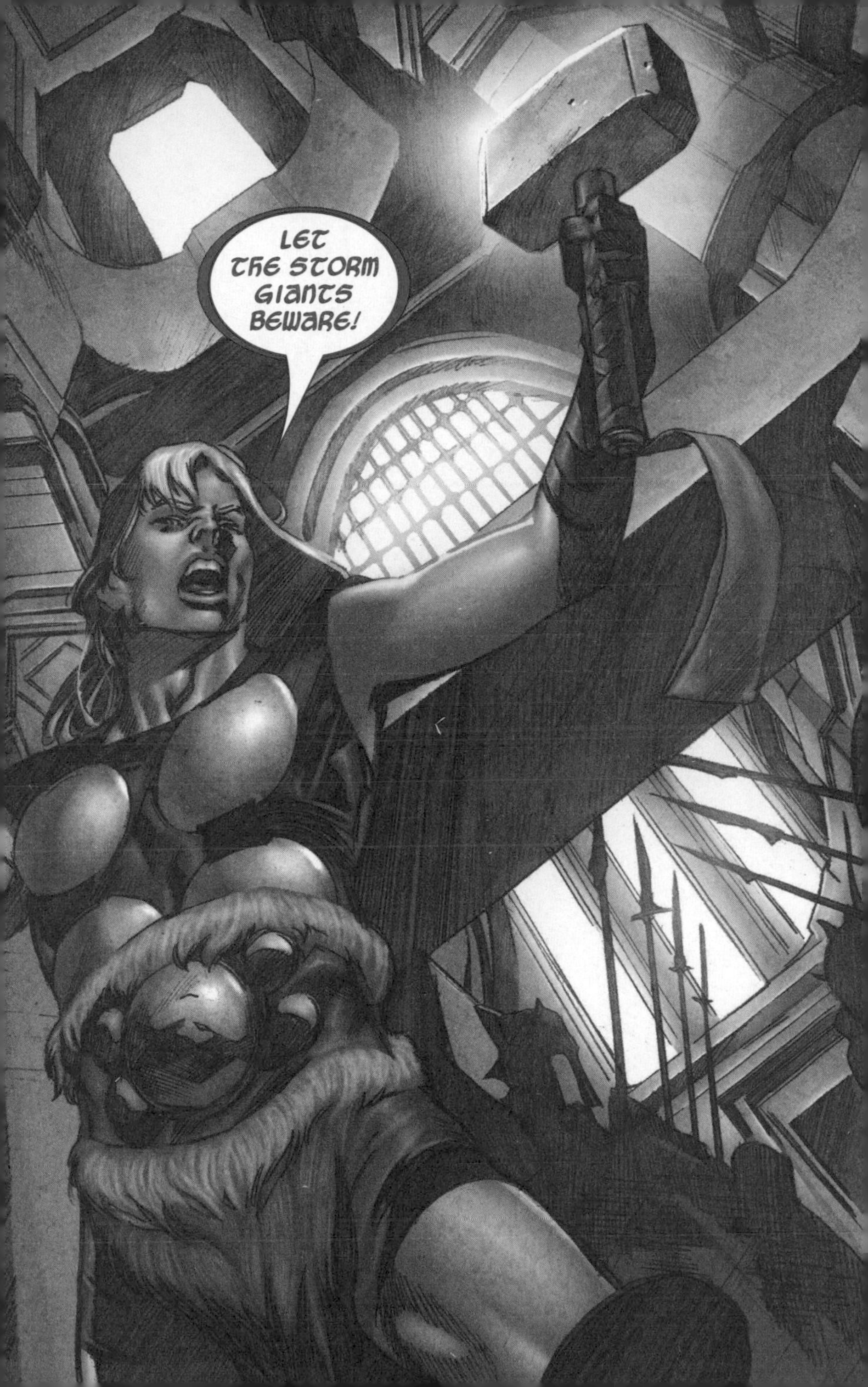
LET THE STORM GIANTS BEWARE!

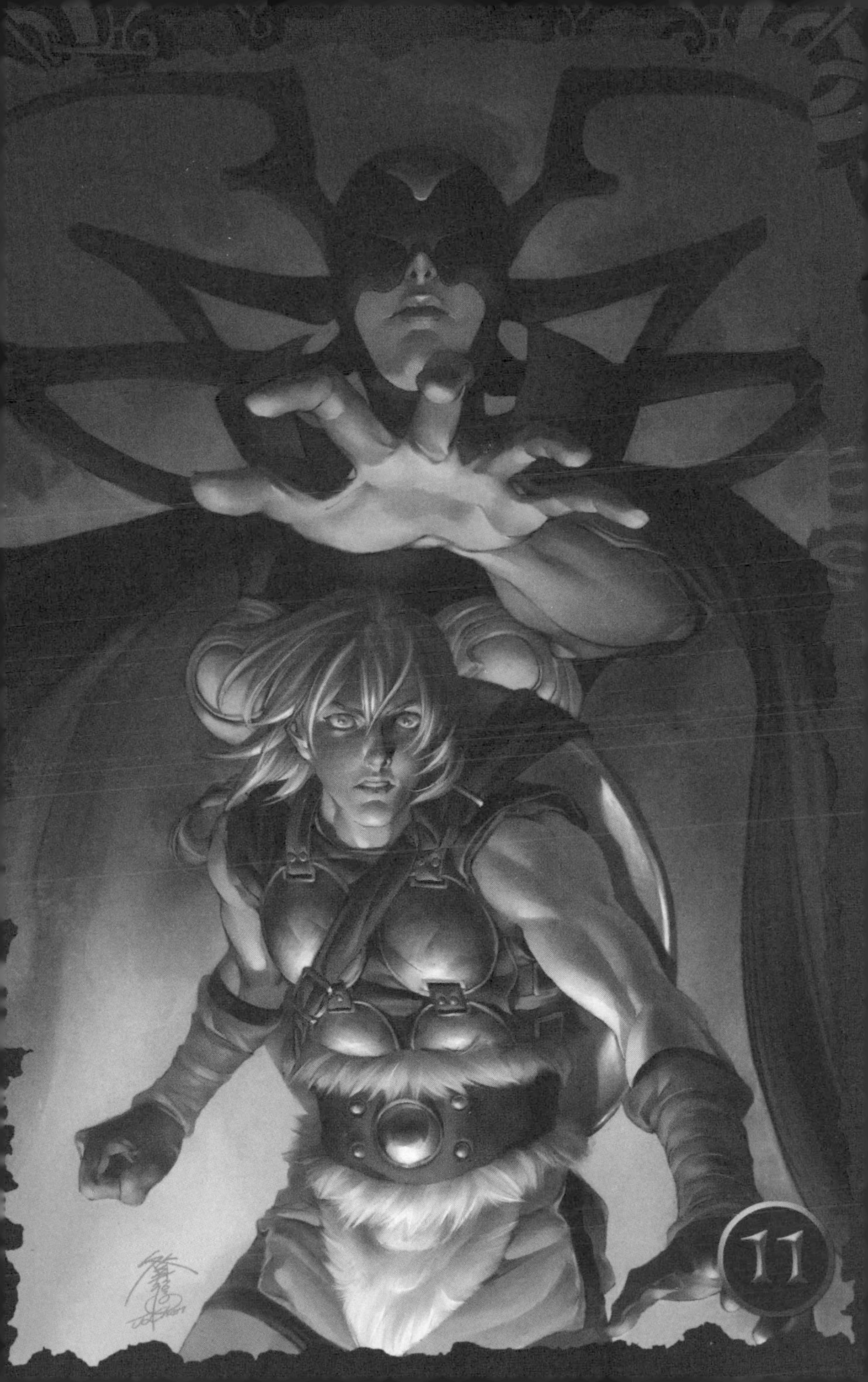
11

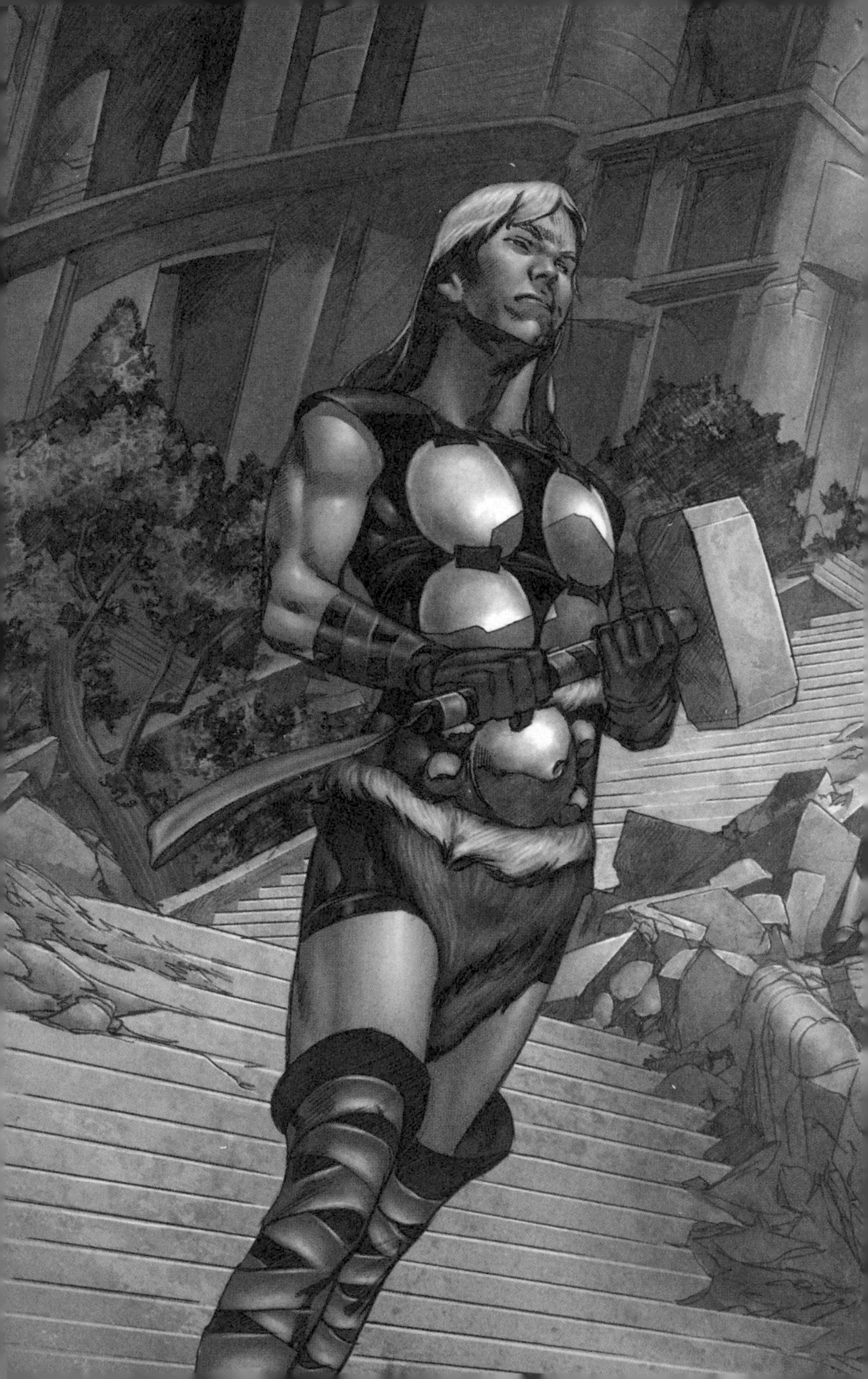

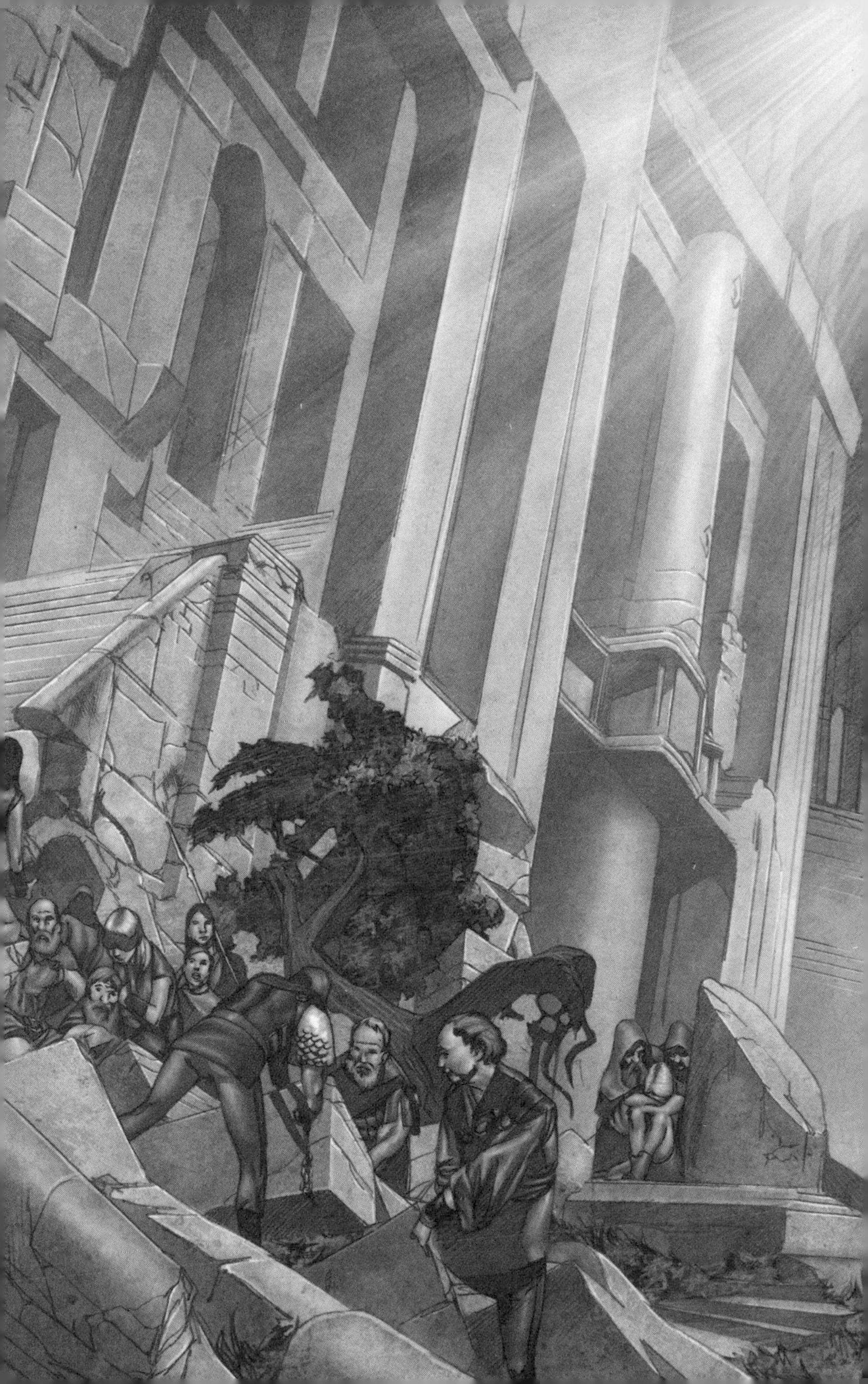

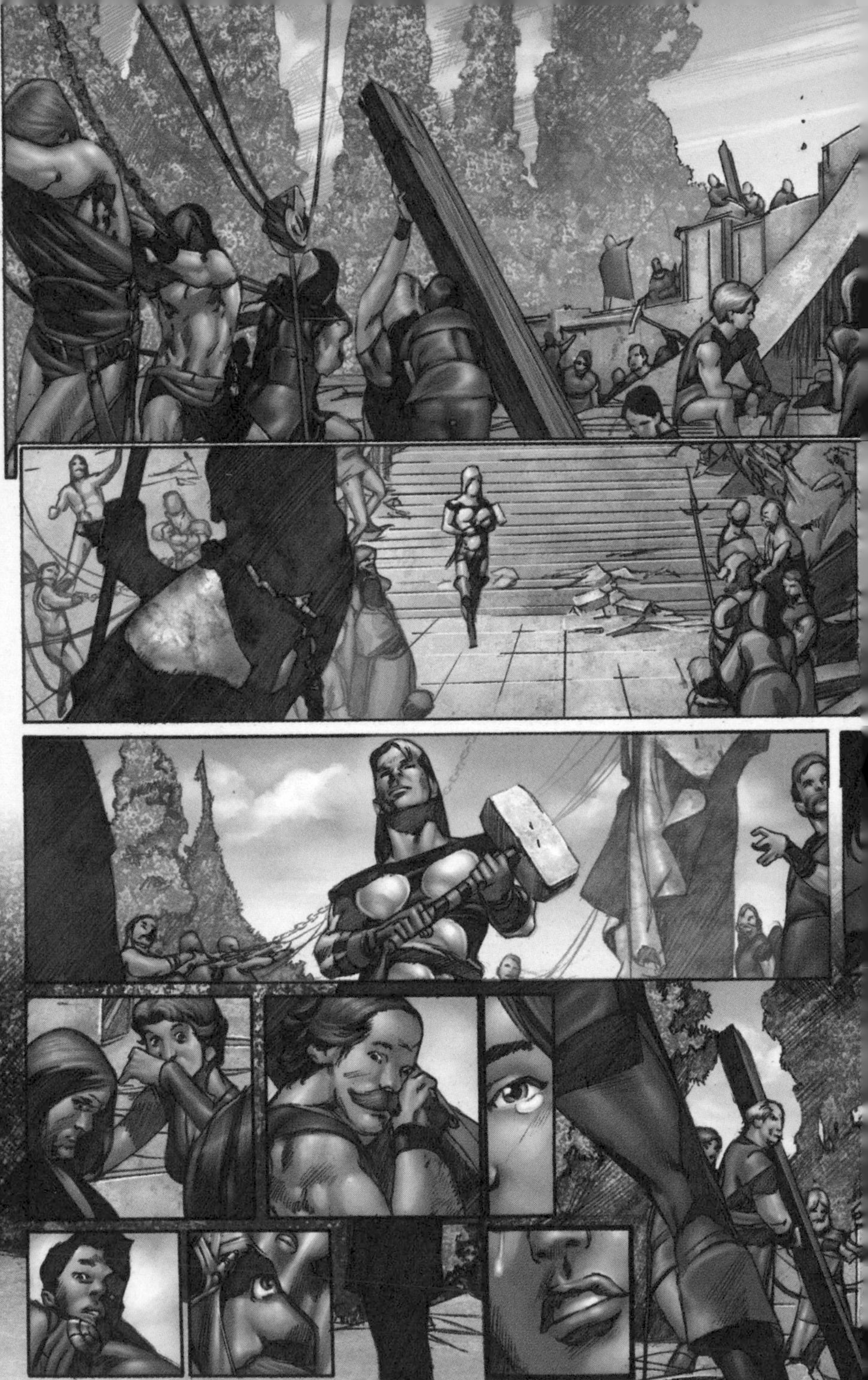

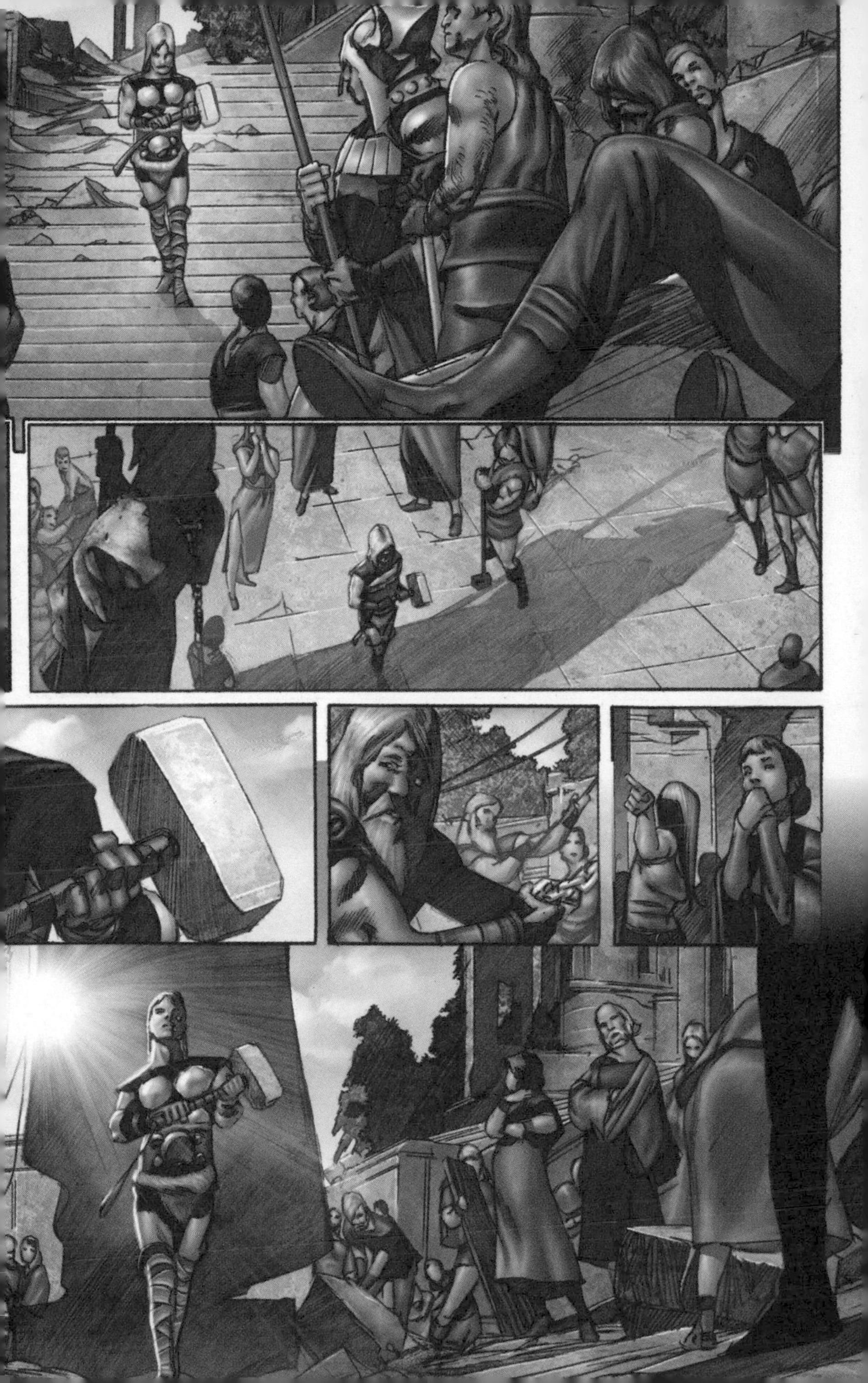

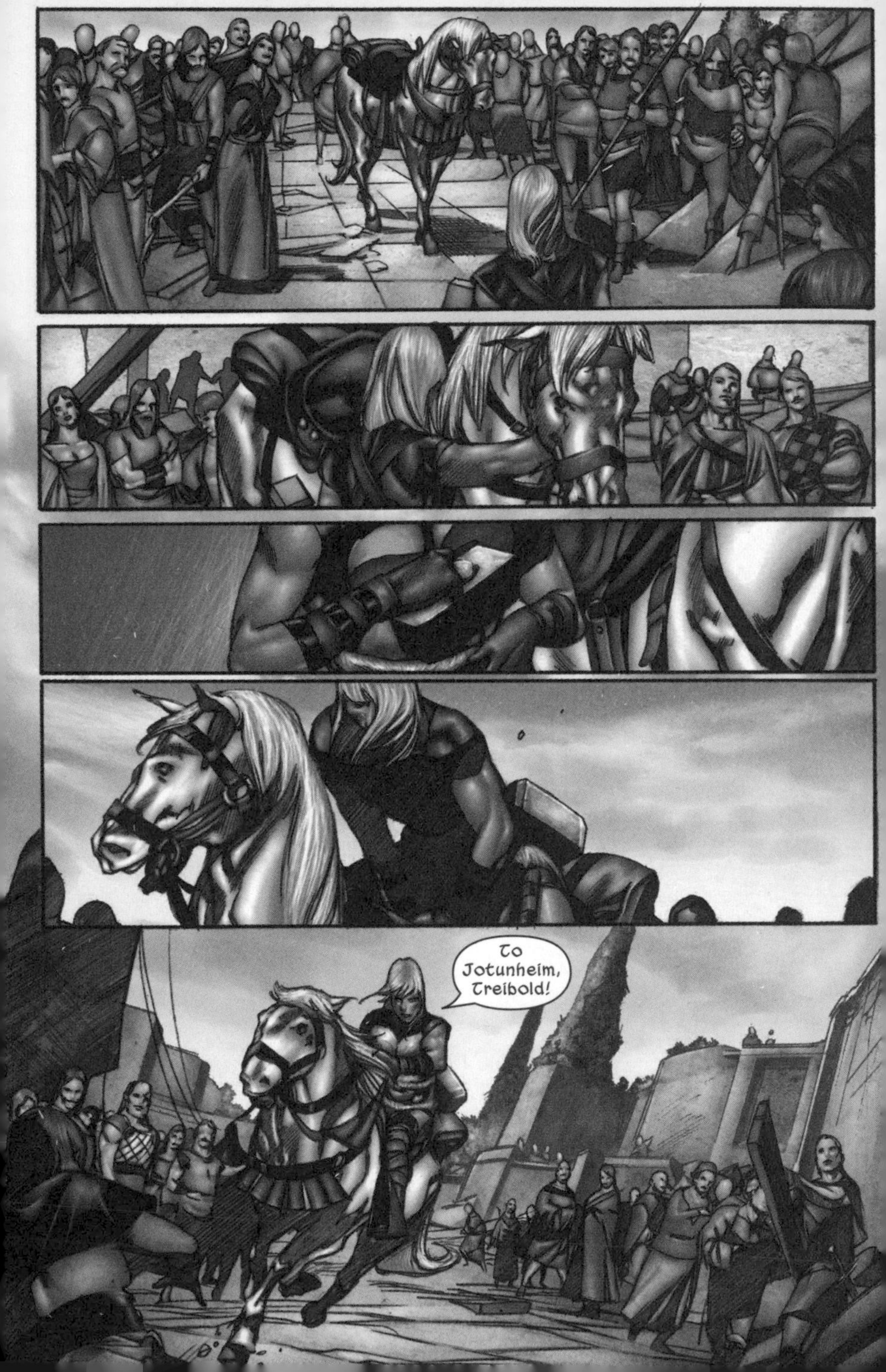
To Jotunheim, Treibold!

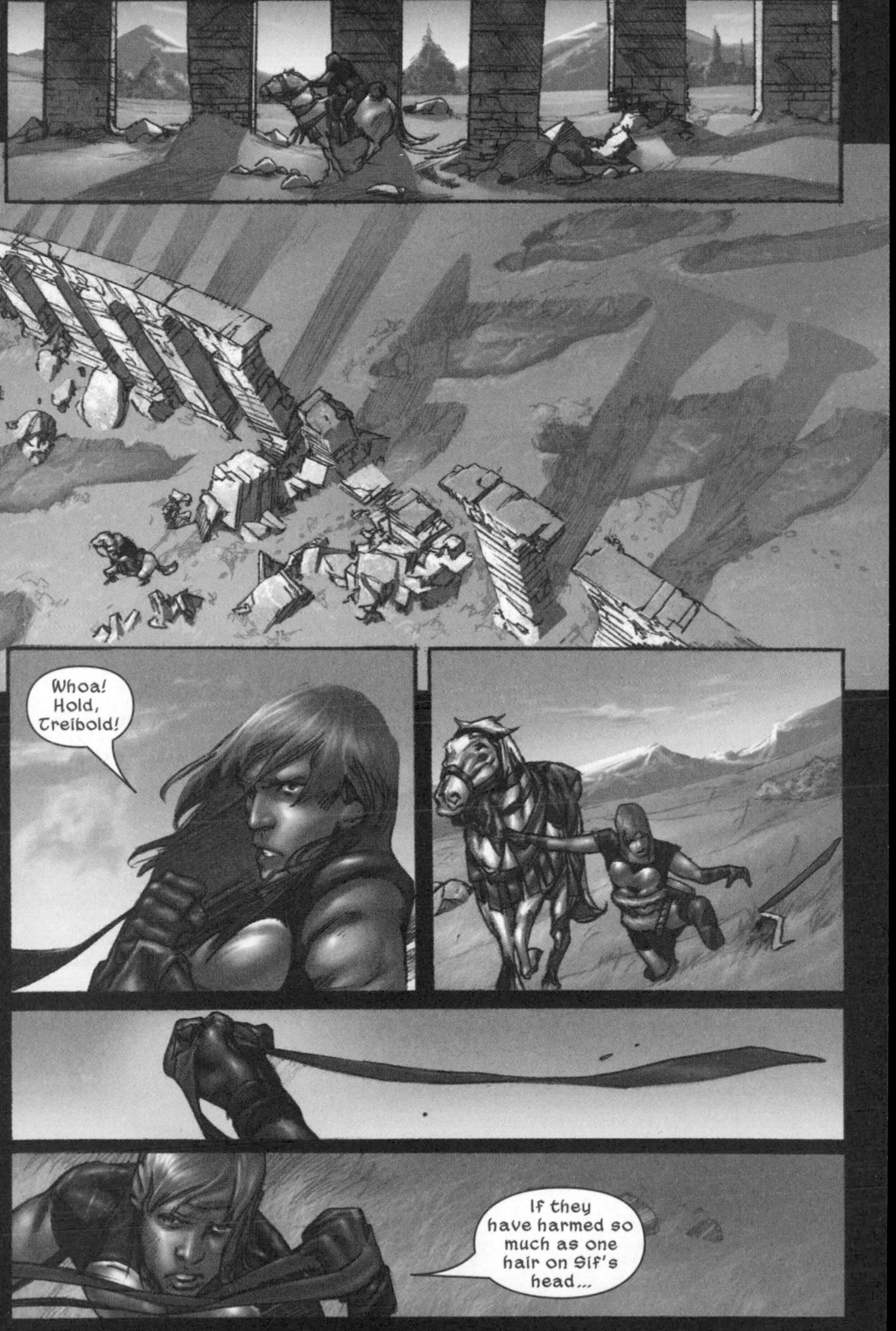
Whoa! Hold, Treibold!
If they have harmed so much as one hair on Sif's head...

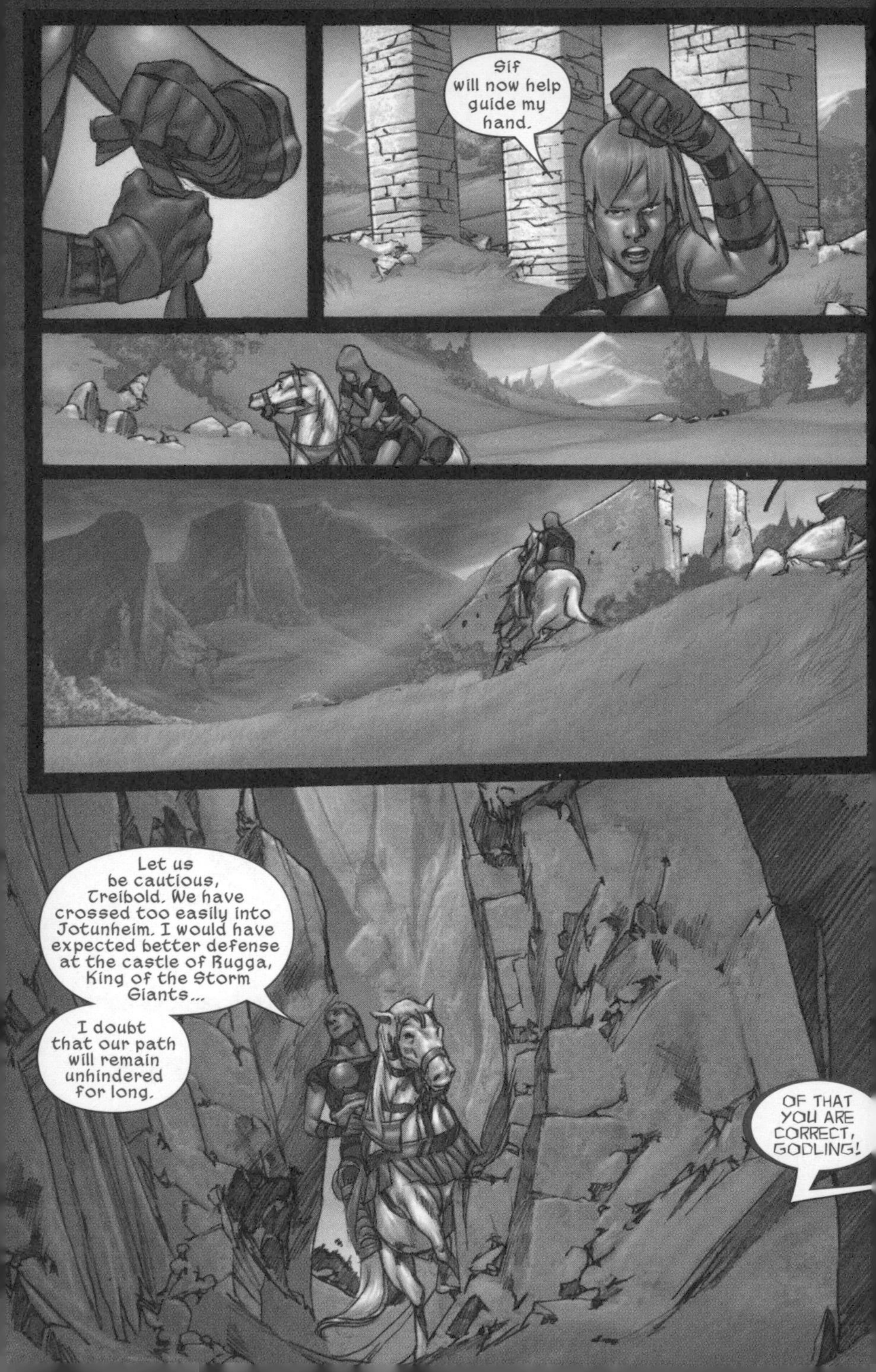
Sif will now help guide my hand.
Let us be cautious, Treibold. We have crossed too easily into Jotunheim. I would have expected better defense at the castle of Rugga, King of the Storm Giants...
I doubt that our path will remain unhindered for long.
OF THAT YOU ARE CORRECT, GODLING!

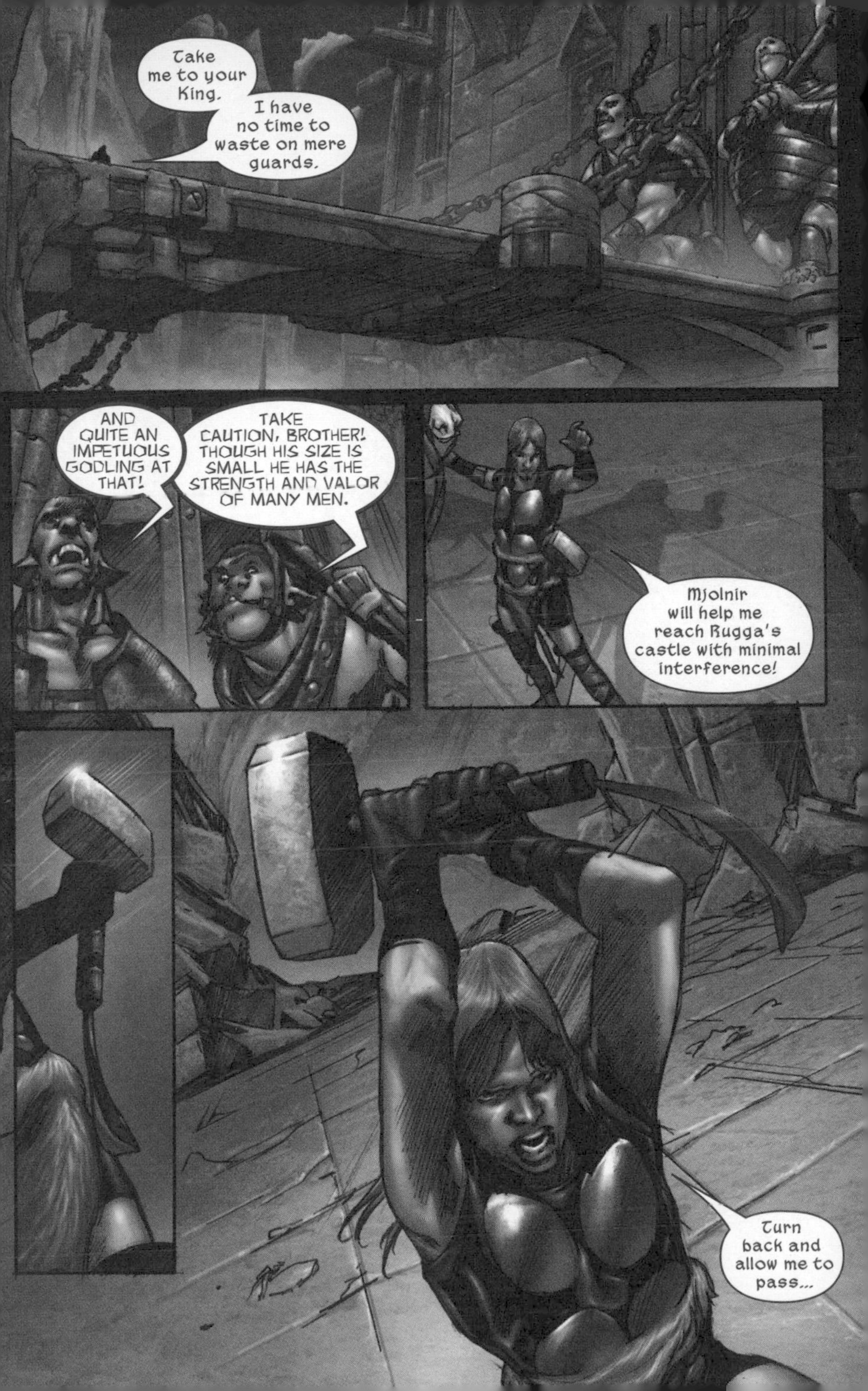
Take me to your King.
I have no time to waste on mere guards.
AND QUITE AN IMPETUOUS GODLING AT THAT!
TAKE CAUTION, BROTHER! THOUGH HIS SIZE IS SMALL HE HAS THE STRENGTH AND VALOR OF MANY MEN.
Mjolnir will help me reach Rugga's castle with minimal interference!
Turn back and allow me to pass...

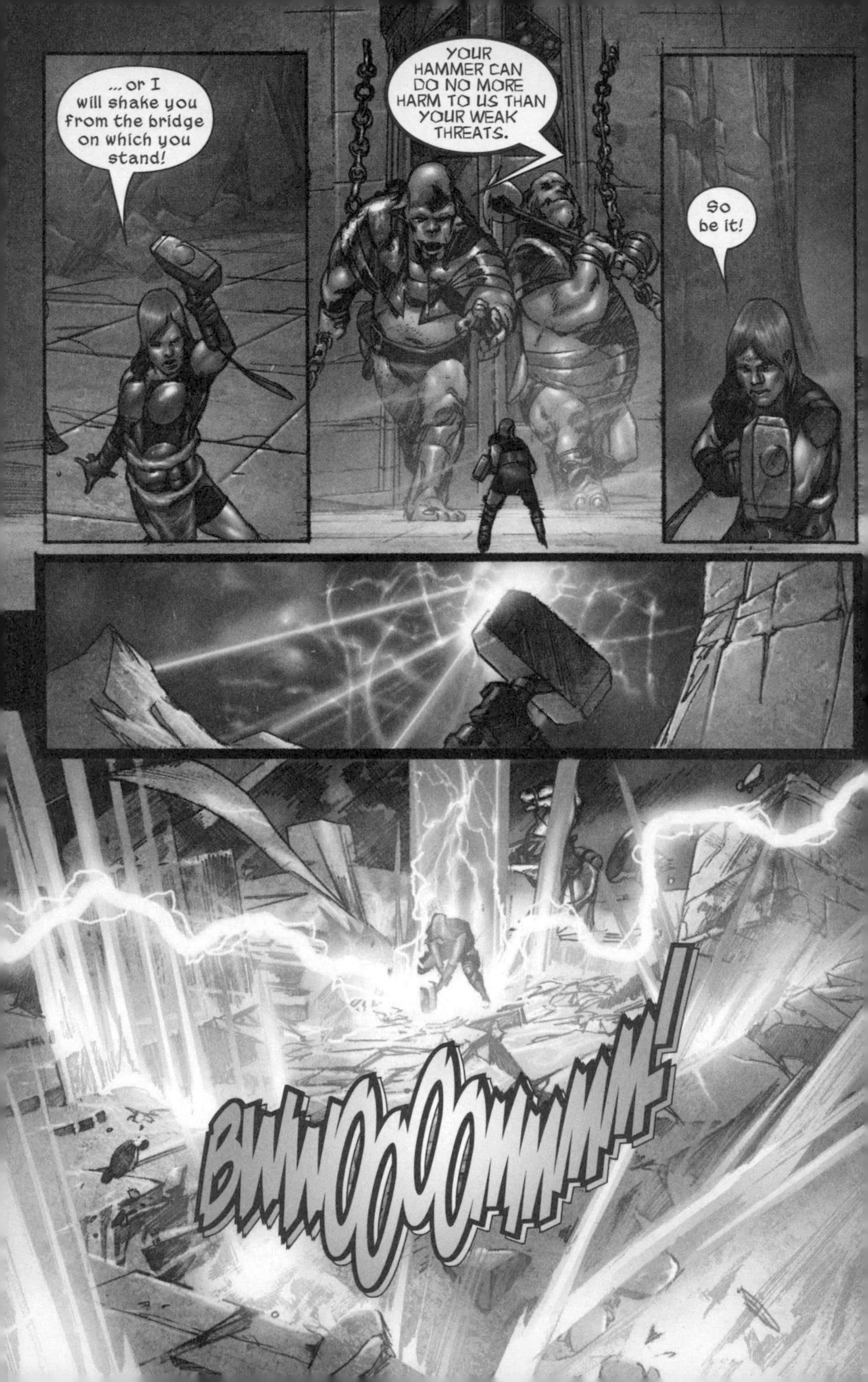
...or I will shake you from the bridge on which you stand!
YOUR HAMMER CAN DO NO MORE HARM TO US THAN YOUR WEAK THREATS.
So be it!
BVVVOOOOOMMMM!

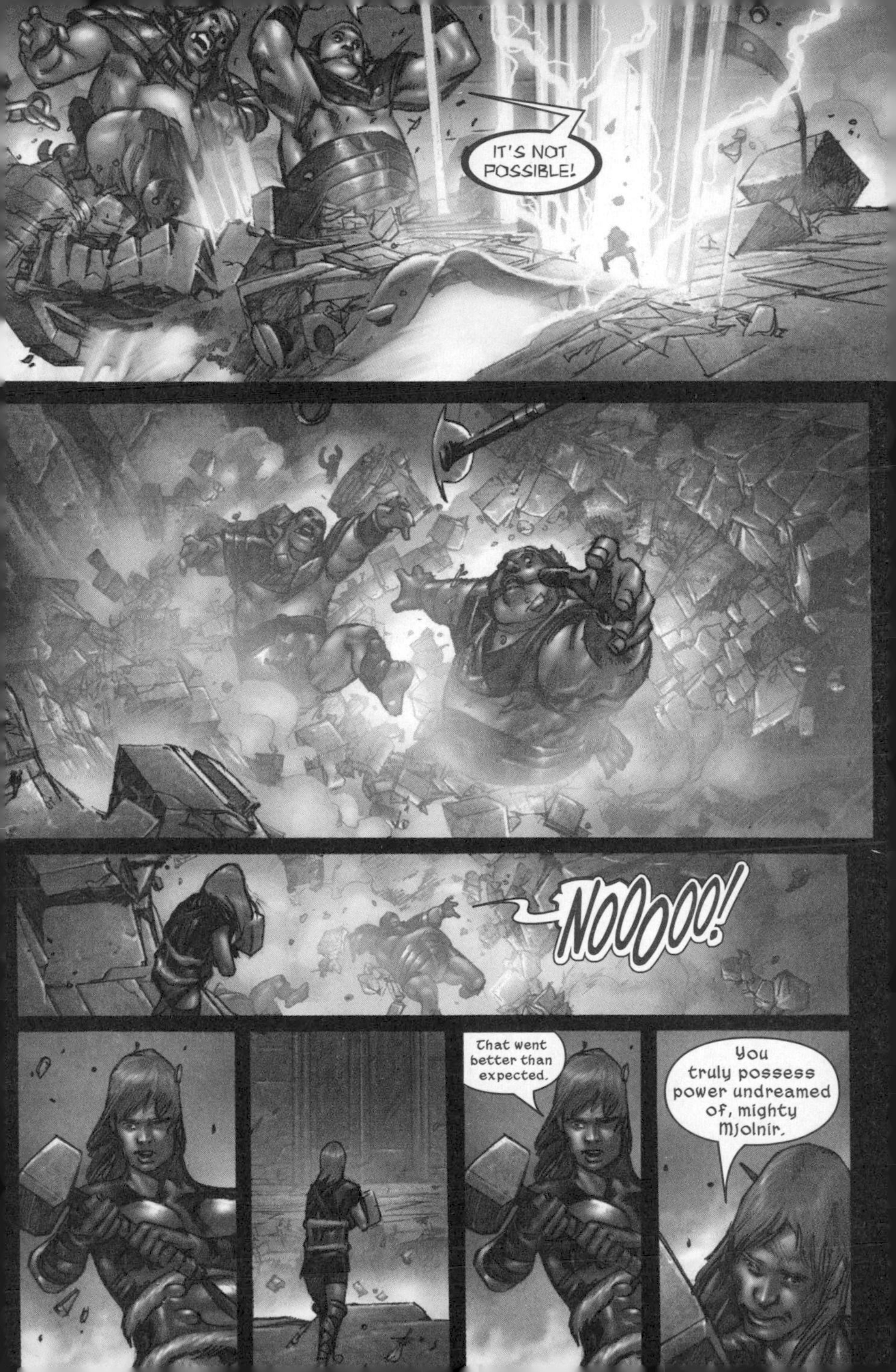
IT'S NOT POSSIBLE!
NOOOOO!
That went better than expected.
You truly possess power undreamed of, mighty Mjolnir.

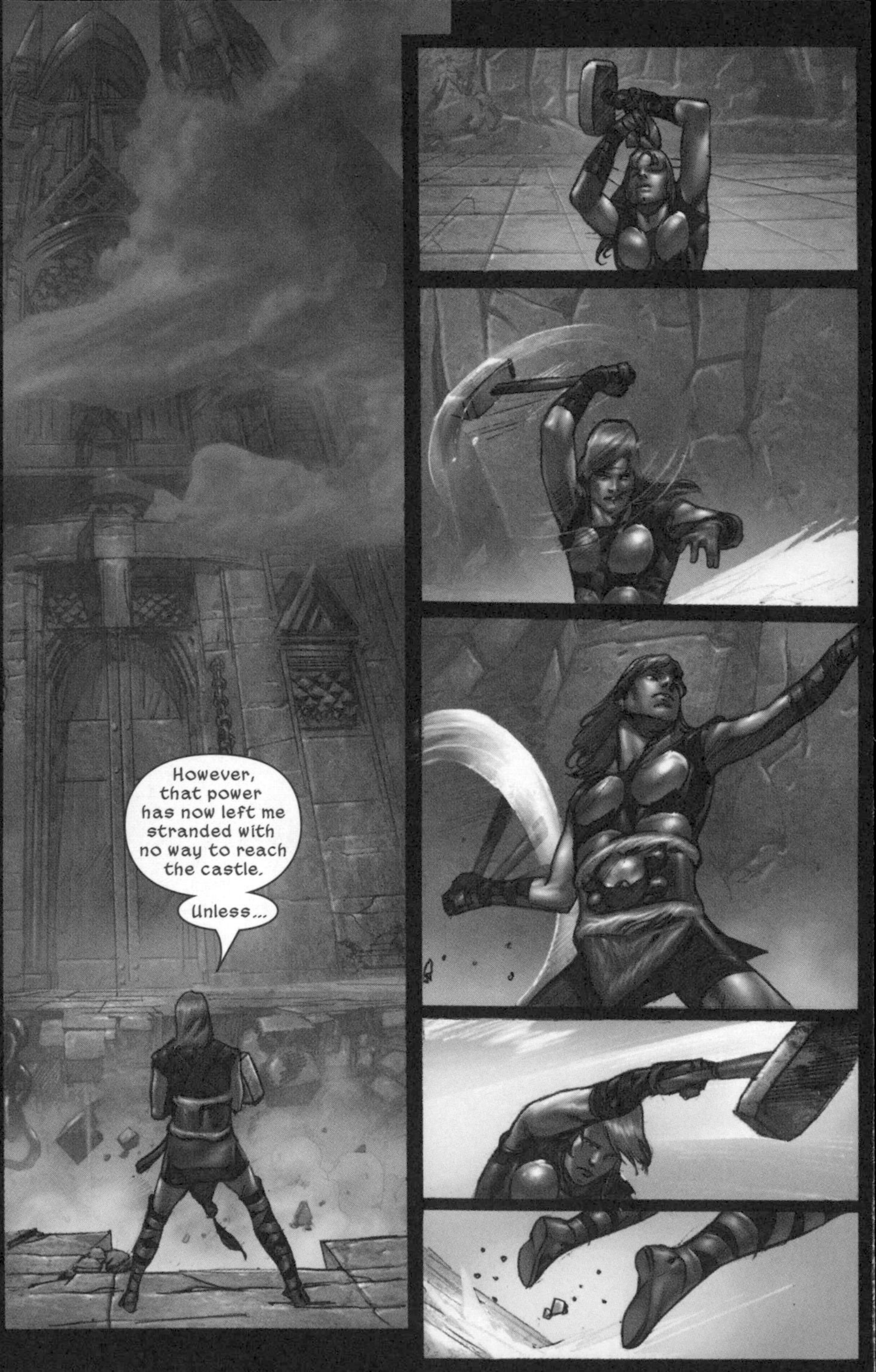
However, that power has now left me stranded with no way to reach the castle.
Unless...

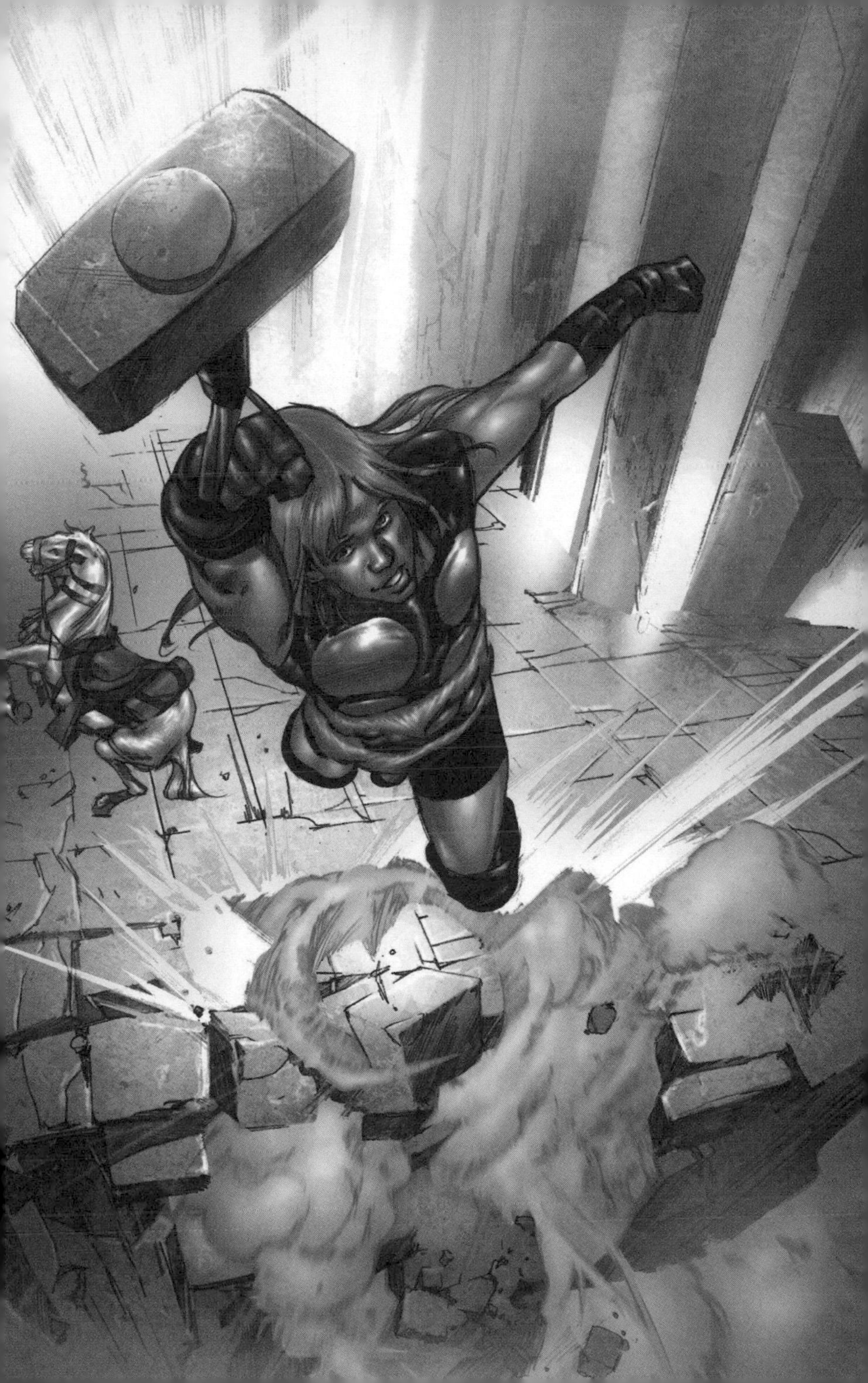

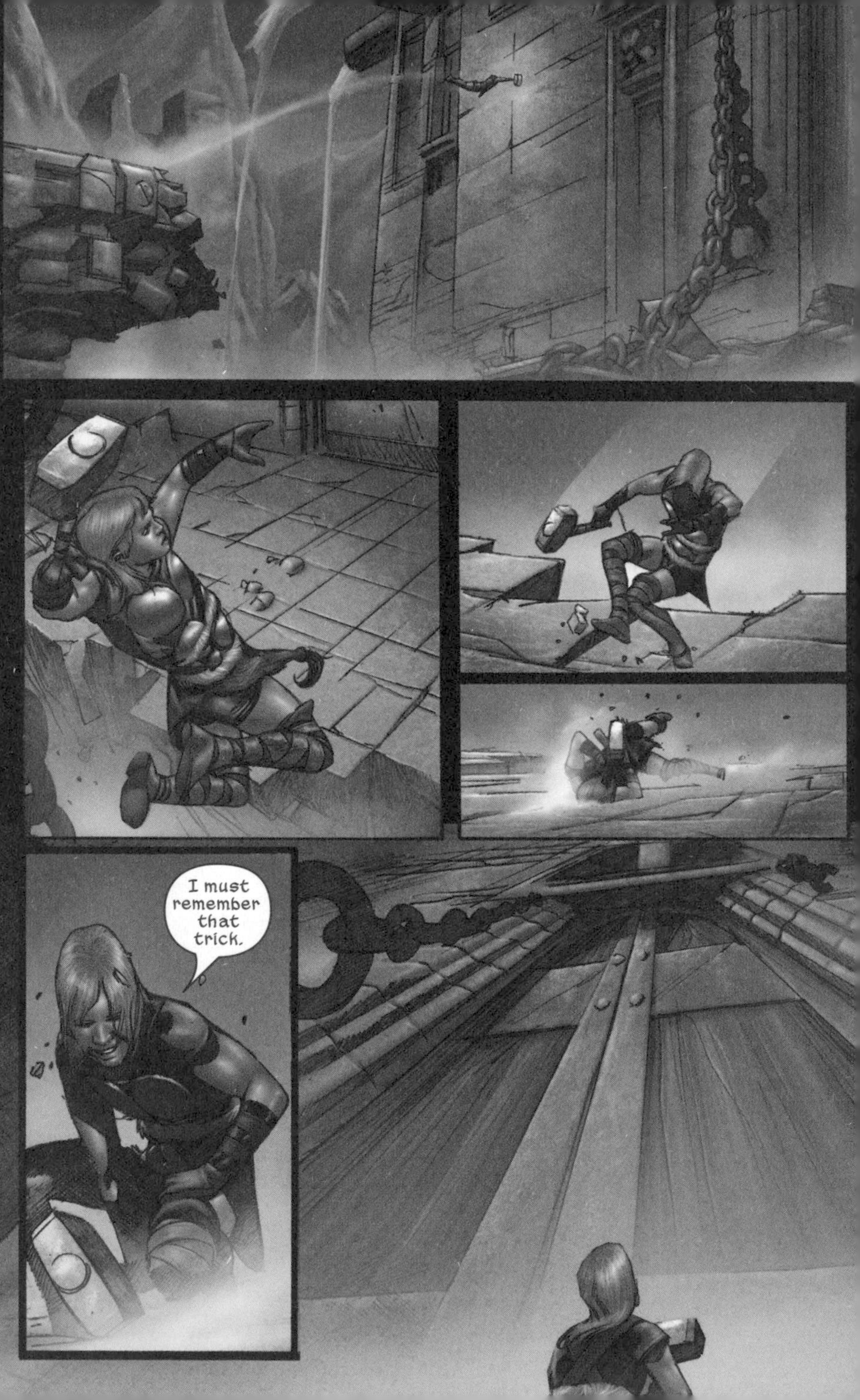
I must remember that trick.

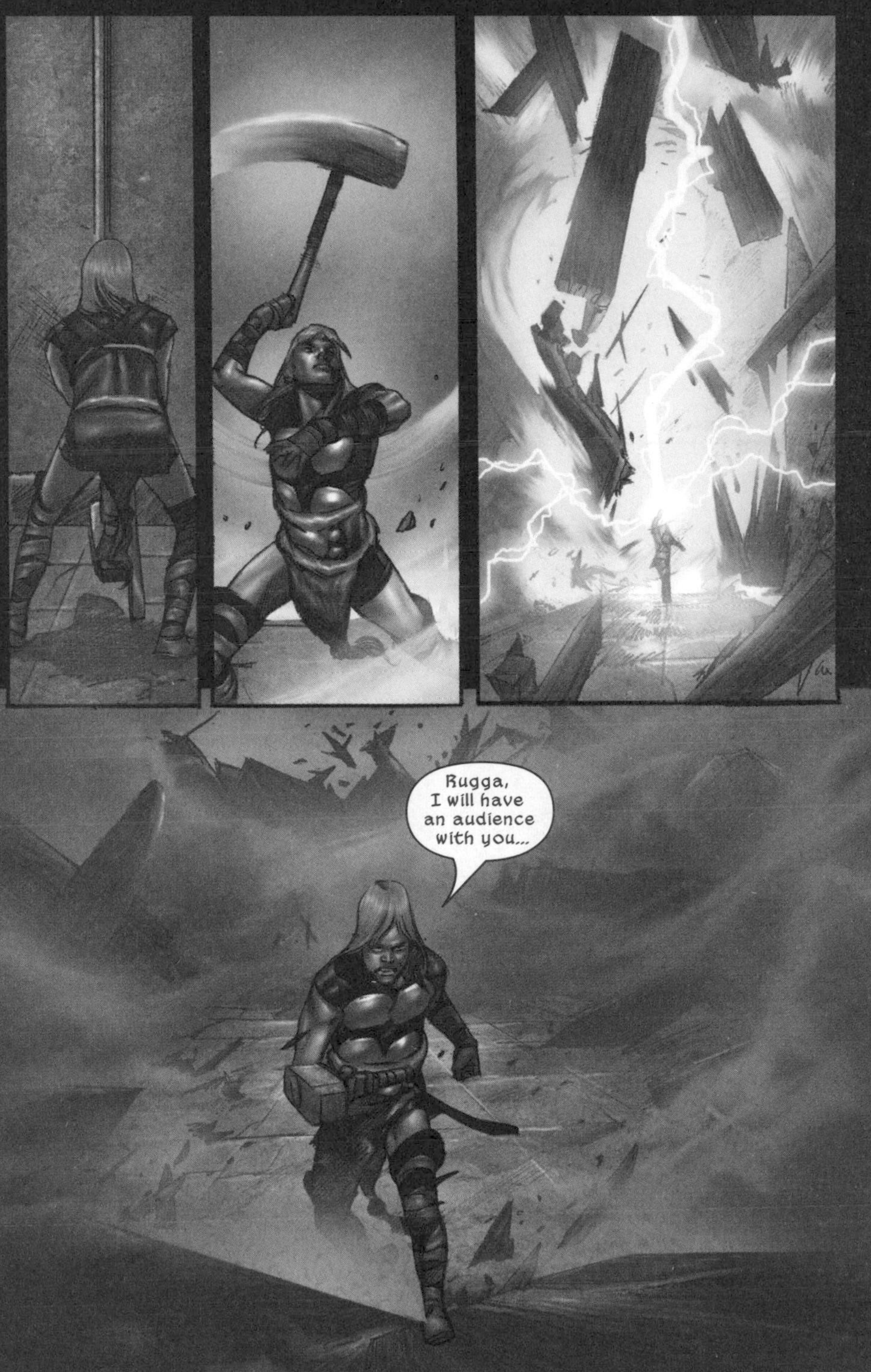
Rugga,
I will have
an audience
with you...

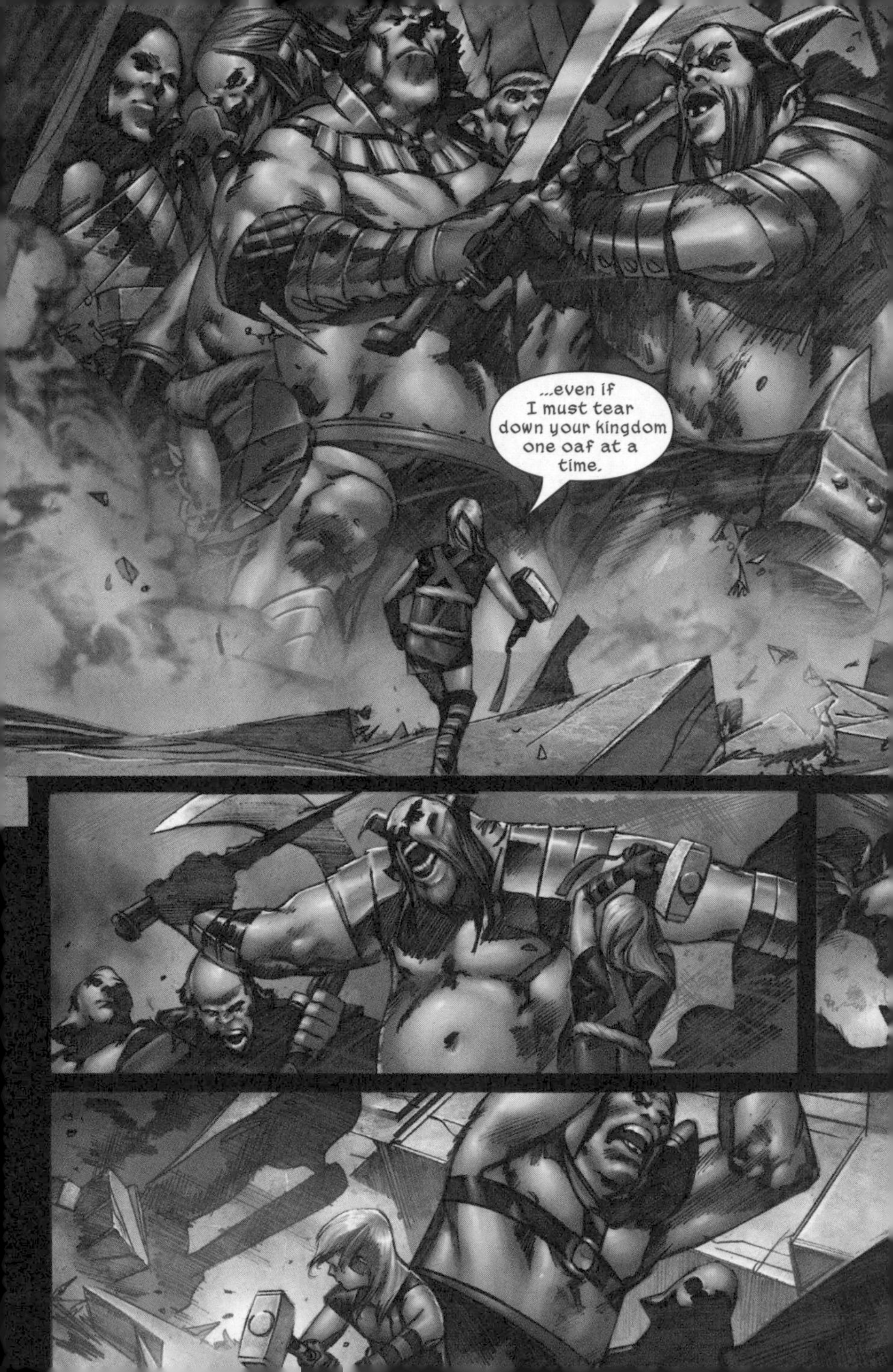
...even if I must tear down your kingdom one oaf at a time.

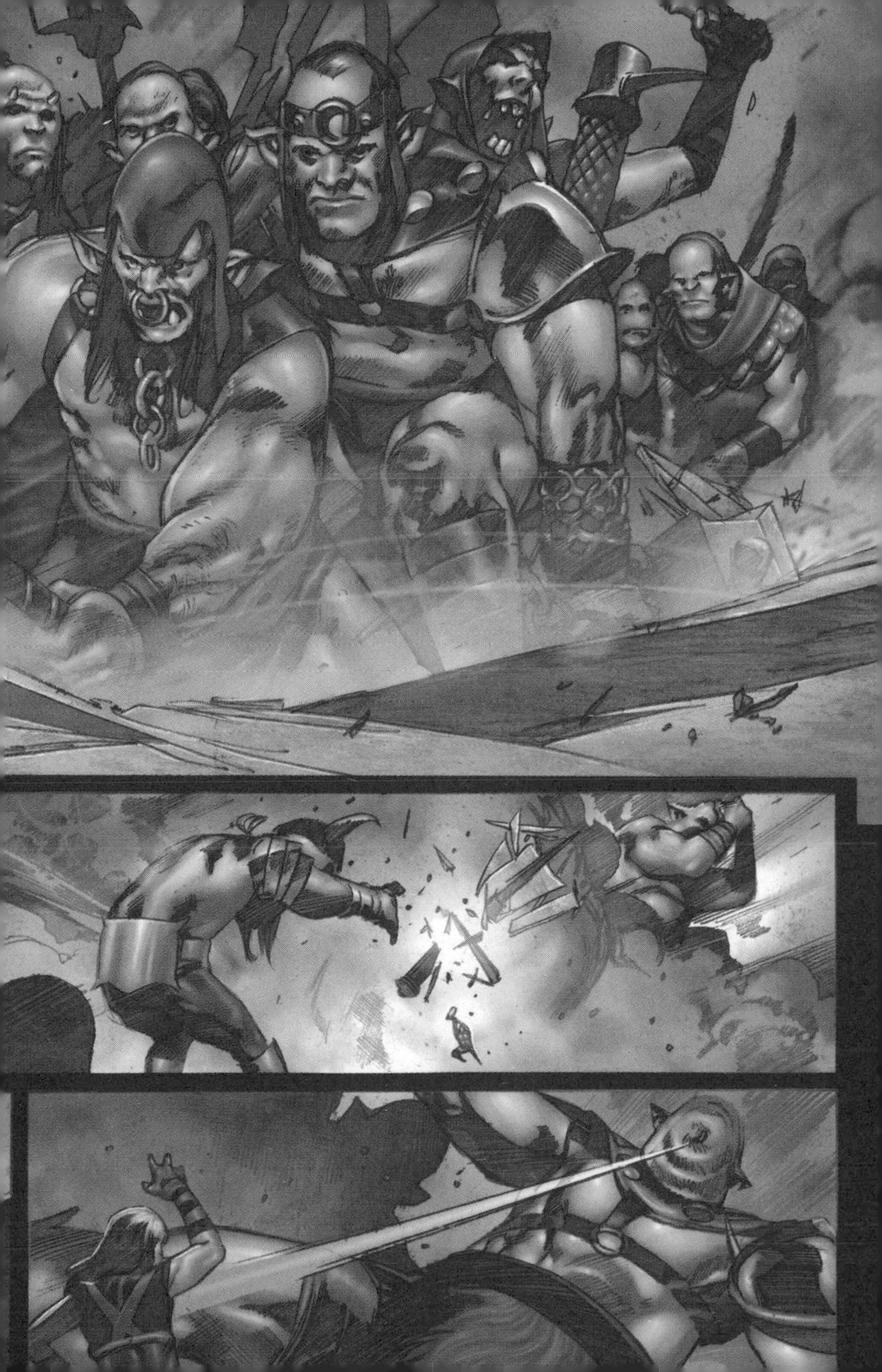

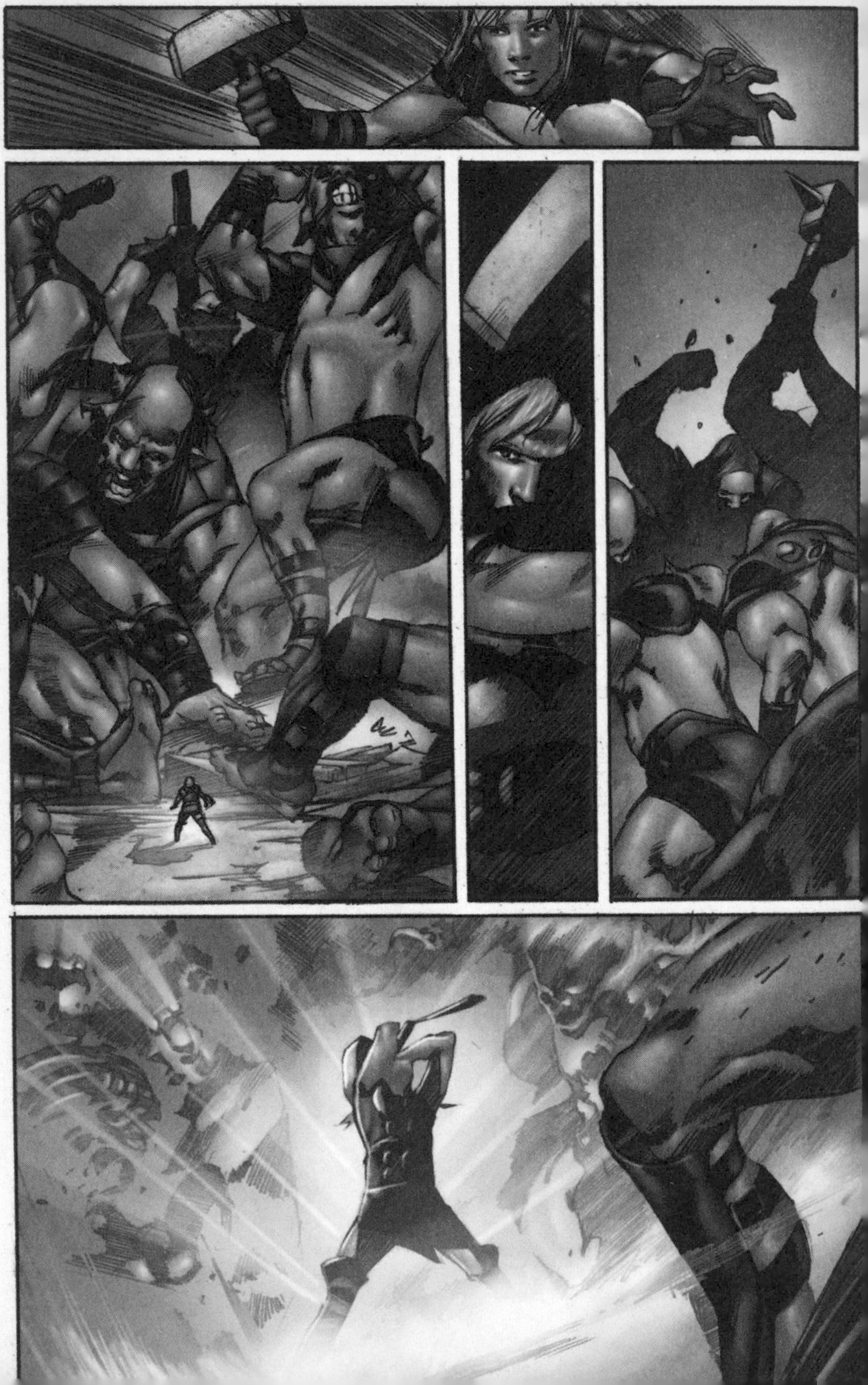

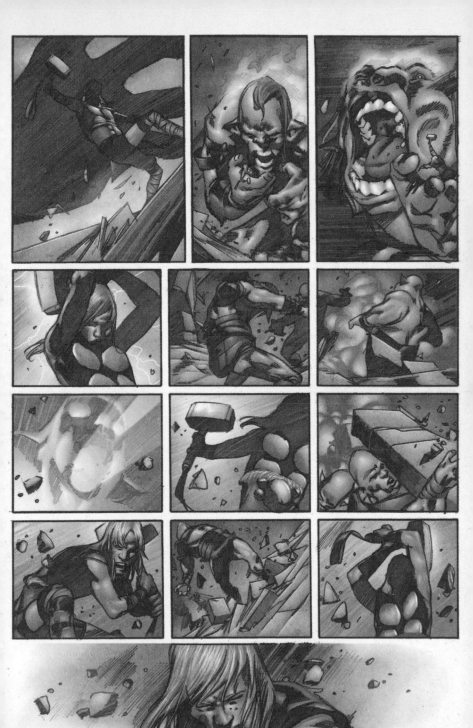

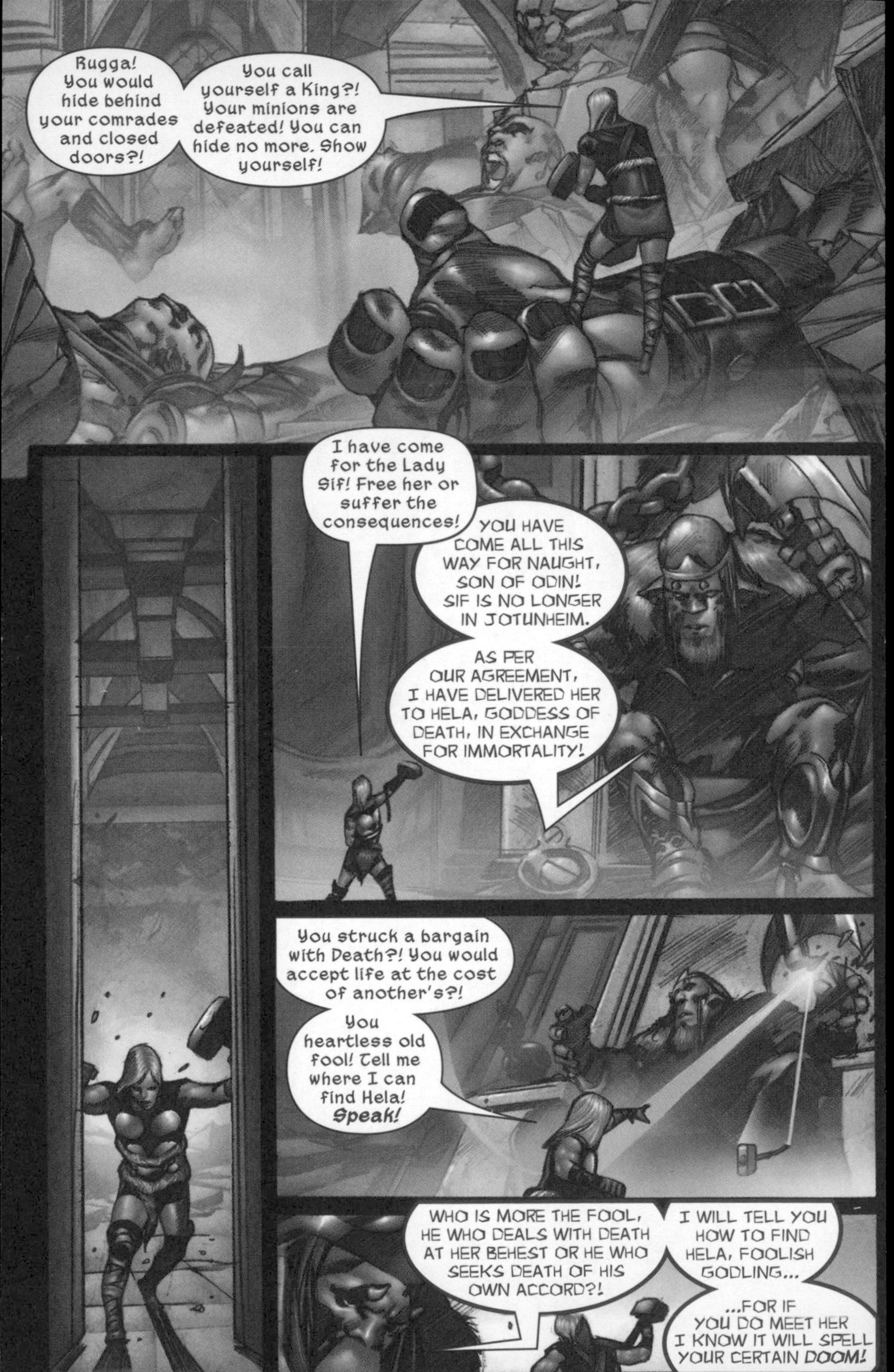
Rugga! You would hide behind your comrades and closed doors?!
You call yourself a King?! Your minions are defeated! You can hide no more. Show yourself!
I have come for the Lady Sif! Free her or suffer the consequences!
YOU HAVE COME ALL THIS WAY FOR NAUGHT, SON OF ODIN! SIF IS NO LONGER IN JOTUNHEIM.
AS PER OUR AGREEMENT, I HAVE DELIVERED HER TO HELA, GODDESS OF DEATH, IN EXCHANGE FOR IMMORTALITY!
You struck a bargain with Death?! You would accept life at the cost of another's?!
You heartless old fool! Tell me where I can find Hela! *Speak!*
WHO IS MORE THE FOOL, HE WHO DEALS WITH DEATH AT HER BEHEST OR HE WHO SEEKS DEATH OF HIS OWN ACCORD?!
I WILL TELL YOU HOW TO FIND HELA, FOOLISH GODLING...
...FOR IF YOU DO MEET HER I KNOW IT WILL SPELL YOUR CERTAIN *DOOM!*

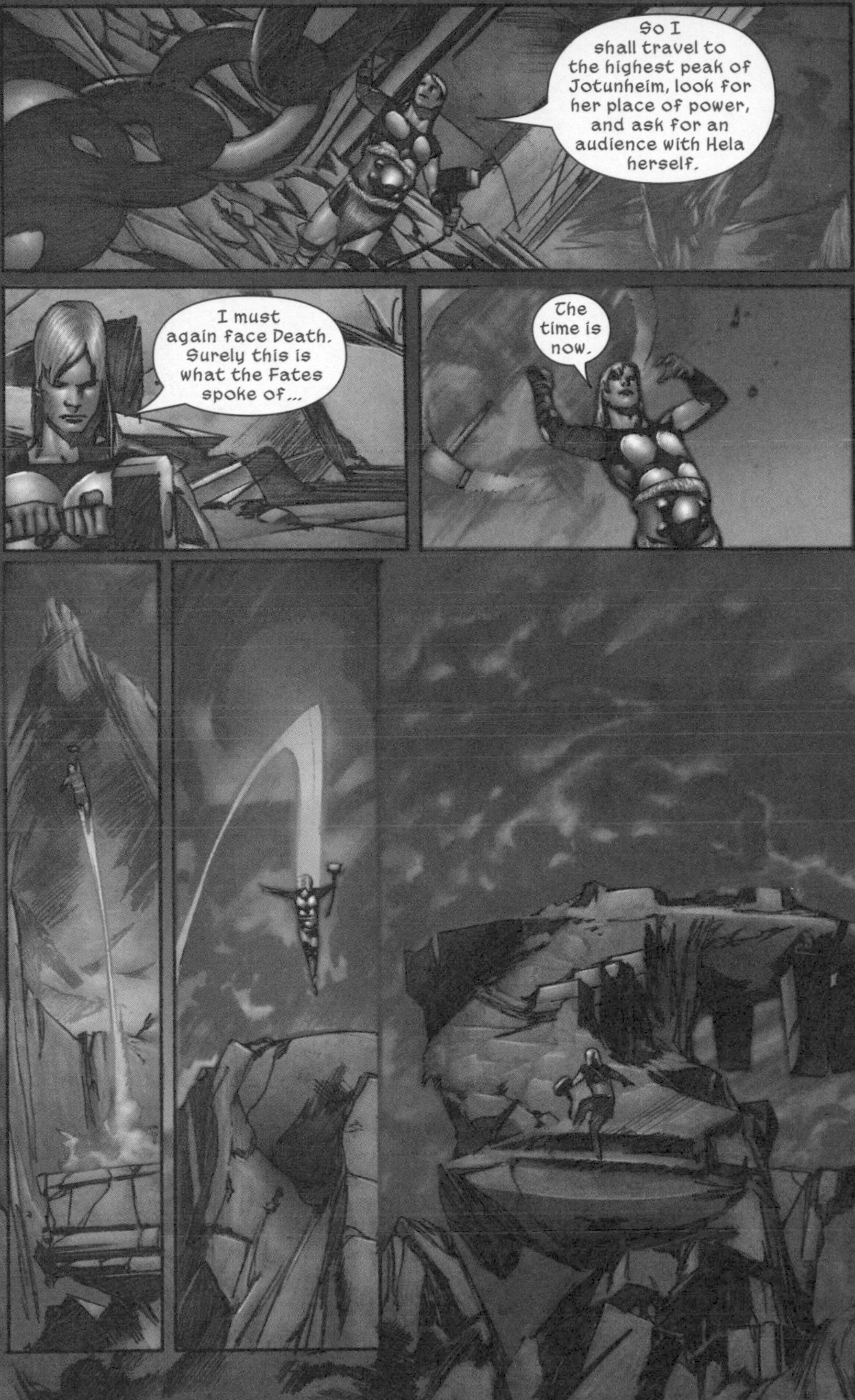
So I shall travel to the highest peak of Jotunheim, look for her place of power, and ask for an audience with Hela herself.
I must again face Death. Surely this is what the Fates spoke of...
The time is now.

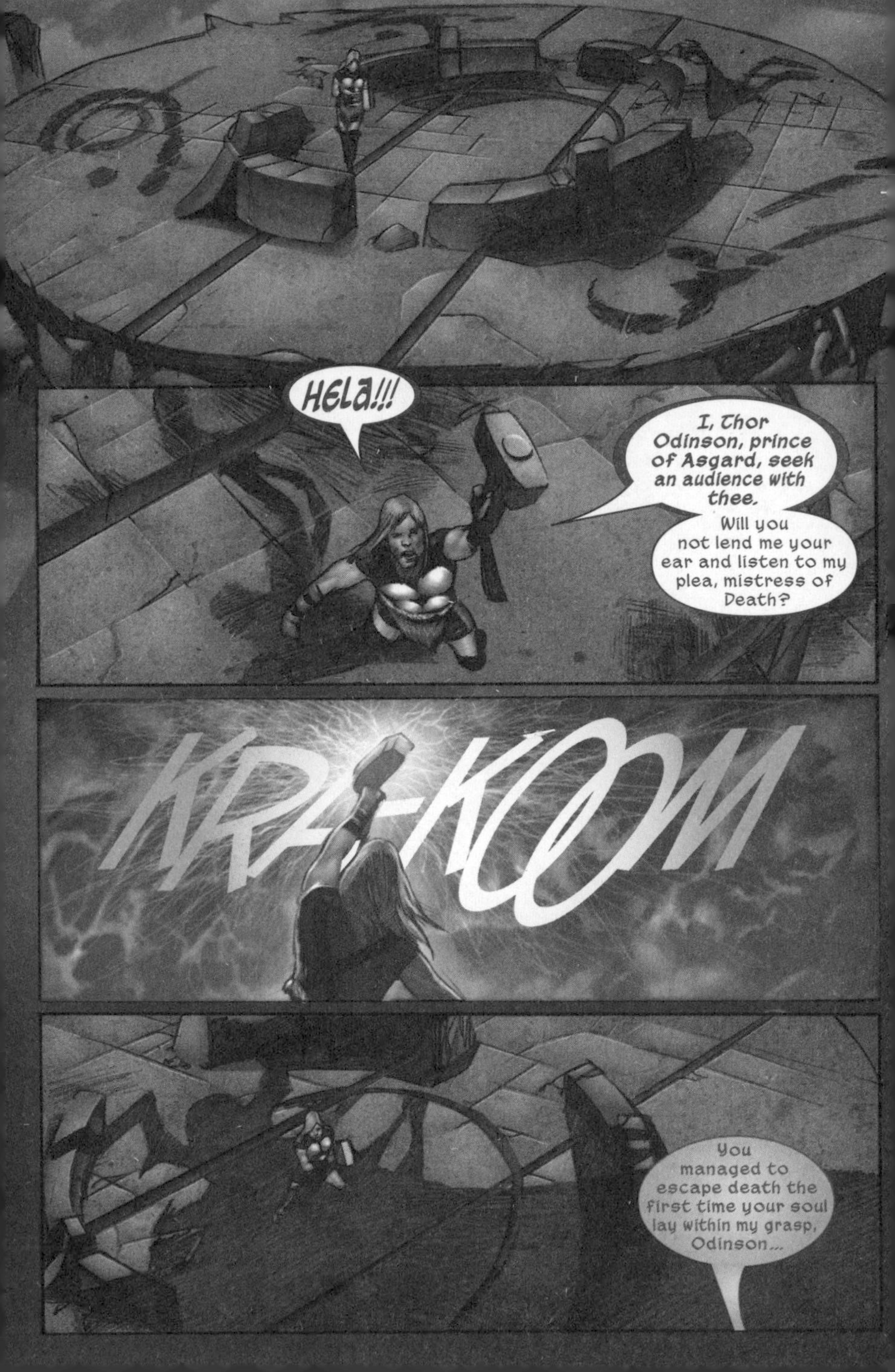
HELA!!!
I, Thor Odinson, prince of Asgard, seek an audience with thee.
Will you not lend me your ear and listen to my plea, mistress of Death?
KRA-KOOM
You managed to escape death the first time your soul lay within my grasp, Odinson...

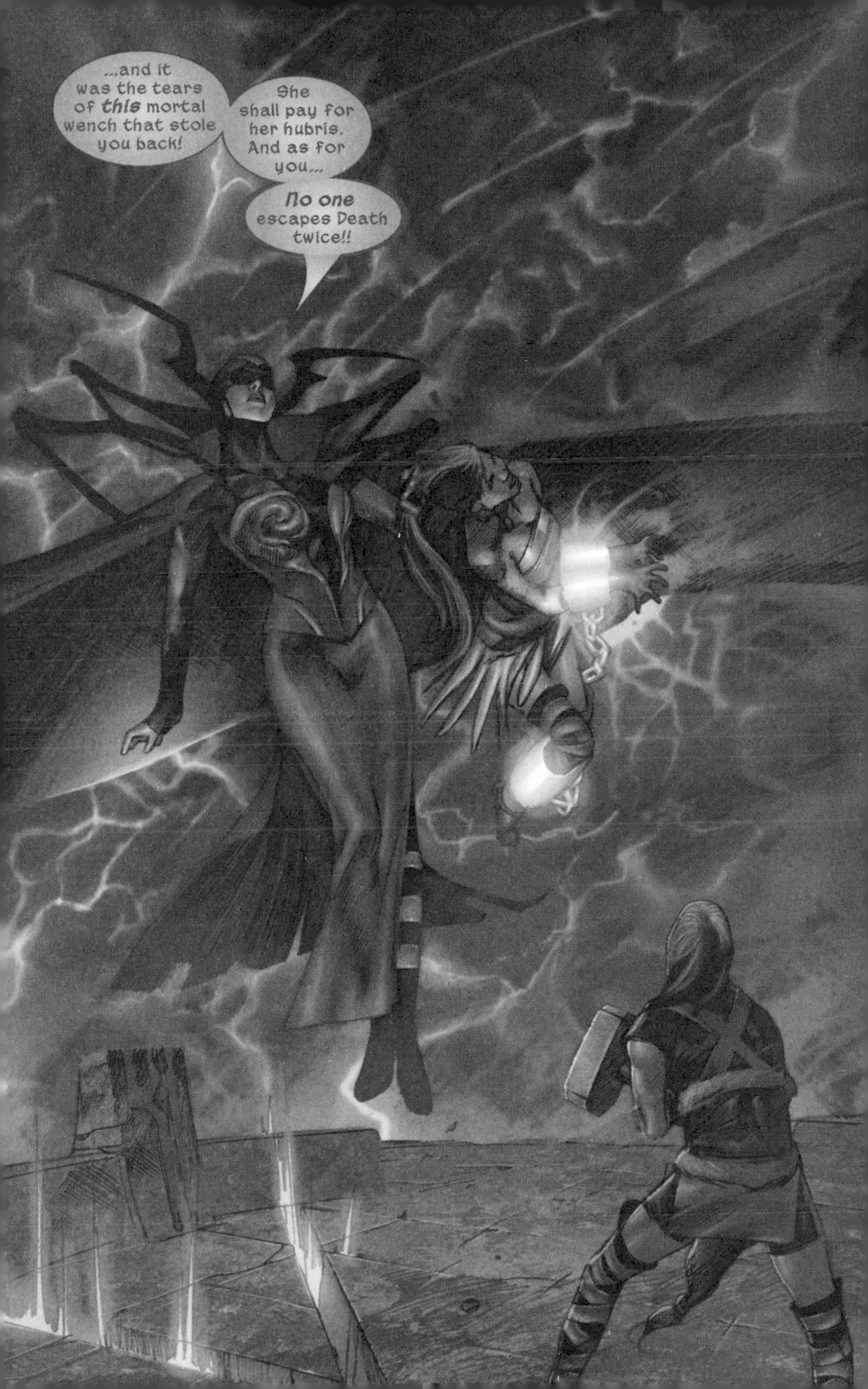
...and it was the tears of *this* mortal wench that stole you back!
She shall pay for her hubris. And as for you...
No one escapes Death twice!!

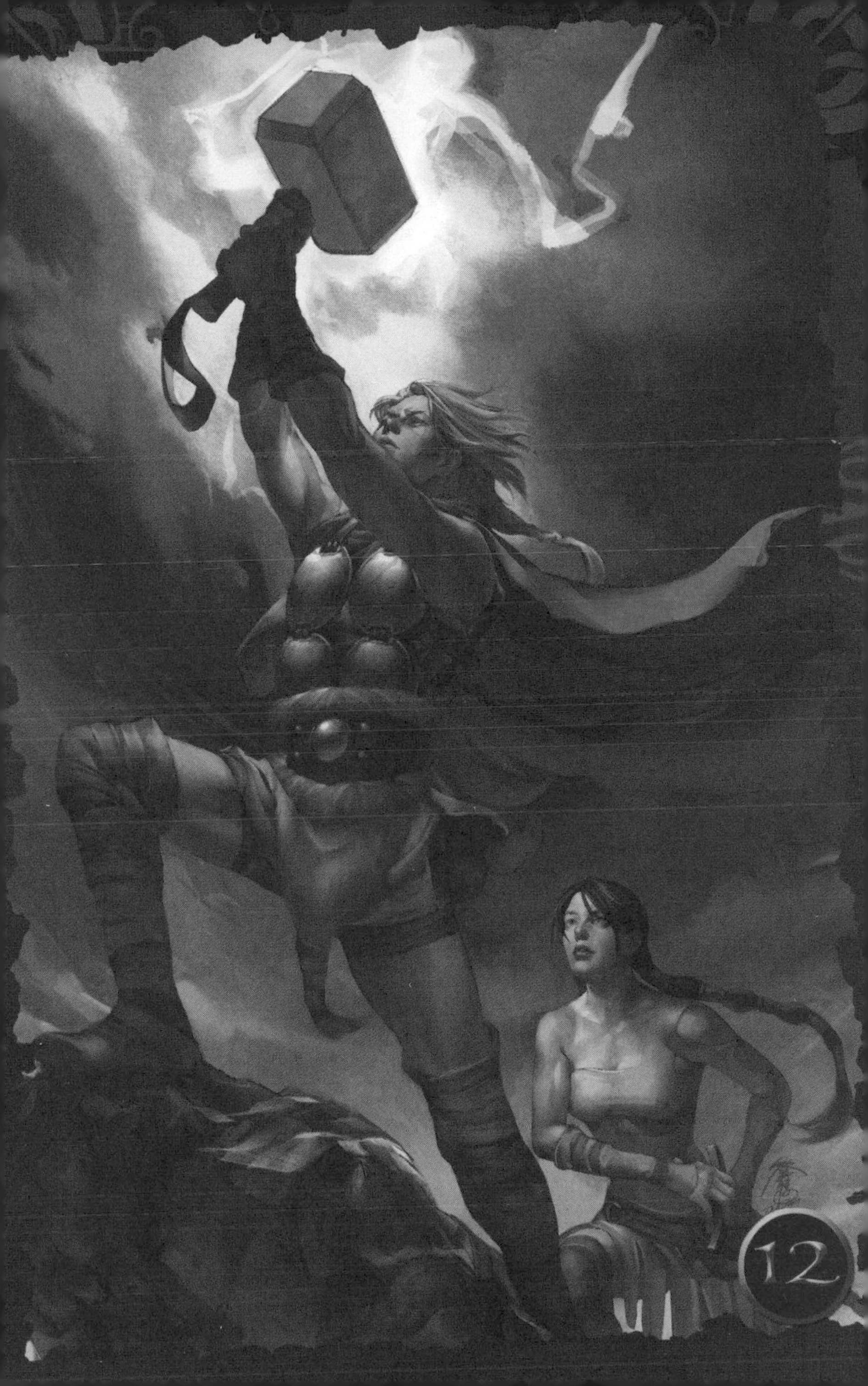
12

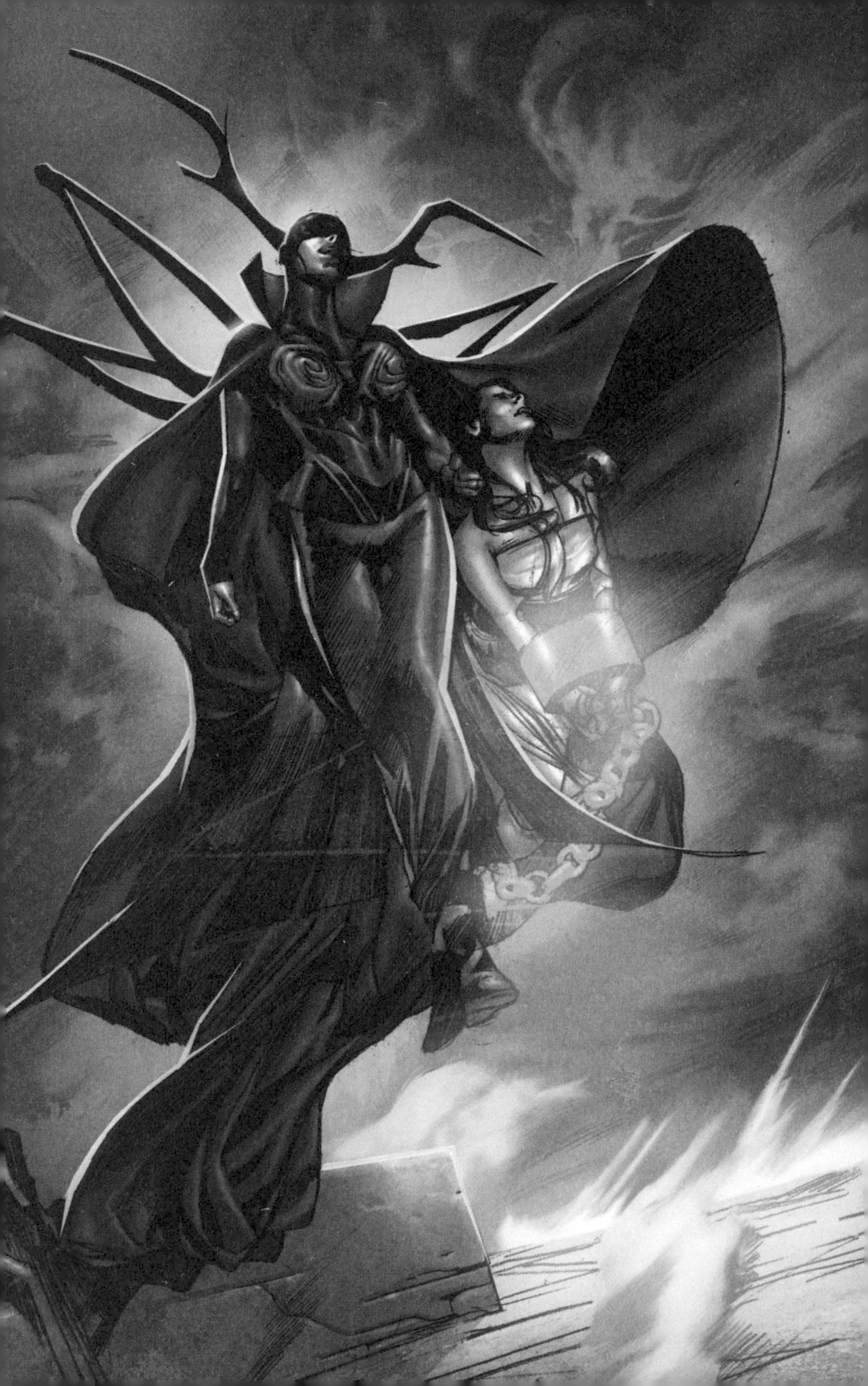

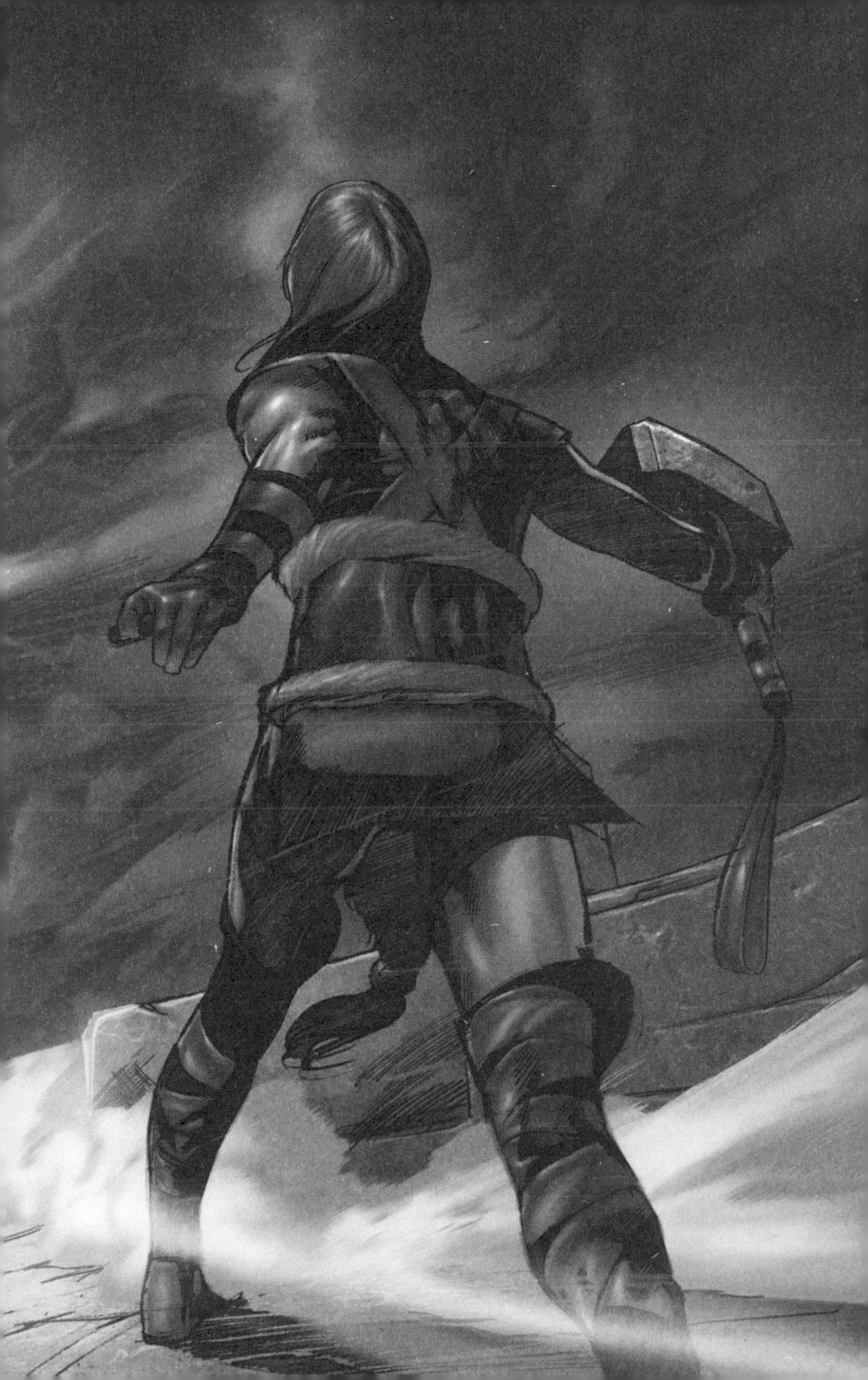

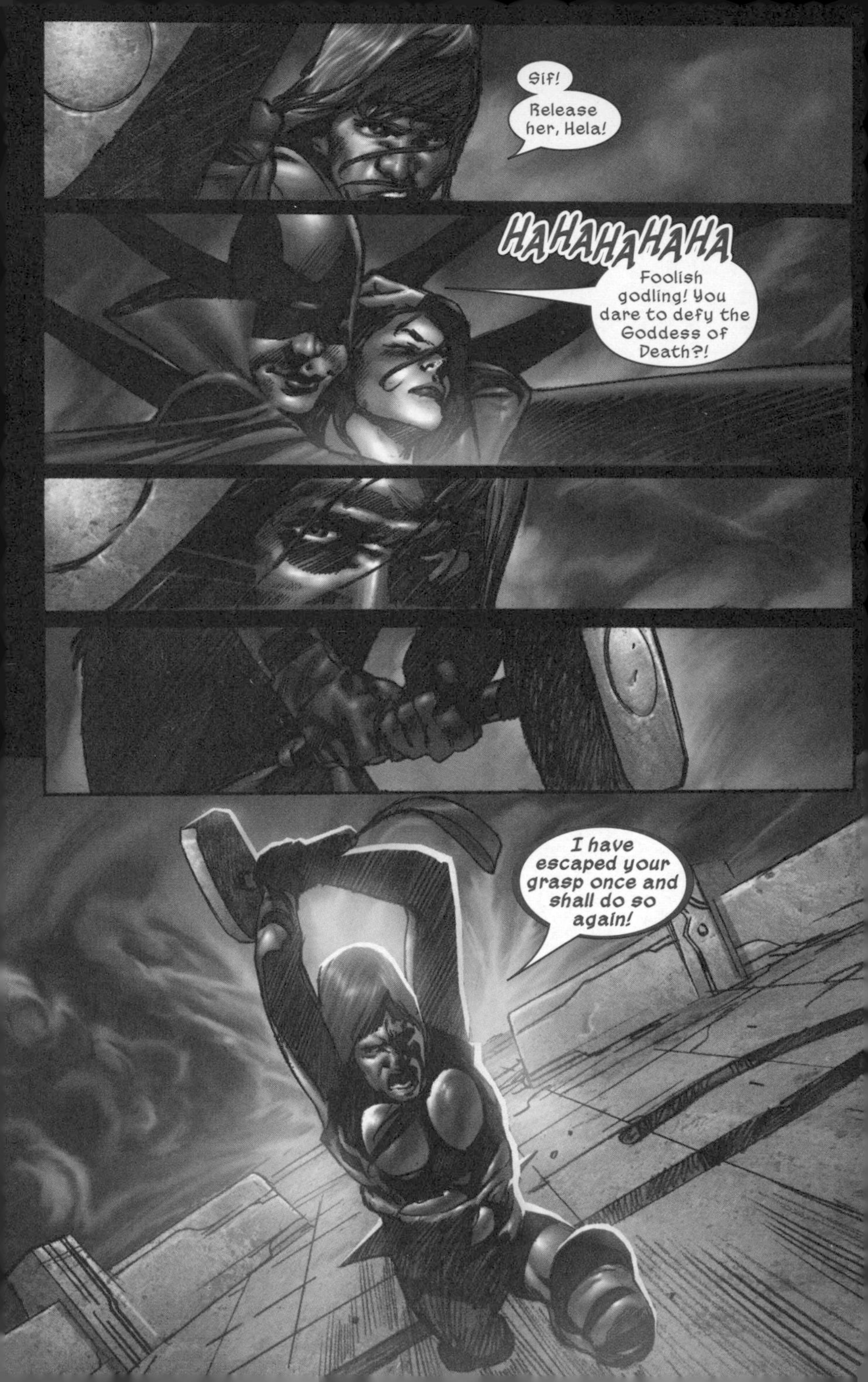
Sif!
Release her, Hela!
HAHAHAHAHAHA
Foolish godling! You dare to defy the Goddess of Death?!
I have escaped your grasp once and shall do so again!

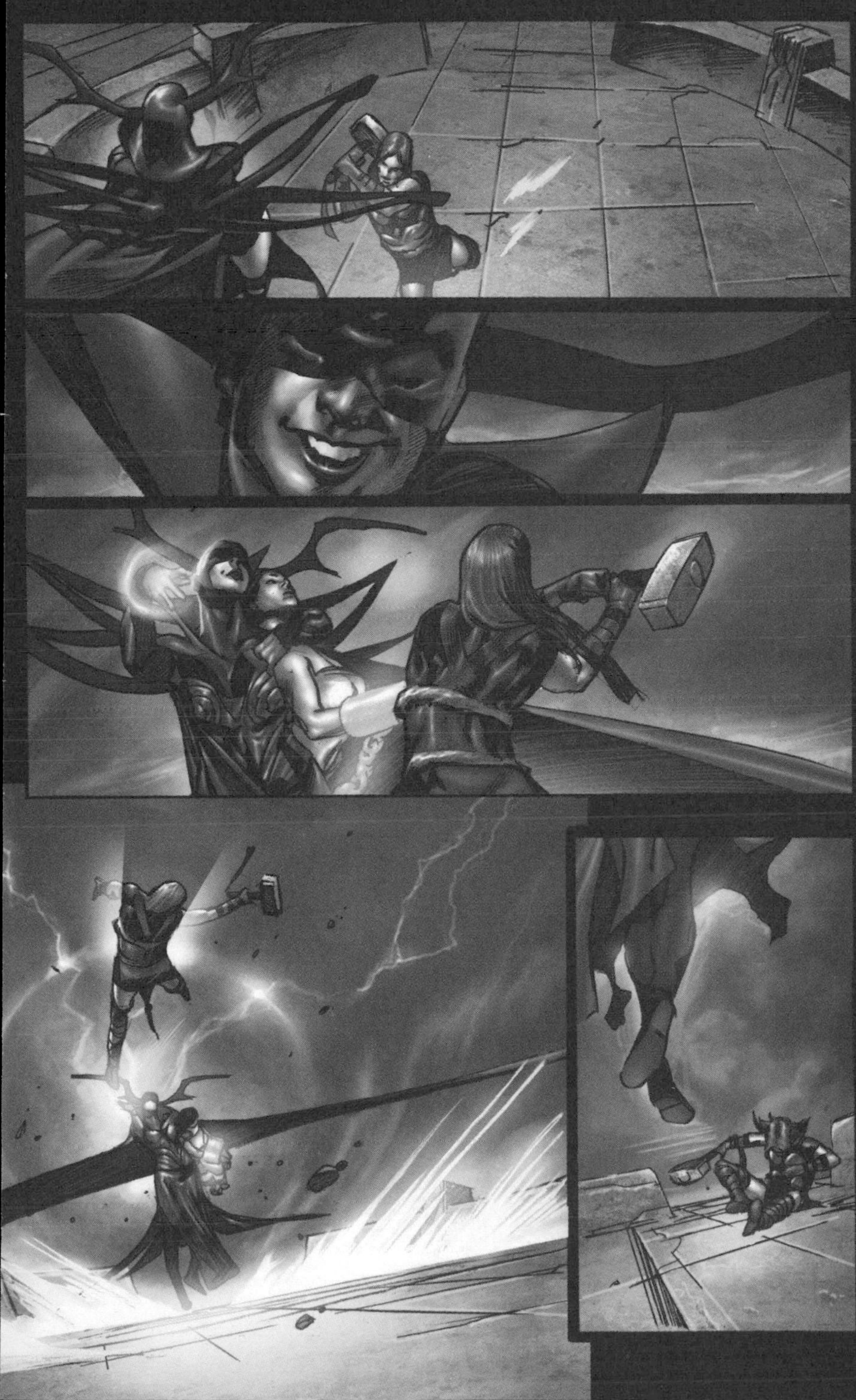

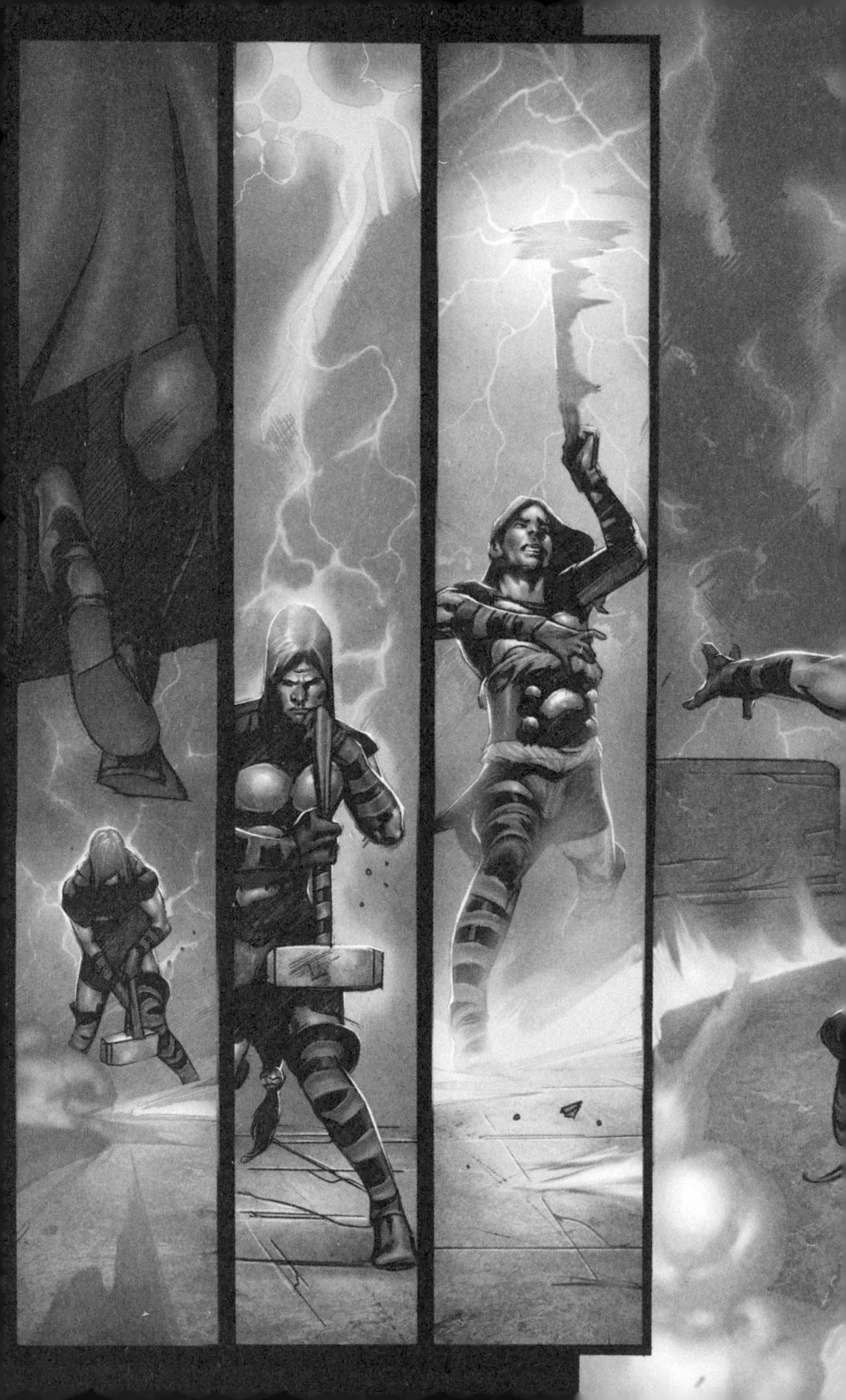

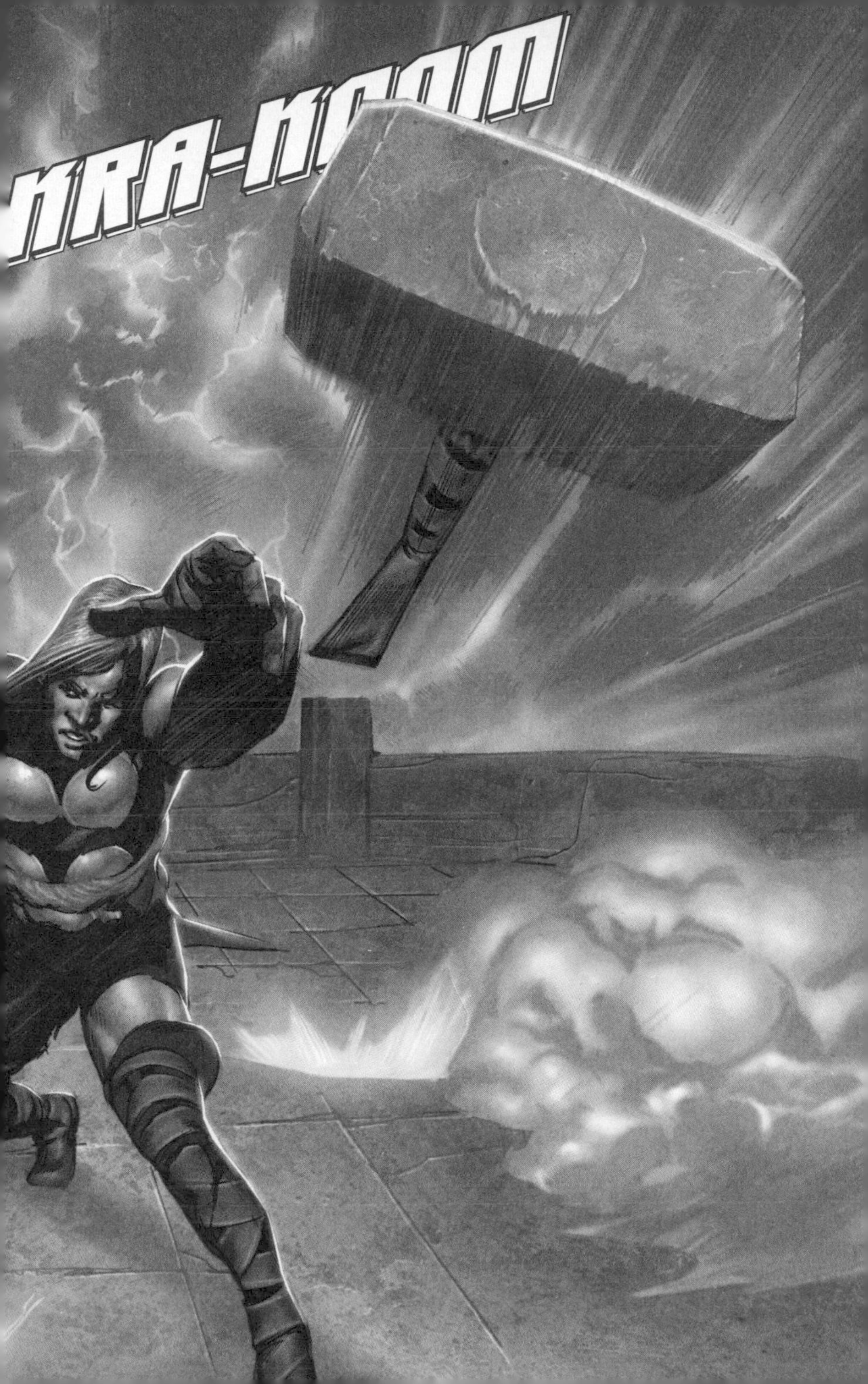
KRA-KOOOM

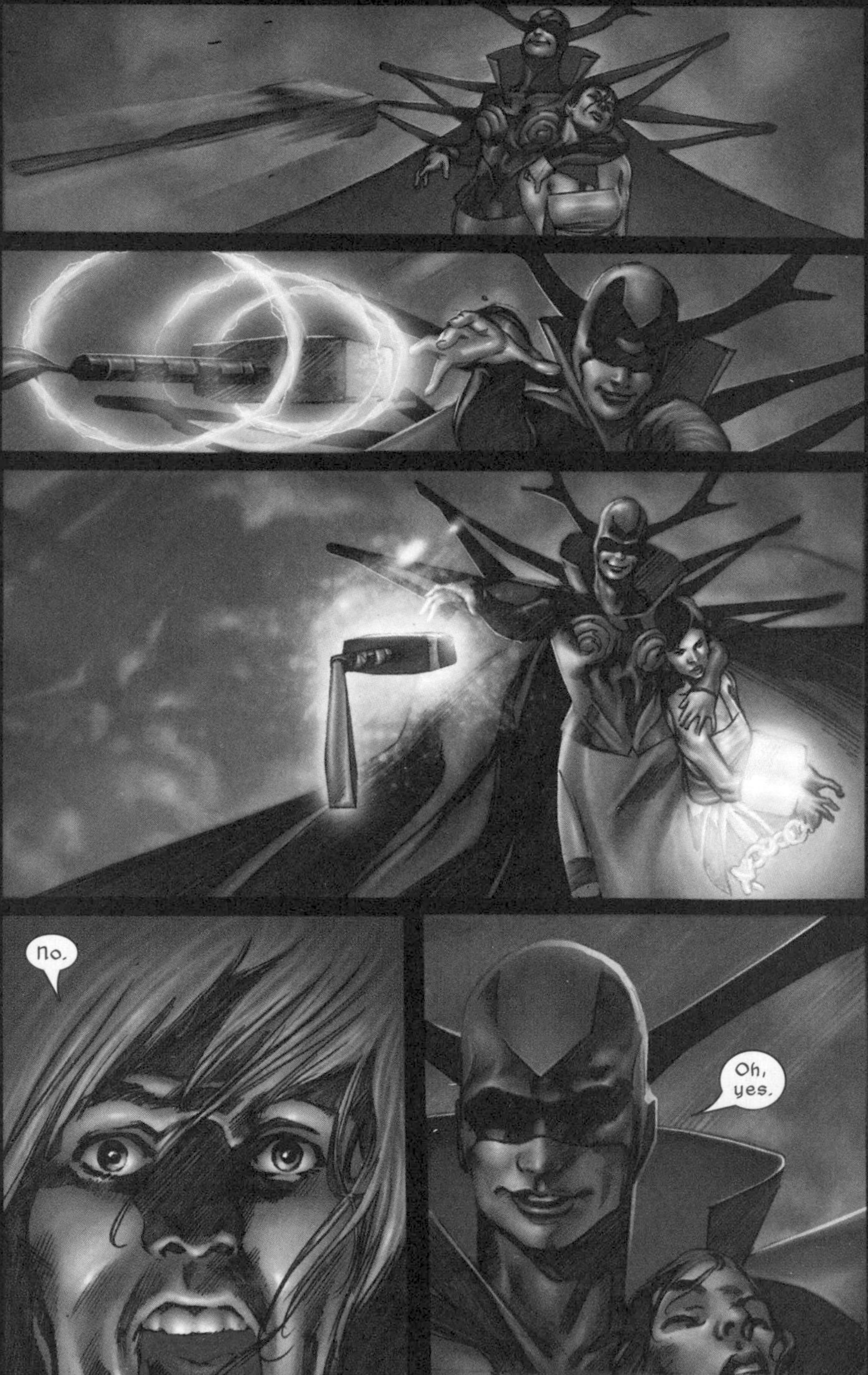
No.
Oh, yes.

You may have survived the icy touch of my hand the first time I came for you, Odinson...
...but that will not happen again!

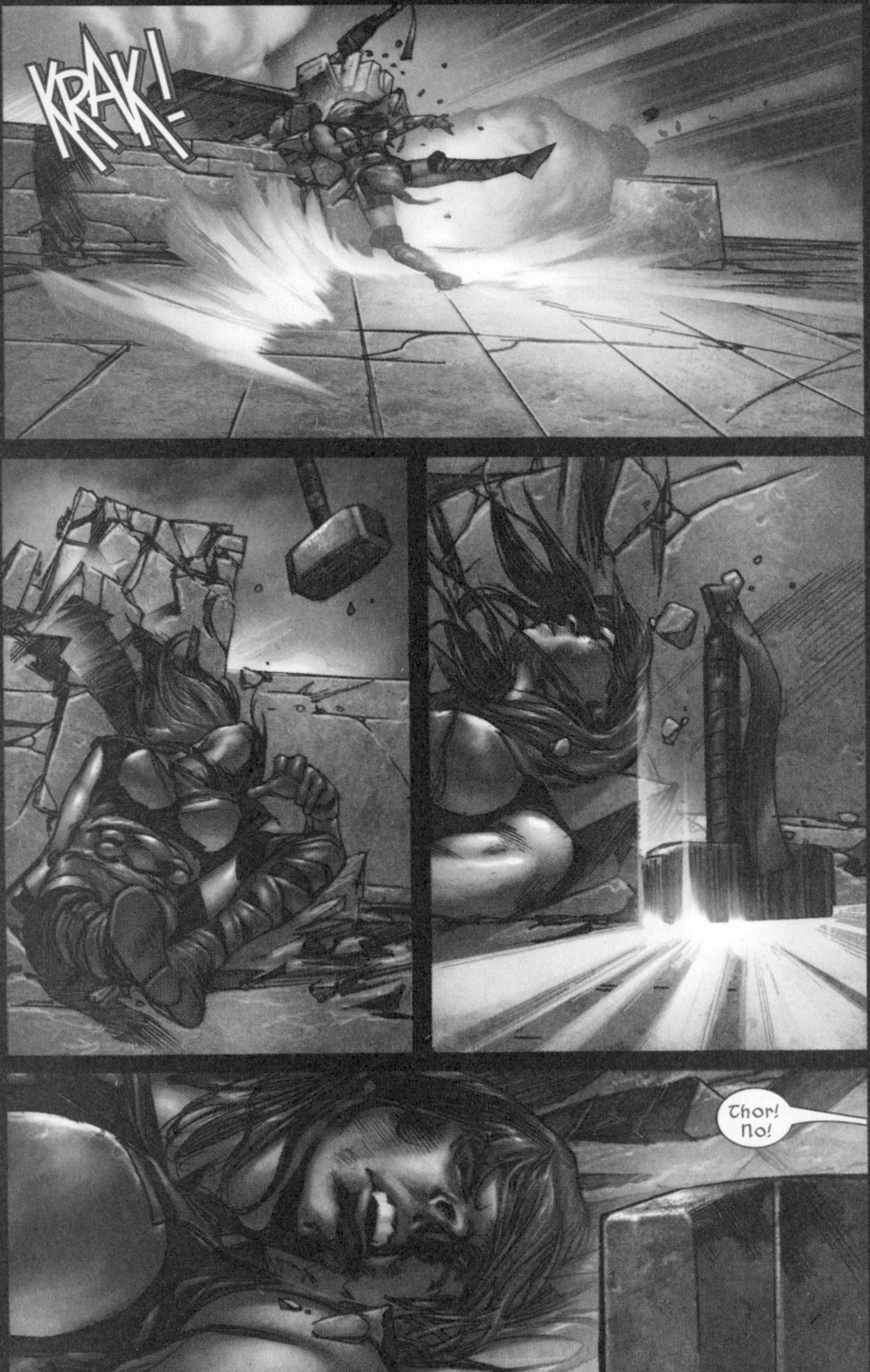
KRAK!
Thor! No!

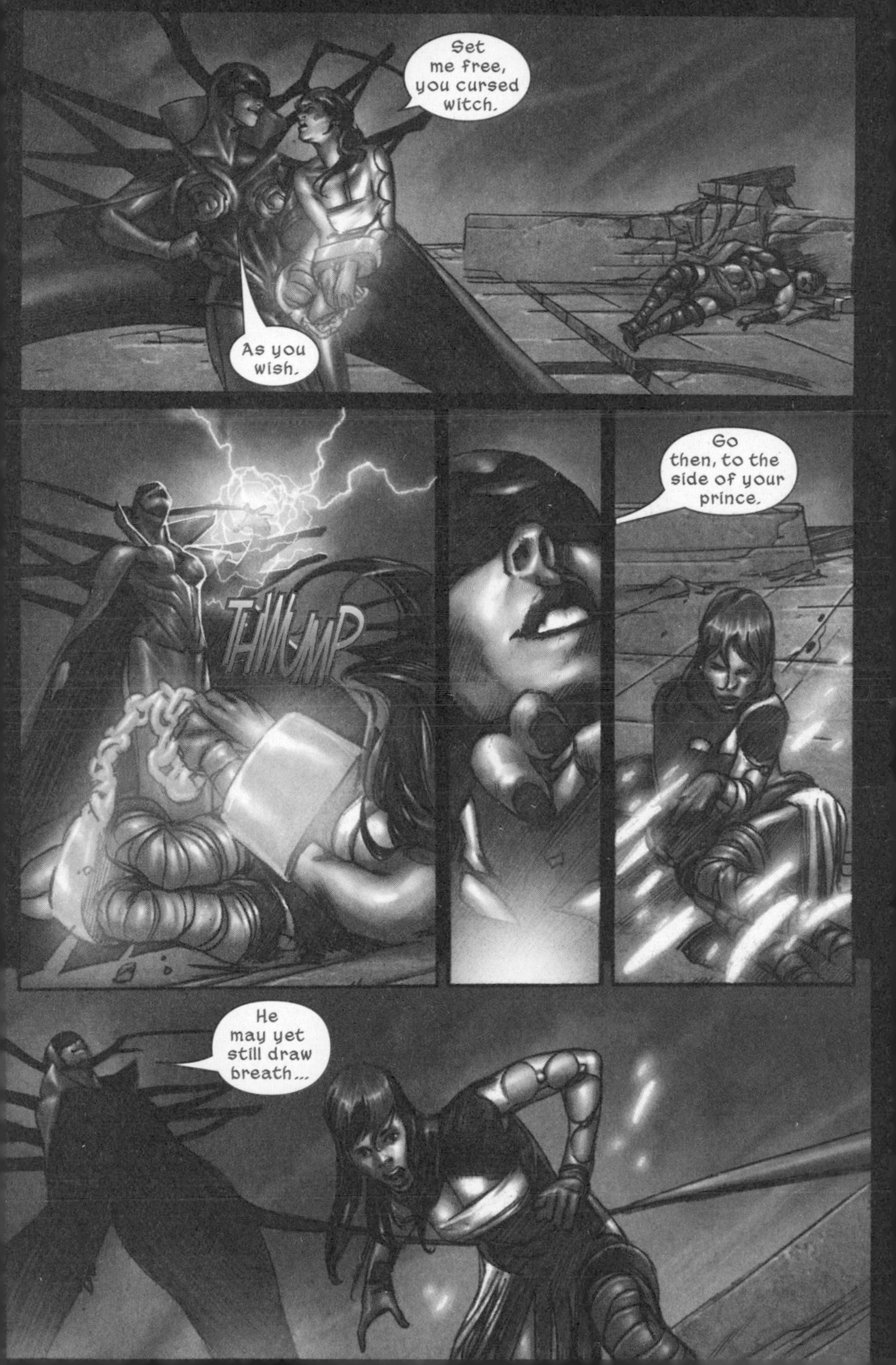
Set me free, you cursed witch.
As you wish.
THWUMP
Go then, to the side of your prince.
He may yet still draw breath...

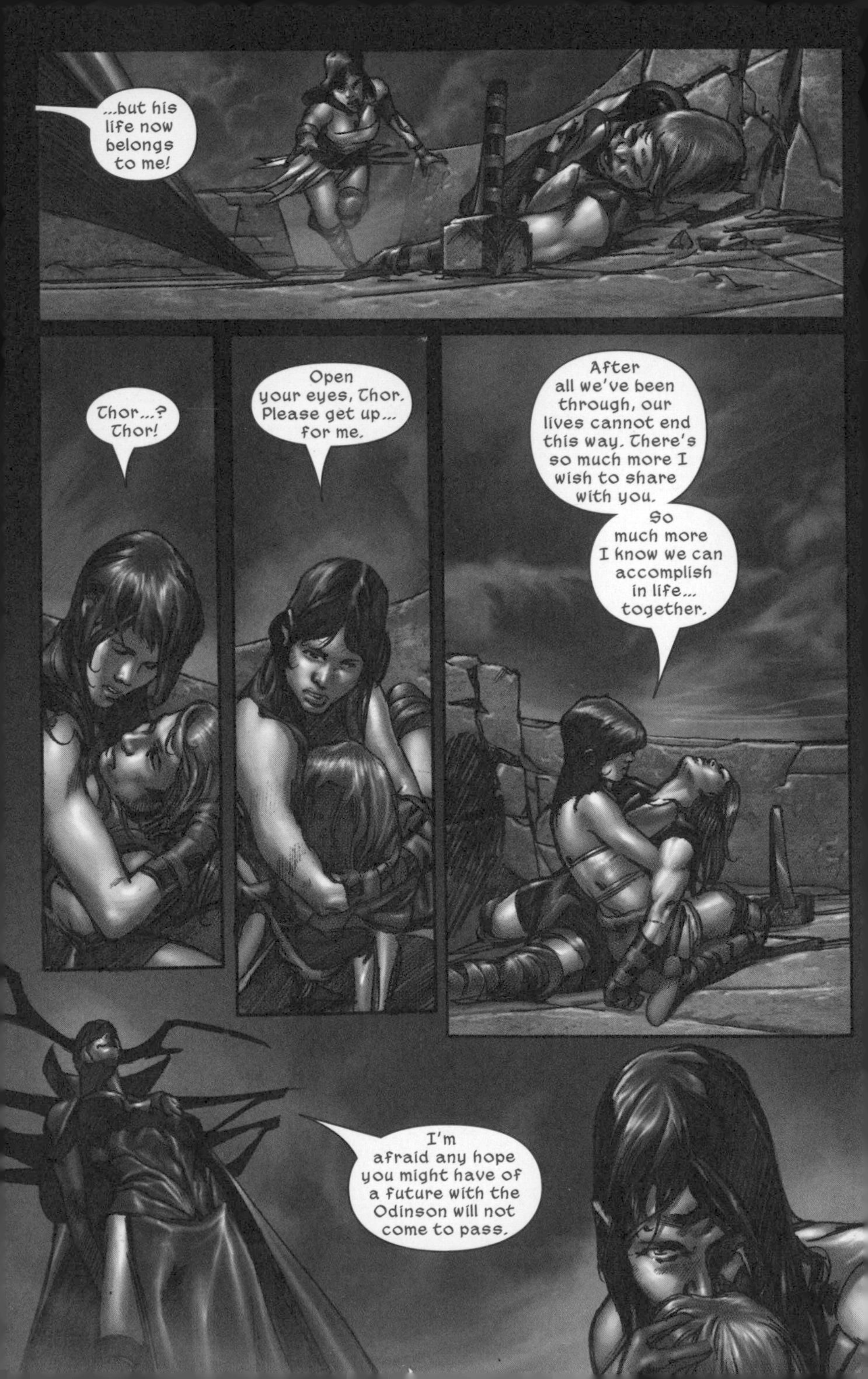
...but his life now belongs to me!
Thor...? Thor!
Open your eyes, Thor. Please get up... for me.
After all we've been through, our lives cannot end this way. There's so much more I wish to share with you.
So much more I know we can accomplish in life... together.
I'm afraid any hope you might have of a future with the Odinson will not come to pass.

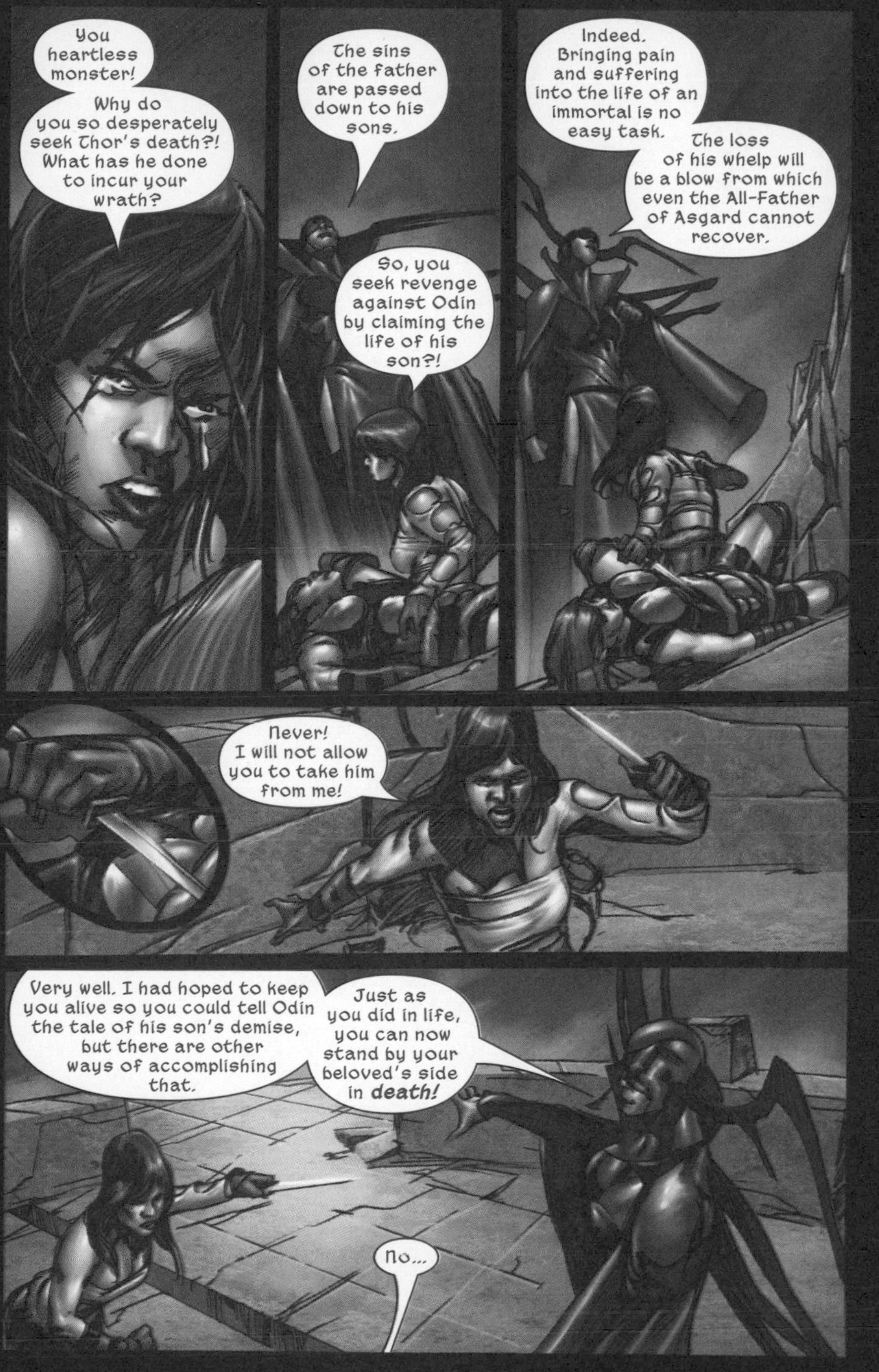

You heartless monster!
Why do you so desperately seek Thor's death?! What has he done to incur your wrath?
The sins of the father are passed down to his sons.
So, you seek revenge against Odin by claiming the life of his son?!
Indeed. Bringing pain and suffering into the life of an immortal is no easy task.
The loss of his whelp will be a blow from which even the All-Father of Asgard cannot recover.
Never! I will not allow you to take him from me!
Very well. I had hoped to keep you alive so you could tell Odin the tale of his son's demise, but there are other ways of accomplishing that.
Just as you did in life, you can now stand by your beloved's side in death!
No...

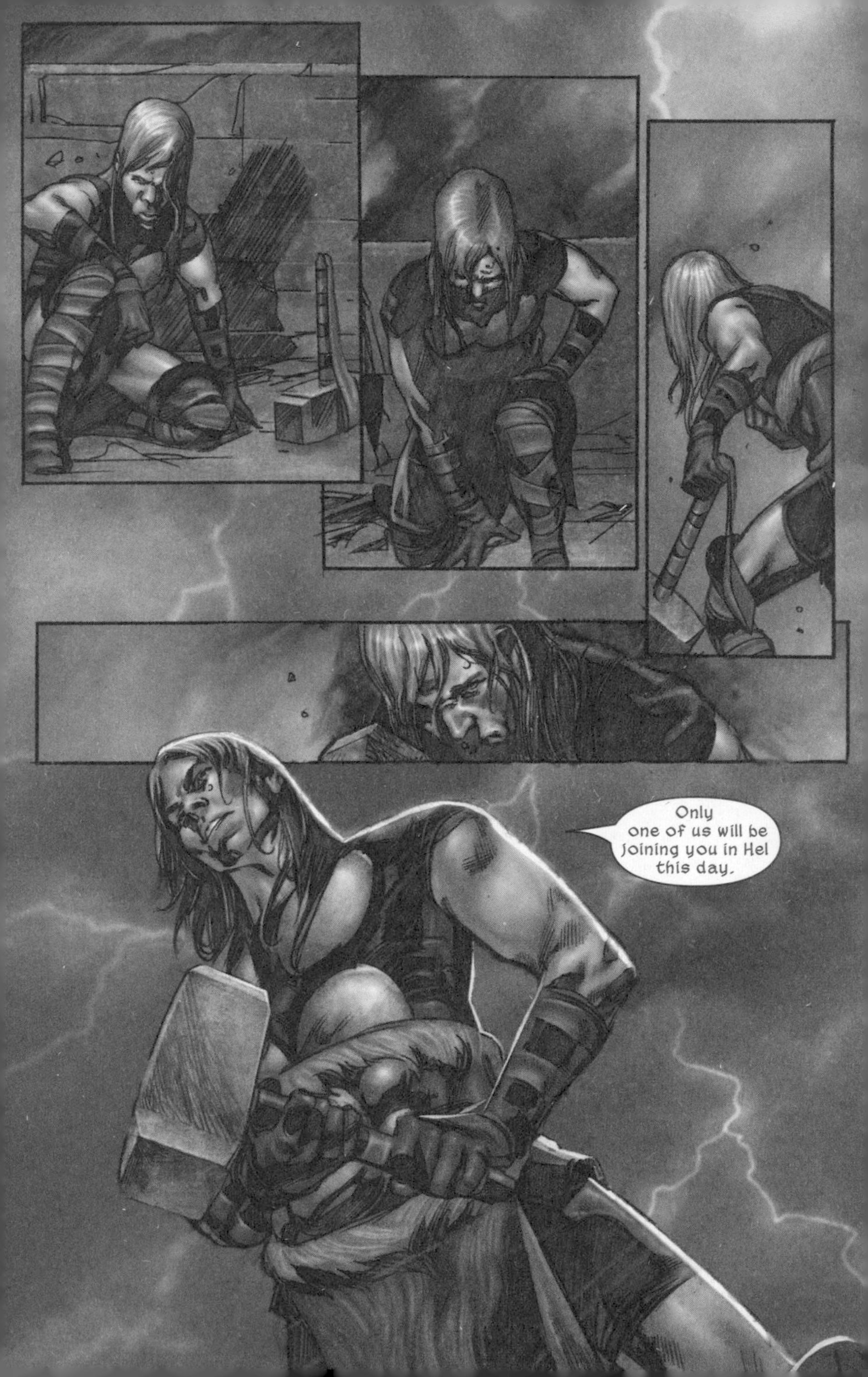
Only one of us will be joining you in Hel this day.

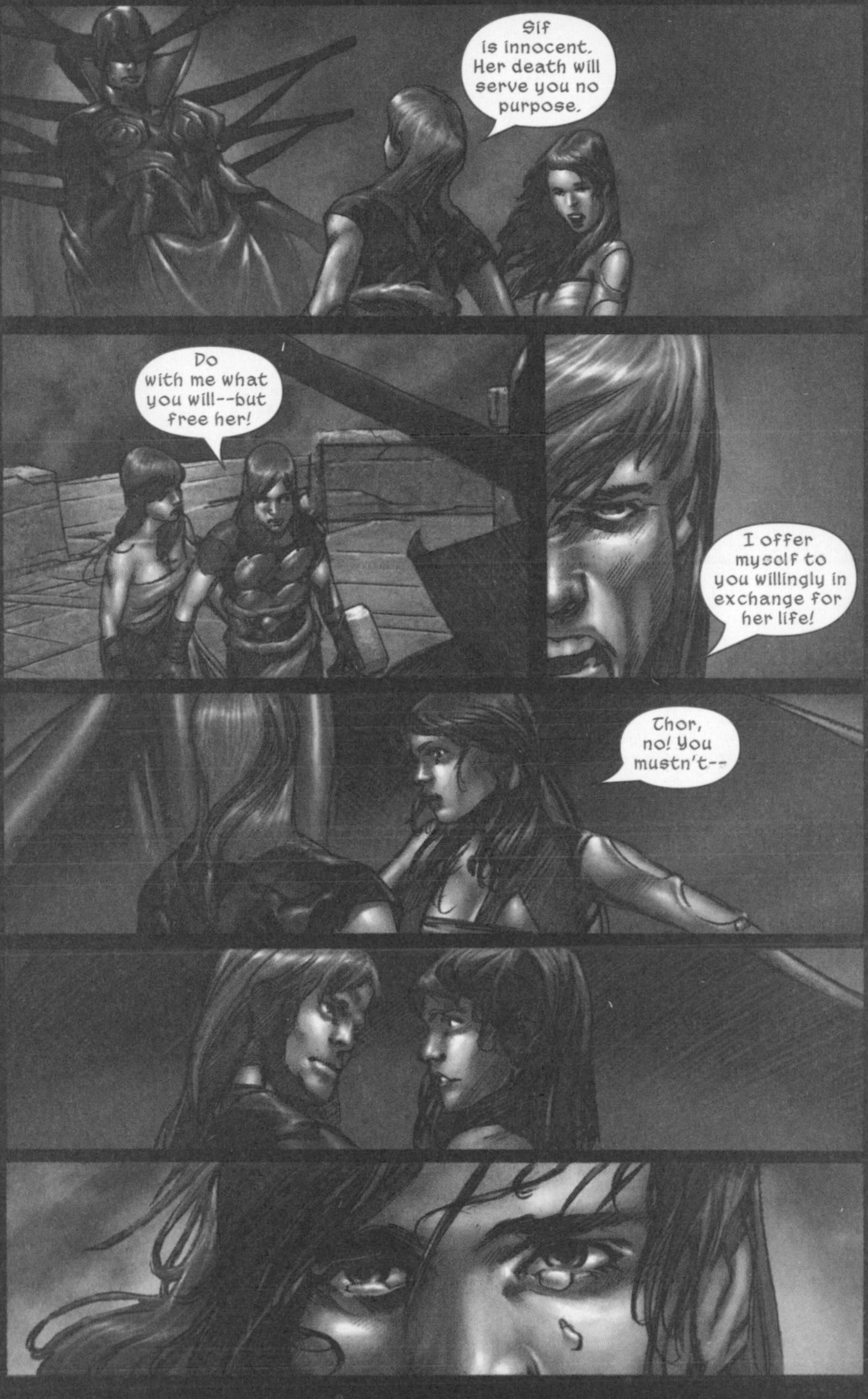
Sif is innocent. Her death will serve you no purpose.
Do with me what you will--but free her!
I offer myself to you willingly in exchange for her life!
Thor, no! You mustn't--

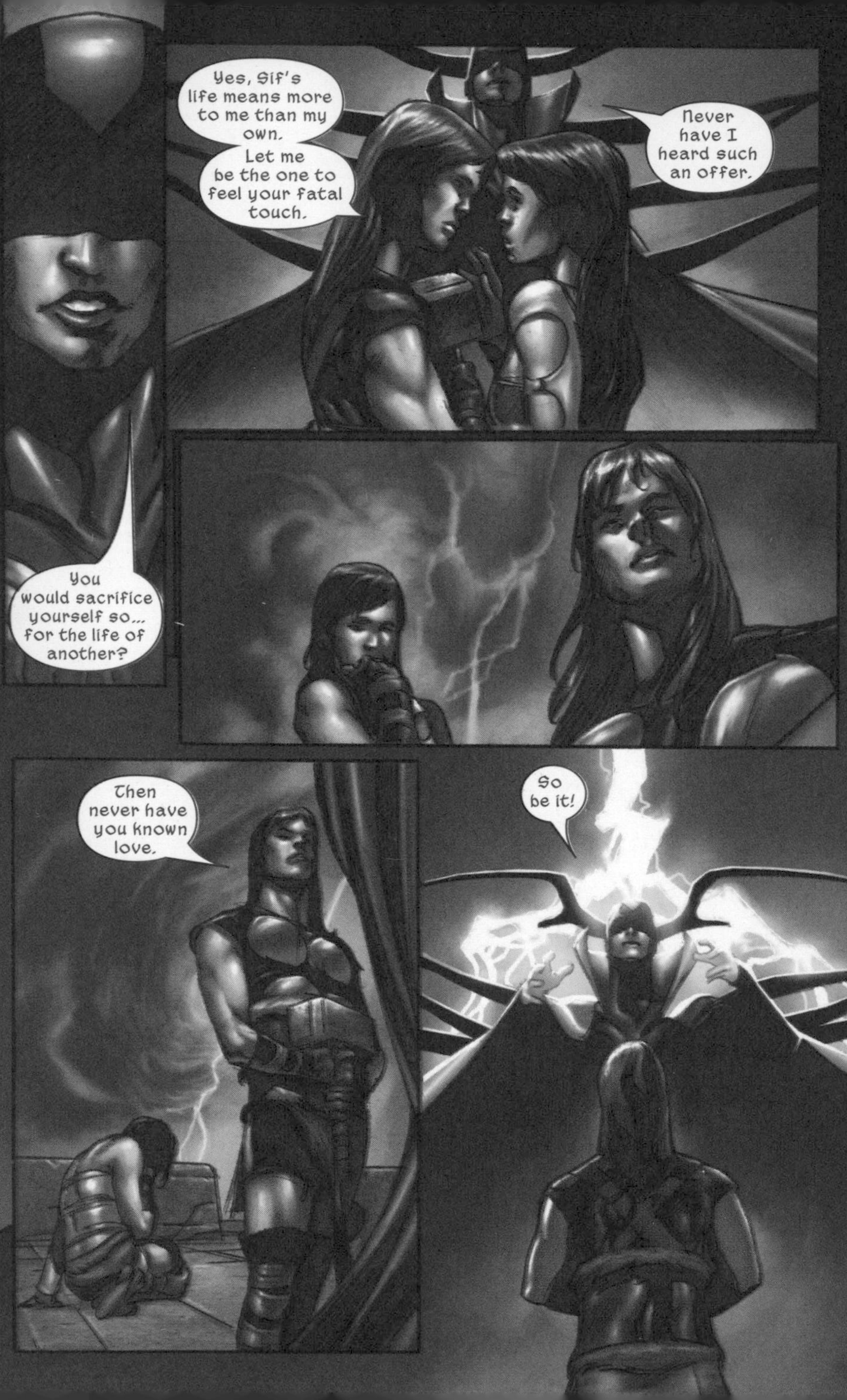
Yes, Sif's life means more to me than my own.
Let me be the one to feel your fatal touch.
Never have I heard such an offer.
You would sacrifice yourself so... for the life of another?
Then never have you known love.
So be it!

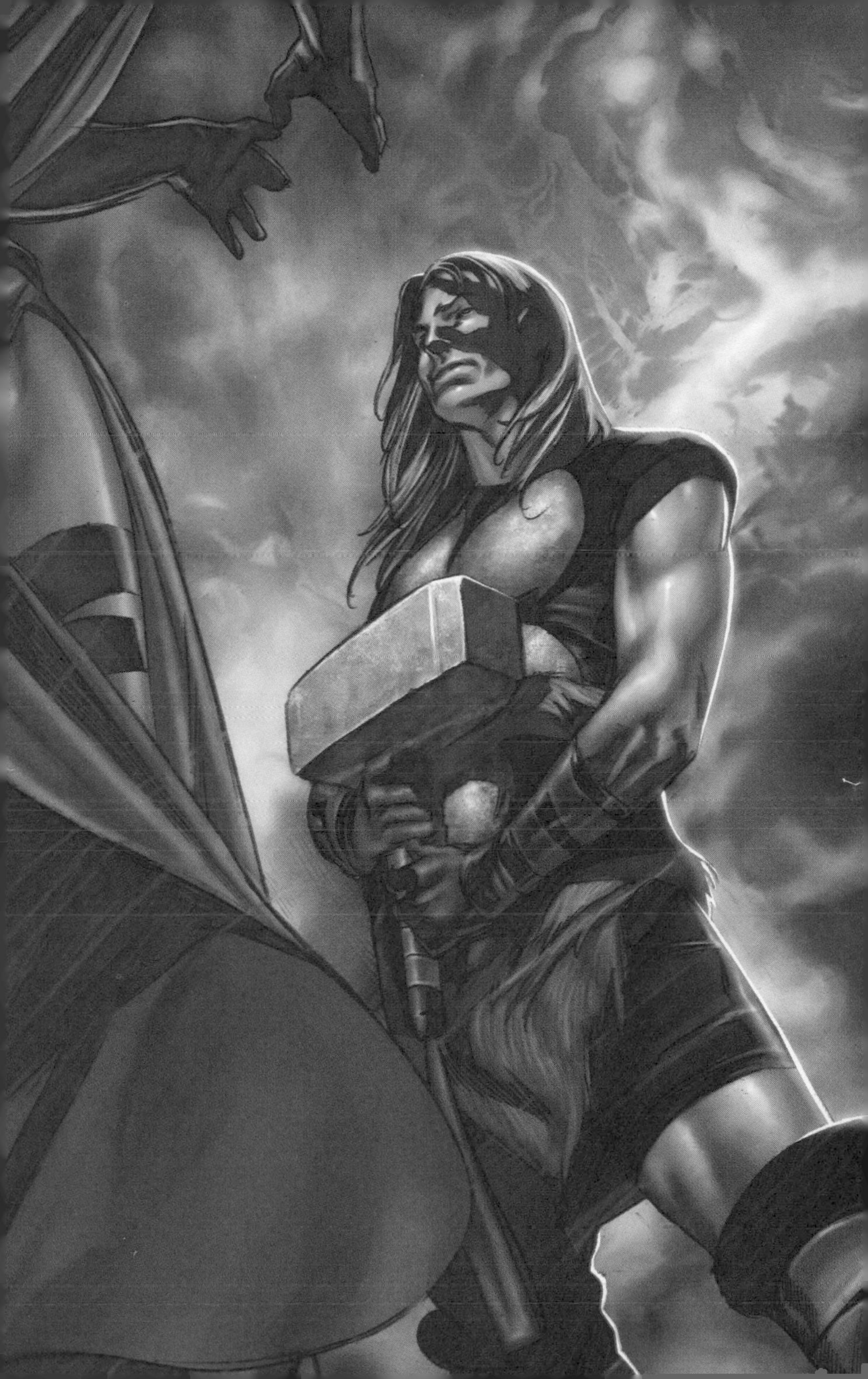

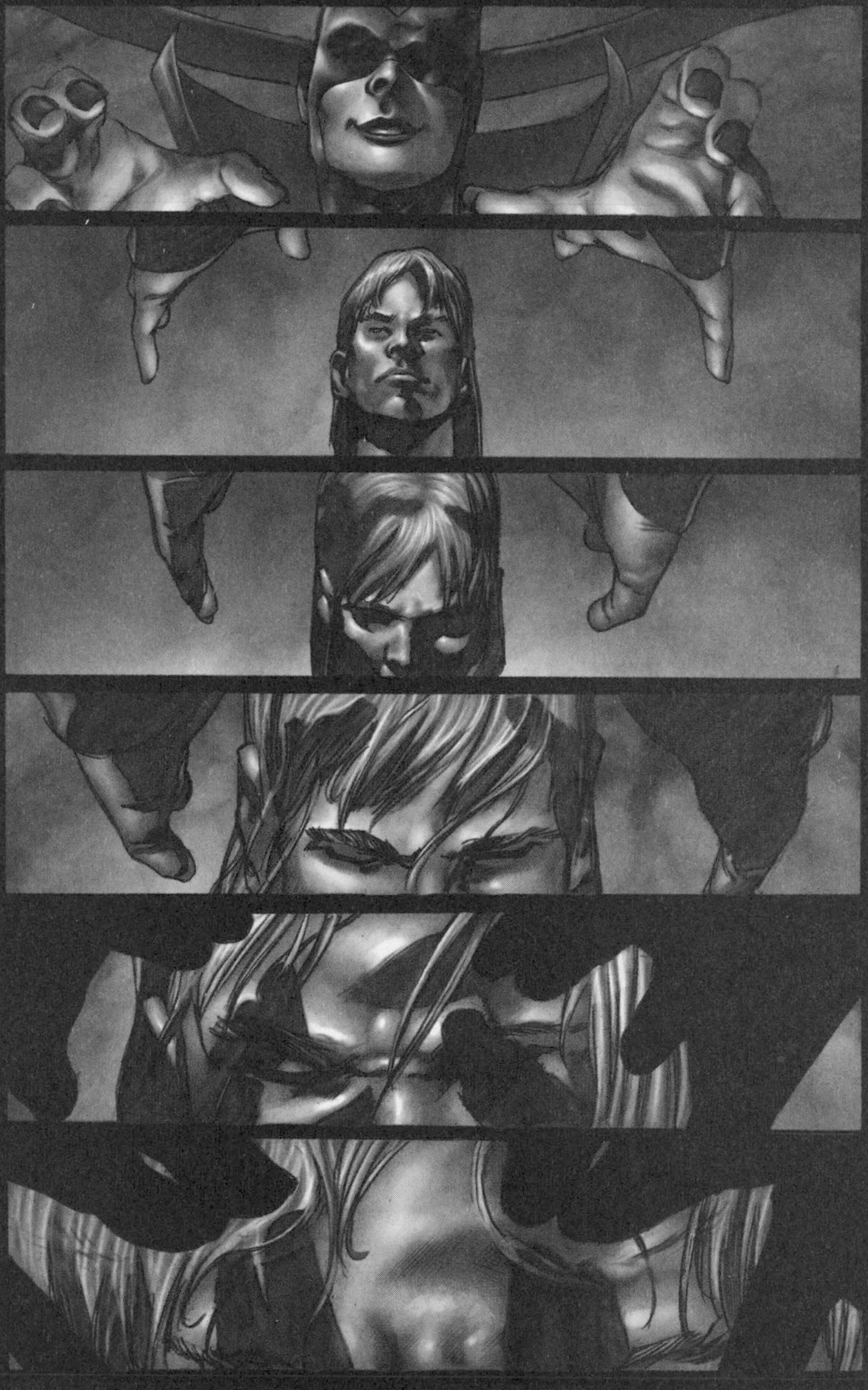

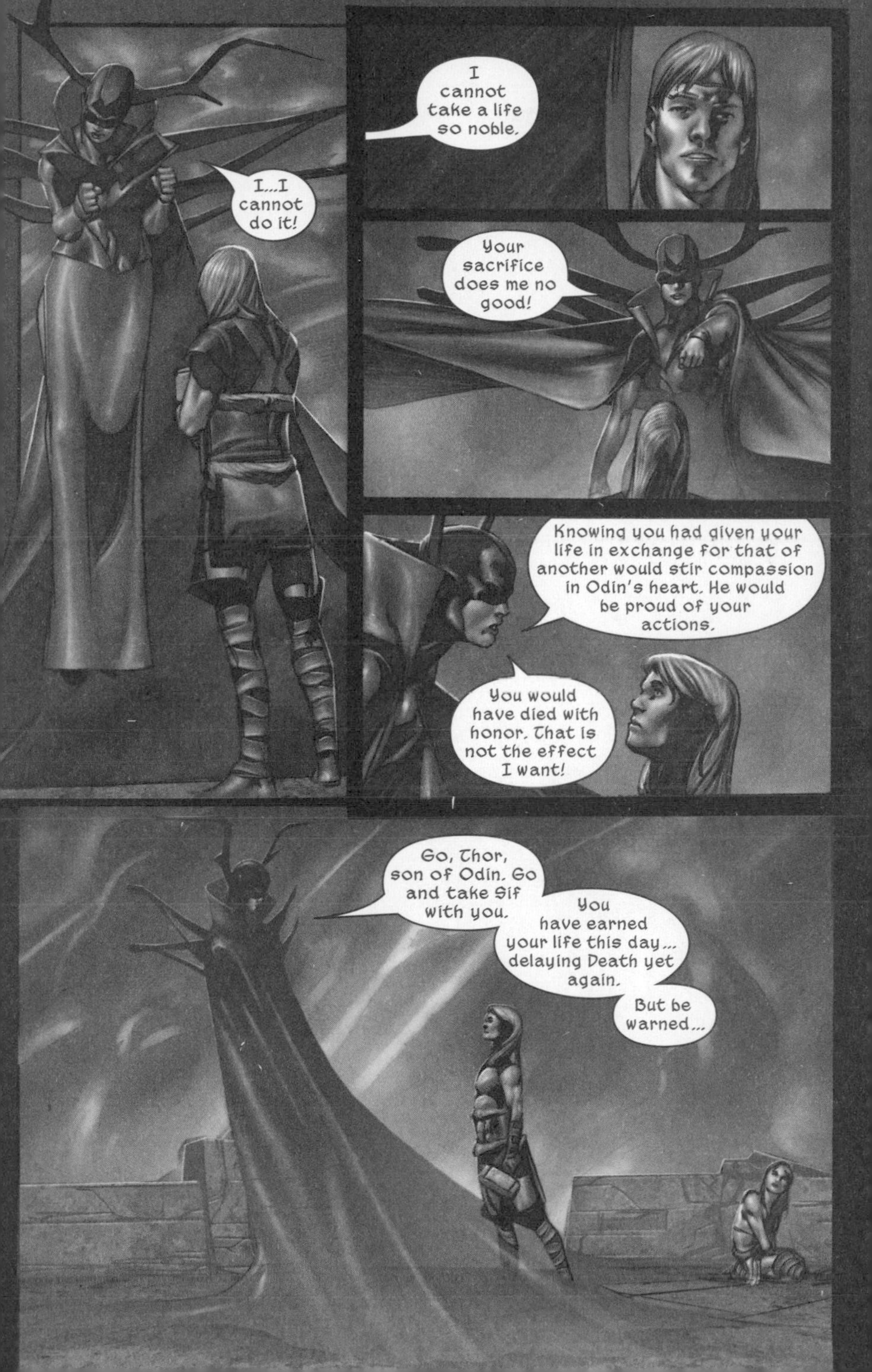
I...I cannot do it!
I cannot take a life so noble.
Your sacrifice does me no good!
Knowing you had given your life in exchange for that of another would stir compassion in Odin's heart. He would be proud of your actions.
You would have died with honor. That is not the effect I want!
Go, Thor, son of Odin. Go and take Sif with you.
You have earned your life this day... delaying Death yet again.
But be warned...

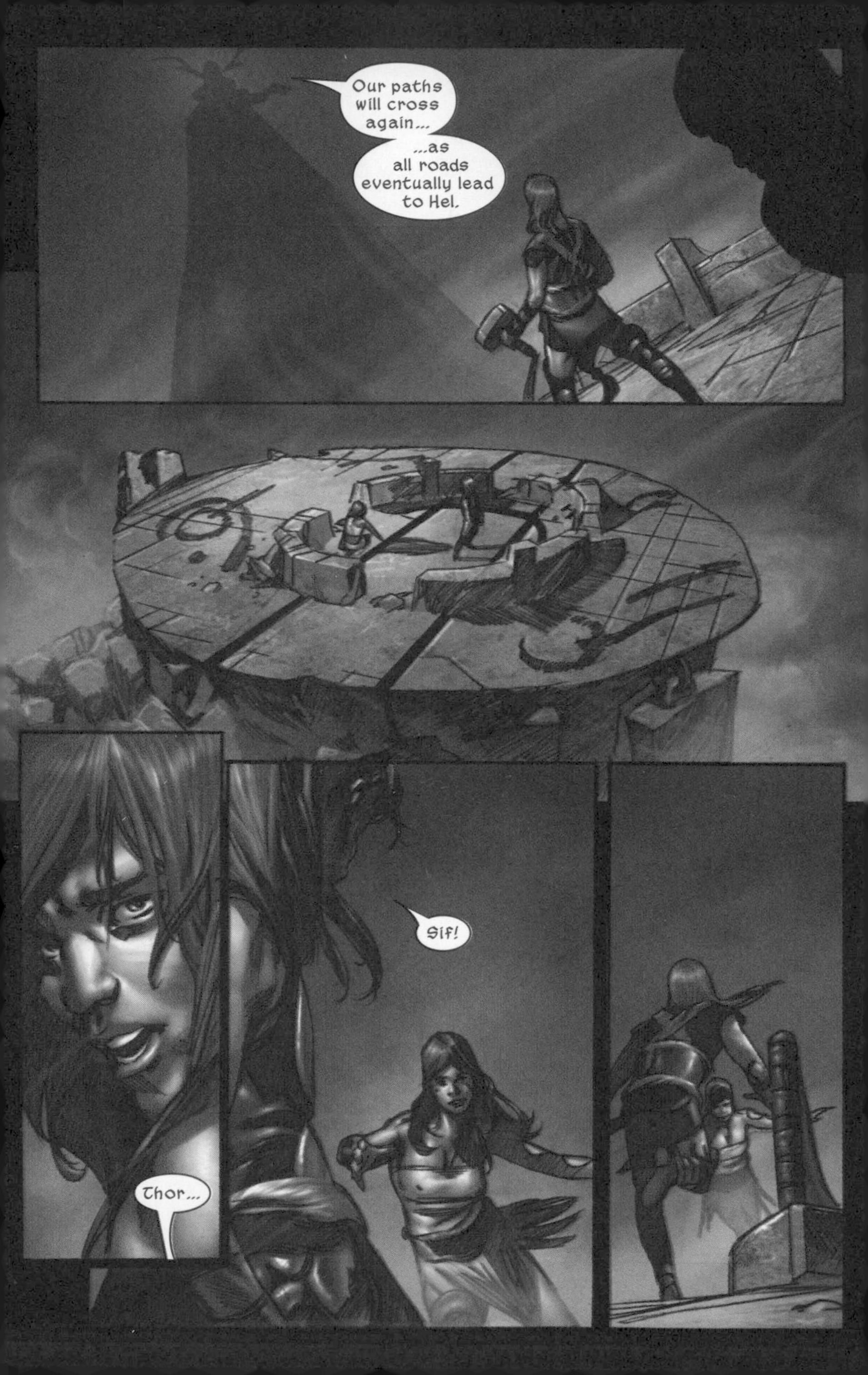
Our paths will cross again...
...as all roads eventually lead to Hel.
Thor...
Sif!

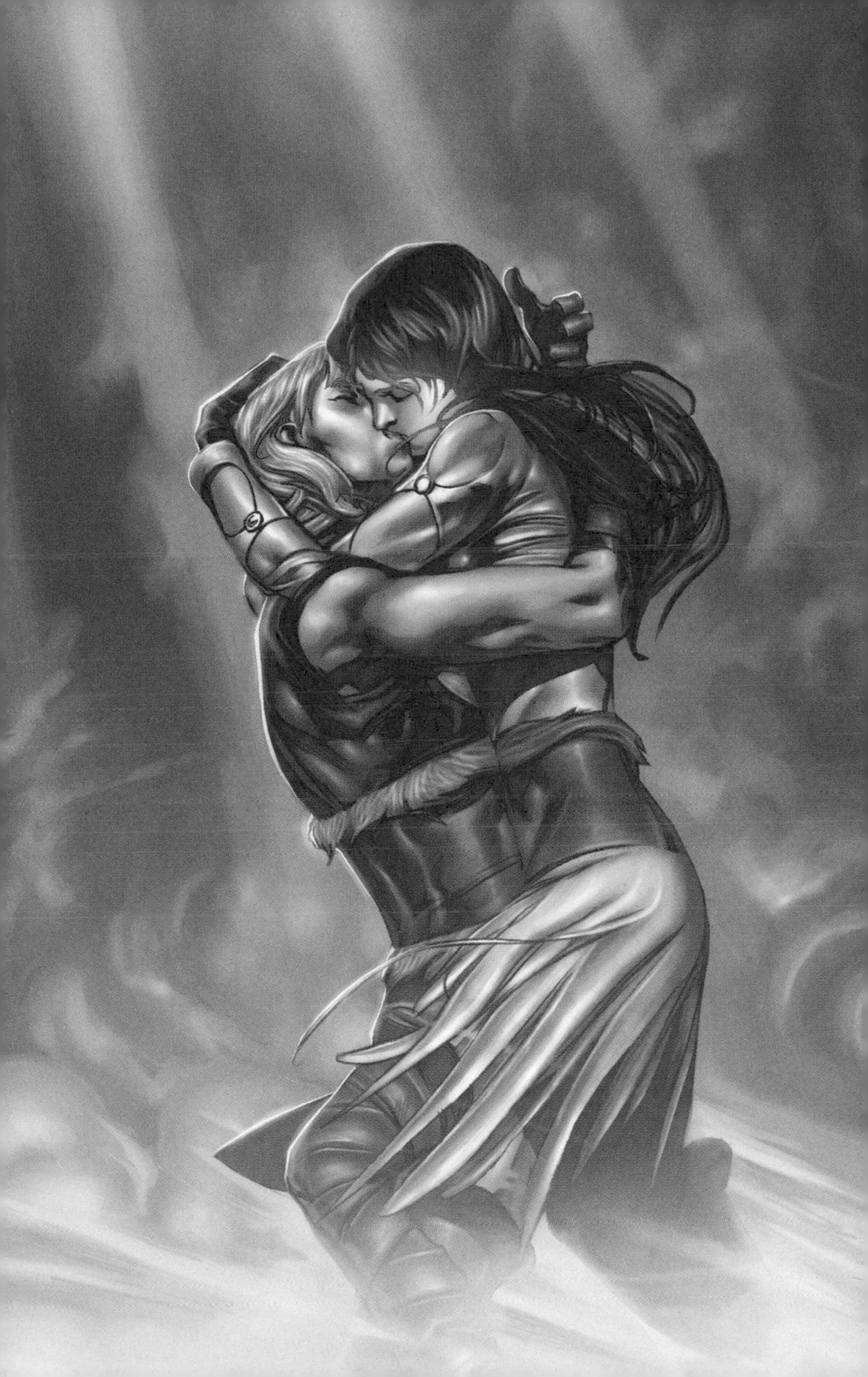

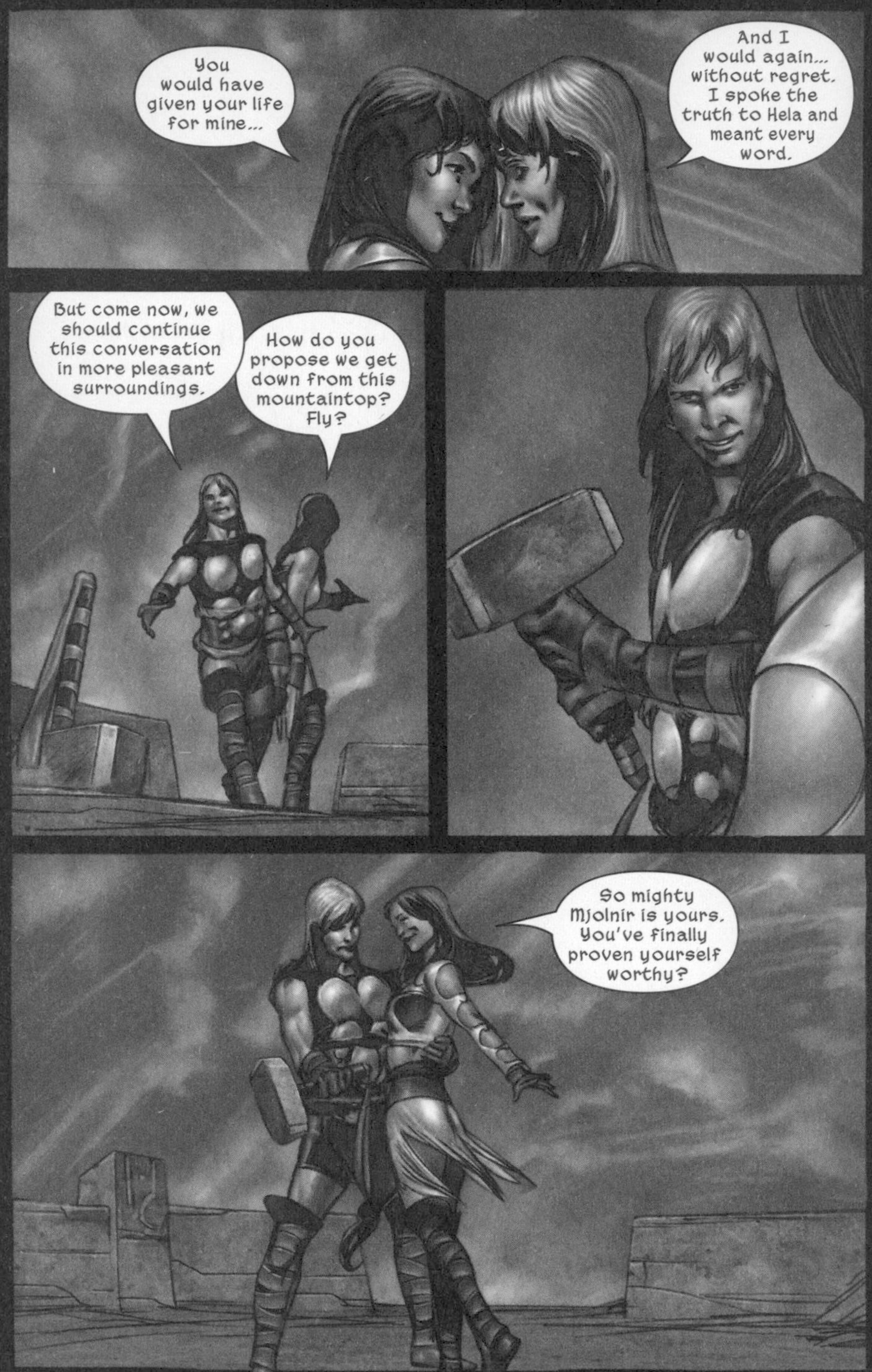
You would have given your life for mine...
And I would again... without regret. I spoke the truth to Hela and meant every word.
But come now, we should continue this conversation in more pleasant surroundings.
How do you propose we get down from this mountaintop? Fly?
So mighty Mjolnir is yours. You've finally proven yourself worthy?

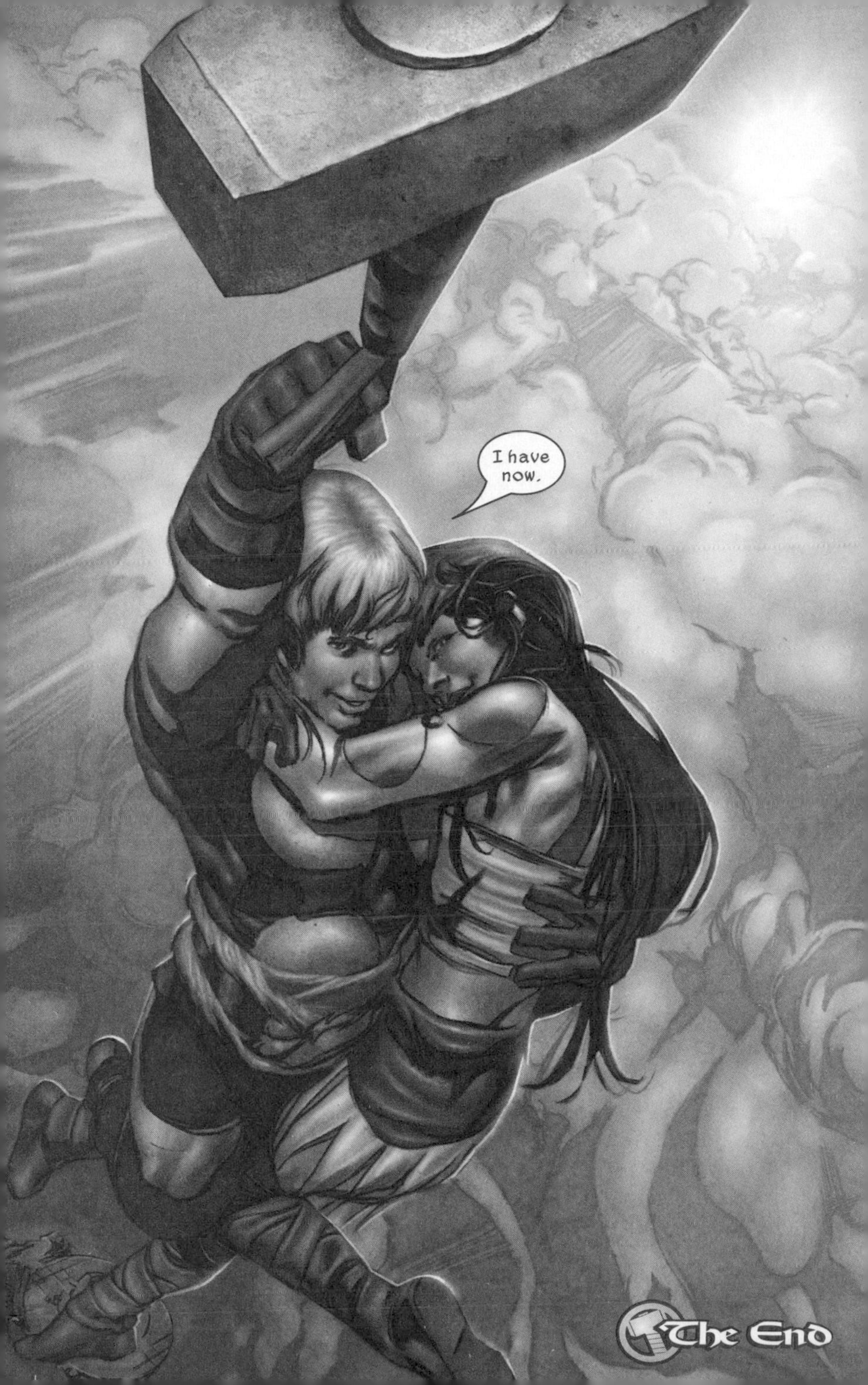
I have now.
The End